Master Plan for the Redemption of Israel

Master Plan for the Redemption of Israel

A Reformation of Messianic Judaism

YEHUDAH RAPUANO

RESOURCE *Publications* • Eugene, Oregon

MASTER PLAN FOR THE REDEMPTION OF ISRAEL
A Reformation of Messianic Judaism

Copyright © 2021 Yehudah Rapuano. All rights reserved. Except for brief quotations in critical publications or reviews, no part of this book may be reproduced in any manner without prior written permission from the publisher. Write: Permissions, Wipf and Stock Publishers, 199 W. 8th Ave., Suite 3, Eugene, OR 97401.

Resource Publications
An Imprint of Wipf and Stock Publishers
199 W. 8th Ave., Suite 3
Eugene, OR 97401

www.wipfandstock.com

PAPERBACK ISBN: 978-1-7252-7805-9
HARDCOVER ISBN: 978-1-7252-7806-6
EBOOK ISBN: 978-1-7252-7807-3

Scripture quotations marked NIV are taken from the Holy Bible, New International Version®, copyright © 1973, 1978, 1984, 2011 by Biblica, Inc.™ Used by permission. All rights reserved worldwide.

Scripture quotations marked NKJV are taken from the New King James Version®, copyright © 1982 by Thomas Nelson. Used by permission. All rights reserved. Scripture quotations marked NRSV are taken from the New Revised Standard Version Bible, copyright © 1989 by the Division of Christian Education of the National Council of the Churches of Christ in the United States of America. Used by permission. All rights reserved.

In scripture citations throughout the text, *Yeshua* is employed in place of *Jesus* and *Messiah* is employed in place of *Christ*.

11/03/21

ON THE COVER: These are the two olive trees and the two lampstands which stand before the Lord of the earth. (Revelation 11:4) The cover art is based on a panel of the fourth century synagogue mosaic floor at Hammat Tiberius in the Galilee. It depicts a Torah arc, (some scholars have suggested the Temple) flanked on either side by a menorah (seven-branched lampstand). Surrounding each menorah are three ritual objects: a shofar (ram's horn), a fire pan (used by the priest to remove coals from the altar), and a lulav (the four species waved on Succoth- the Feast of Tabernacles). The olive trees were added to either side of the panel. These symbols are intended here to visually represent the two components of the Tanakh (Old Testament Scriptures), the Law and the Prophets.

For my amazing wife, Maribeth, my severest critic and my most encouraging supporter: Thanks for all the many late nights you stayed up with me contemplating these wonders and discussing them (Proverbs 27:17).

Contents

List of Abbreviations		ix
Preface		xi
1	The Promise	1
2	And So All Israel Will Be Saved	9
3	The Torah: A Schoolmaster to Lead Us to Messiah	24
4	From the Foundation of the World: The Meaning of Sacrifice	39
5	The Two Realms	58
6	The Covenant	73
7	Until Heaven and Earth Pass Away	99
8	Free From the Law	107
9	Grafted in . . . to What?	119
10	What They Came Up with at Yavneh	145
11	The Restoration	163
12	The Master Plan Revealed	181
13	Recognizing Our Times	198
14	Israel Coming Alive!	209
15	Messianic Judaism Comes of Age	223
16	Revealing Joseph to the Sons of Israel	231
17	It Is No Dream	255
Bibliography		267
Subject Index		271
Scripture Index		275

List of Abbreviations

ANES	*Ancient Near Eastern Studies*
Her.	*Philo of Alexandria, Quis Rerum Divinarum Heres Sit*
KJV	King James Version
NIV	New International Version
NKJV	New King James Version
PEQ	*Palestine Exploration Quarterly*
RSV	Revised Standard Version

Preface

THE REDEMPTION IS NOW!

BEYOND ALL THAT THE Jewish people as individuals or as a nation have accomplished in our world, a day will soon dawn for Israel that will brilliantly outshine even the most glorious moment of its past, a day beyond all dreams and exceeding our capacity even to imagine it. The sons of Jacob shall yet be bearers of the full measure of salvation to mankind, even as it was promised to the patriarch Abraham!

The redemption of Israel is not in some distant future but has in fact already begun in our day! However, because of our limited human perspective, it is difficult for us to perceive where we actually stand in history.

A THRESHOLD IN TIME

When we look at events happening in the world around us there is an overwhelming sense that we are standing at an enormously important threshold in time. Unfortunately, locked as we are in our own era, we are incapable of perceiving our place within the greater scheme of history. Here the Bible comes to our aid. It opens to us a window through which we are able to view the past as well as the future. When Daniel read the words of Jeremiah, he understood when the Babylonian captivity of the Jewish People would come to an end (Dan 9:2). By studying the writings of the prophet, he recognized God's plan for Israel and understood his timing. Equipped with this knowledge, Daniel took action that changed the course of history.

THE MASTER PLAN

God has a plan whose aim is the redemption of Israel as a nation, a transformation so pervasive that it will extend to all peoples of the earth. The blueprint of this plan is revealed in amazing detail in the pages of the Scriptures. There are three stages to the redemption of Israel. The first stage, the return of the Jewish people to the land of Israel, is nearly complete. The second stage, the spiritual transformation of Israel, is already in progress. The third and final stage will culminate in a total regeneration of Israel and through it the rebirth and renewal of mankind itself.

In recent years a growing number of Jewish people are awakening to the understanding that Yeshua (Jesus) is the long-promised Messiah of Israel. However, this number represents yet but a trickle of individuals. If only we could realize how this trickle has the potential to become a flood! A major reason why we have been ineffective in sharing the message of the Messiah is that we have failed to recognize God's plan for the Jewish people. By ignoring his plan, we have in fact been unwittingly working against it. We are consequently fighting our way upstream. Like Paul on his way to Damascus, while striving hard to do God's will, we are actually opposing his very purposes. Before we can be effective in sharing the good news with the Jewish people, we need to have a grasp of the master plan, to look ahead and see how it all turns out. By carefully studying the Scriptures, we can, like Daniel, step out of our own time, so to speak. From this unique vantage point we will be able to soberly assess our place in the greater scheme of history and at the same time, looking forward, get a glimpse of our future goal. With this insight we will be ready to work *with* God's plan in order to be effective now rather than finding ourselves, as it were, "kicking against the goads."

REFORMING MESSIANIC JUDAISM

Messianic Judaism desperately needs direction, self-awareness of its purpose, and specific goals. Messianic Jews very much require a clear, unified, single vision. An understanding of the master plan will go a long way toward fulfilling these needs. On the way to our destination, we will examine the scriptural basis for Messianic Judaism, and we will touch upon a number of important doctrinal issues all in light of the master plan. But, make no mistake! This is no dry, armchair theology. Rather, it is a call to action. The intended purpose of this book is to incite a revolution through insight and revelation!

THE GREATEST STORY EVER TOLD: THE FINAL CHAPTER

The call of Abraham, many centuries ago, initiated a journey that has extended throughout the ages. It continues today as we move toward the culminating point in history. When we think of Bible times, we tend to picture in our minds very distant ages of the past, yet some of the greatest occurrences in the Bible were written about in the future tense. Many of the most important events and most astounding miracles are still yet to happen. The greatest story ever told is in fact an unfinished drama waiting to be completed. The final chapter, the most exciting episode, has yet to be written into the pages of history.

In the chapters that follow you are about to discover the master's plan of the ages for Israel's redemption. There are some readers who will awaken to a special inner call to join in the quest, a challenge that if answered will certainly change the direction of their lives. This, then, is an invitation to come along on a journey of discovery, one that, as it unfolds, is undoubtedly the greatest real-life adventure of all time.

1

The Promise

SOUND THE SHOFAR!

AT CRUCIAL MOMENTS IN their ancient history, the Israelites would blow the *shofar*, the ram's horn. Its shrill, eerie timbre pierced the air, stirring the spirits of God's people with courage and striking fear into the hearts of those who hated them. It was a call to war and it was a call to repentance. It was a shout of praise to the God of Israel and it was a desperate plea to him for rescue! Psalms 47:1–5 proclaims:

> *1:* O clap your hands, all ye people; shout unto God with the voice of triumph.
> *2:* For the Lord most high is terrible; he is the great king over all the earth.
> *3:* He shall subdue the people under us, and the nations under our feet.
> *4:* He shall choose our inheritance for us, the excellency of Jacob whom he loved. Selah.
> *5:* God is gone up with a shout, the Lord with the sound of a trumpet [*shofar*].[1]

The ram's horn has always been a symbol of the redemption of Israel. However, nowhere in the Scriptures is it ever explained why this is. According to tradition the blowing of the ram's horn is to be a reminder of the binding of

---

1. Ps 47:1–5 (KJV).

Isaac, the son of Abraham.[2] In the telling of this heart-wrenching tale we get a glimpse for the first time in Scripture of God's wonderful master plan for the redemption of Israel, and so it is here that our journey will begin.

THE PROMISE

Abraham was a man with a promise. When the Creator of the universe spoke to him to leave his native city of Ur in Mesopotamia and sent him on a voyage to the land of Canaan, God gave Abraham a marvelous promise that would extend far beyond his own time into eternity.

> *1:* Now the Lord said to Abram, "Go from your country and your father's house to the land that I will show you. *2:* And I will make of you a great nation, and I will bless you, and make your name great, so that you will be a blessing. *3:* I will bless those who bless you, and him who curses you I will curse; and by you all the families of the earth shall bless themselves."[3]

The entire promise was not revealed to Abraham all at once, but was rather disclosed periodically at crucial junctures in the life of the patriarch each time with increasing clarity. The promise comprised specific blessings to Abraham that dealt with his particular needs. His greatest concern at the time was that he was without an heir. God promised him a son from whom he would have many offspring. At the time he was a wandering nomad, God swore that his descendants would possess the land of Canaan, and that they would be delivered from the enemies who would threaten them.

Yet within the promise to Abraham there was embedded a much greater hope. It did not merely deal with the temporal needs of the patriarch but envisioned the ultimate destiny of his descendants: the redemption of the people of Israel. Moreover, the clause in the promise that by Abraham all the families of the earth would be blessed foreshadowed no less than the complete restoration of the fallen human race![4] The final disclosure of the promise came when Abraham had faithfully carried out preparations to obey God's command to him to offer up his son, Isaac, as a sacrifice upon the altar. It is by far the hardest thing a father has ever been asked to do. God bid him to give up that which was most dear to him, his only beloved son, whom he had waited and pined for, the one who was more precious to

---

2. Gen 22:1–18.
3. Gen 12:1–3 (RSV).
4. See Rom 4–5, especially 5:18–21.

him than life itself. Let us recall this crucial episode in sacred history and so catch in it a glimpse of God's plan for the redemption of his people.

THE BINDING OF ISAAC

God instructs Abraham to take his son to a specific mountain in the land of Moriah in order to sacrifice him as a burnt offering. Early in the morning, Abraham takes his son along with two servants and, after a three-day journey, arrives at the spot. Abraham leaves instructions for the servants to stay behind. He places the wood for the sacrifice on his son, Isaac. (This curious detail that was faithfully recorded in Scripture seems trivial, yet we shall see that it was in fact quite significant.) As the two set off for the place of sacrifice, Abraham with knife and fire in hand and Isaac carrying the wood, the young man is perplexed. He sees that his father is about to offer a sacrifice and yet there is no animal anywhere to be found.

> *7:* And Isaac said to his father Abraham, "My father!" And he said, "Here am I, my son." He said, "Behold, the fire and the wood; but where is the lamb for a burnt offering?" *8:* Abraham said, "God will provide himself the lamb for a burnt offering, my son."[5]

More than simply reassuring Isaac, sparing his son from knowing his fate until the very last, Abraham was in fact speaking prophetically. They arrive at the place; Abraham builds an altar, places the wood on the altar, binds Isaac, and lays him on the wood. Then he takes up the knife to slay his son. Suddenly, the Angel of the Lord calls to him to stop.

> *12:* He said, "Do not lay your hand on the lad or do anything to him; for now I know that you fear God, seeing you have not withheld your son, your only son, from me."[6]

Abraham looks up, and seeing a ram caught in the thicket by its horns offers it up instead.

> *15:* And the angel of the Lord called to Abraham a second time from heaven, *16:* and said, "By myself I have sworn, says the Lord, because you have done this, and have not withheld your son, your only son, *17:* I will indeed bless you, and I will multiply your descendants as the stars of heaven and as the sand which is on the seashore. And your descendants shall possess

---

5. Gen 22:7–8 (RSV).
6. Gen 22:12 (RSV).

> the gate of their enemies, *18:* and by your descendants shall all the nations of the earth bless themselves, because you have obeyed my voice."[7]

In order to truly understand the meaning of this rather strange and intriguing story we must pay close attention to its details. Behind the scene of this story lurks a vexing question that demands an answer. God had promised Abraham that he would have many descendants and that they would come from Isaac, yet God had commanded Abraham to sacrifice him. How could Abraham possibly think to receive descendants from Isaac if his son was dead? He had already made up his mind to kill Isaac and did not foresee that the Angel of the Lord would stay his hand. The book of Hebrews in verses 11:17–19 informs us that Abraham was fully convinced that God the all-powerful was in fact able to raise Isaac back to life. Consequently, it must not be overlooked that Abraham expected that not only Isaac would be resurrected, but that through him all of Abraham's future descendants would receive life as well.

THE PLACE

The place of the sacrifice was not selected arbitrarily. It was specifically chosen by God himself. In addition to the name Mount Moriah, it has been called by other names as well: the mountain of the Lord and Mount Zion. Many years in the future, the city of Jerusalem would sprawl out beneath this hill. Upon this mount would stand the Temple of the God of Israel, the place of his earthly dwelling. A glorious future still awaits this mountain in connection with the role it shall yet play in the coming redemption of Israel.

> *7:* And he [God] will destroy on this mountain the covering that is cast over all peoples, the veil that is spread over all nations. *8:* He will swallow up death for ever, and the Lord GOD will wipe away tears from all faces, and the reproach of his people he will take away from all the earth; for the Lord has spoken. *9:* It will be said on that day, "Lo, this is our God; we have waited for him, that he might save us. This is the Lord; we have waited for him; let us be glad and rejoice in his salvation."[8]

Thus it is prophesied that God will one day remove death once and for all on this mountain. This was not meant in a spiritual or allegorical sense only. It will literally occur as a consequence of Israel's redemption.

7. Gen 22:15–18 (RSV).
8. Isa 25:7–8 (RSV).

Another crucial point is that the animal caught in the thicket was a ram and not a lamb. This again may easily be overlooked as a trifling detail, yet this too, as we shall see, is very significant. The prophetic word that God would provide himself the lamb was not entirely fulfilled by the ram in the thicket. This is underlined by the fact that Abraham spoke of the coming of the lamb in the future tense and that his words thereafter became a proverb in Israel.

> *14:* So Abraham called the name of that place The Lord will provide; as it is said to this day, "On the mount of the Lord it shall be provided."[9]

THE LAMB

In fact, the entire promise of redemption hinged upon the coming of the Lamb. The story of the binding of Isaac envisions another episode in the Scriptures that occurred in the same vicinity around two thousand years later. At that time, another father, in this case God himself, led his only begotten Son to the place of sacrifice. Like Isaac, he carried the wood of the sacrifice on his back to the place of slaughter, this time the beam of a Roman cross. Like Isaac, he was bound and placed on the wood of the sacrifice, his father intent on slaying him. But unlike Isaac, he did not find escape and was not spared; for he was not only the chosen Son; he himself was also the promised Lamb of whom Abraham had prophesied. Isaiah also prophesied of him hundreds of years before his birth:

> *4:* Surely he has borne our griefs and carried our sorrows; yet we esteemed him stricken, smitten by God, and afflicted. *5:* But he was wounded for our transgressions, he was bruised for our iniquities; upon him was the chastisement that made us whole, and with his stripes we are healed. *6:* All we like sheep have gone astray; we have turned every one to his own way; and the Lord has laid on him the iniquity of us all. *7:* He was oppressed, and he was afflicted, yet he opened not his mouth; *like a lamb that is led to the slaughter, and like a sheep that before its shearers is dumb, so he opened not his mouth.* *8:* By oppression and judgment he was taken away; and as for his generation, who considered that he was cut off out of the land of the living, stricken for the transgression of my people? *9:* And they made his grave with the wicked and with a rich man in his death, although he

---

9. Gen 22:14 (RSV).

had done no violence, and there was no deceit in his mouth. *10:* Yet it was the will of the Lord to bruise him; he has put him to grief; when he makes himself an offering for sin, he shall see his offspring, he shall prolong his days; the will of the Lord shall prosper in his hand; *11:* he shall see the fruit of the travail of his soul and be satisfied; by his knowledge shall the righteous one, my servant, make many to be accounted righteous; and he shall bear their iniquities. *12:* Therefore I will divide him a portion with the great, and he shall divide the spoil with the strong; because he poured out his soul to death, and was numbered with the transgressors; yet he bore the sin of many, and made intercession for the transgressors."[10]

The Scriptures also foretold with amazing accuracy other details regarding the Lamb, including his lineage, the miraculous circumstances and place of his birth,[11] and even the precise date of his coming, 483 scriptural years after the command to return and build Jerusalem.[12] These prophecies all found fulfillment in the person of Yeshua of Nazareth, of whom it was proclaimed, "Behold, the Lamb of God, who takes away the sin of the world!"[13]

As the Lamb, he was innocent and undeserving of death. Thus, after three days in the tomb, he was raised again to life by the power of God. Through the resurrection of Yeshua, God laid the foundation of a new creation completely free from sin and death. Furthermore, God promised that Yeshua would inherit the throne of David his forefather; he would reign from Mount Zion in Jerusalem, and his kingdom would be worldwide and everlasting.

WHEN DID ABRAHAM SEE YESHUA'S DAY?

Yeshua addressing the Jews of his time made an astonishing statement. He told them, "Your father Abraham rejoiced that he was to see my day; he saw it and was glad."[14] How was it that Abraham "saw" Yeshua's day some two thousand years in the future? Was it by means of a prophetic vision? And when in the lifetime of the patriarch did this occur? Is it not likely that Abraham foresaw the coming of Yeshua the Messiah at that crucial moment

---

10. Isa 53:4–12 (RSV), emphasis added.
11. Isa 7:14; 9:6–9; Mic 5:2 (verse 1 in the Hebrew text).
12. Dan 9:24–26.
13. John 1:29 (RSV).
14. John 8:56 (RSV).

when the Angel of the Lord stayed his hand and he, looking up, saw the ram caught in the thicket? In a sudden flash of absolute clarity he would have understood that the Lamb whom God would provide on the mount would, like Isaac, be his own offspring, and yet somehow at the same time God's own Son. He would have perceived that, like the ram, Yeshua would be a substitute, an atonement, upon the altar for Abraham and his descendants. He would have realized that it would be through Yeshua's death and resurrection that he and his descendants would find redemption, protection from their enemies, escape from death, and the hope of eternal life. Abraham saw Yeshua's day. By this revelation he tasted the hope of eternal life and he rejoiced because he had found the joy of his salvation. We are told of Abraham, "And he believed the Lord; and he [God] reckoned it to him as righteousness."[15] The apostle Paul tells us in the book of Romans 4:23–25:

> 23: But the words, "it was reckoned to him," were written not for his sake alone, 24: but for ours also. It will be reckoned to us who believe in him that raised from the dead Yeshua our Lord, 25: who was put to death for our trespasses and raised for our justification.[16]

While many individual Jewish people throughout the ages have embraced Yeshua, the nation of Israel rejected him as a false Messiah. His coming did not bring the long-expected peace and redemption for which Israel had hoped. Far from it; since that time the Jewish people have faced unprecedented hardship, a two thousand-year exile from the land of Israel, and terrible suffering, often at the very hands of those who claimed to be Yeshua's followers. Many explanations have been attempted for why this is, yet, as we shall see in the next chapter, none is more astonishing than the reason given by Scripture itself.

If indeed the blowing of the *shofar* is a reminder of the binding of Isaac, then we may thus have our explanation of why it is a symbol of Israel's redemption. It evidently recalls that very moment when it suddenly all came together for Abraham when he saw the substitute for his son, the ram caught in the thicket, and understood the fullness of the promise when he saw Yeshua's day and rejoiced. In that moment, he perceived the plan for the redemption of Israel. In that moment, by faith, Abraham himself trusted in Yeshua and experienced the joy of personal redemption.

The promise, then, envisioned important elements concerning Israel's redemption: the place where the redemption will occur, Jerusalem, and

---

15. Gen 15:6 (RSV).
16. Rom 4:23–25(RSV).

more specifically, Mount Zion; resurrection, and a new eternal creation free from death, tears; and most importantly, the Lamb, Yeshua who is both the sacrifice for atonement and the king who will rule his people with perfect justice and peace.

THE SHOFAR AND THE PROPHETIC VOICE

Although the *shofar* is blown without a complete grasp of its true meaning, God is of course fully aware of its significance. He knows the sequence of future events that will eventually lead to Israel's acceptance of Yeshua as the Messiah. Hence, whenever the *shofar* is sounded it brings to his remembrance his promise to Abraham that, through the atonement of Yeshua, he will defend and redeem his people, Israel, and establish them in their own land.

> 42: "For thus says the Lord: Just as I have brought all this great evil upon this people, so I will bring upon them all the good that I promised them."[17]

Scripture assures us that there is yet coming a day when a trumpet shall sound in the heavens.[18] At that time God will keep his promise to Abraham. He will usher in his kingdom of everlasting peace; he will destroy the enemies of the Jewish people; he will establish his eternal dwelling on Mount Zion in Jerusalem; he will put an end to death forever, and will finally complete his plan for the redemption of the nation of Israel!

---

17. Jer 32:42 (RSV).
18. 1 Thess 4:16; 1 Cor 15:52; Rev 10:7.

2

And So All Israel Will Be Saved

HA TIKVAH—THE HOPE

THE MODERN REGATHERING OF the Jewish people into their ancient homeland and the reunification of Jerusalem under Jewish sovereignty in the year 1967 are unmistakably the fulfillment of biblical prophecy. God foretold through his prophets in ancient times that he would yet again restore the Jewish people to their homeland.[1] Through the dark night of the exile, in the midst of pogrom and holocaust, the Jewish people remembered God's words, drawing from them hope and strength to endure. The steadfast confidence of Israel in the promise of restoration in the face of millennia of suffering is expressed in the words of the Zionist hymn *Hatikvah*, which has become the Israeli national anthem.

> *Our hope is not yet lost,*
> *The hope of two thousand years,*
> *To be a free people in our land,*
> *The land of Zion and Jerusalem.*[2]

It was with this same trust in the faithfulness of God toward Israel that Paul the apostle addressed the Gentile believers in Yeshua of his day at Rome, in the eleventh chapter of his masterpiece, the Epistle to the Romans:

---

1. E.g., Isa 11:11; Ezek 37.
2. Imber, *Hatikva*.

> *25:* Lest you be wise in your own conceits, I want you to understand this mystery, brethren: a hardening has come upon part of Israel, until the full number of the Gentiles come in, *26:* and so all Israel will be saved . . .[3]

PAUL THE APOSTLE

Paul the apostle started out as Saul of Tarsus, a Pharisee and a student of Gamliel I.[4] The story of how he persecuted Jewish believers in Yeshua until he himself encountered Yeshua in a blinding light on the road to Damascus[5] is one of the most familiar stories to readers of the New Testament. As the good news of the Messiah was beginning to go forth throughout the world, God called Paul to be an apostle (one who is sent) to the uncircumcised.[6] His knowledge of the Torah, God's Law, and his excellent understanding of its true meaning made him the preeminent exponent of the doctrine of grace, which laid the theological foundation for the inclusion of the Gentiles into the body (congregation) of Messiah. In spite of this, Paul never lost his Jewish identity or the deep love that he had for his people. In the two chapters leading up to the eleventh chapter of his Letter to the Romans, he wrote:

> *2:* . . . I have great sorrow and unceasing anguish in my heart. *3:* For I could wish that I myself were accursed and cut off from Messiah for the sake of my brethren, my kinsmen by race. *4:* They are Israelites, and to them belong the sonship, the glory, the covenants, the giving of the law, the worship, and the promises . . .[7]
> *1:* Brethren, my heart's desire and prayer to God for them is that they may be saved.[8]

How ironic it is that in our day, when we are seeing the Jewish people returning from the diaspora, the insight of this "apostle to the Gentiles" holds so many keys needed for our understanding of the restoration and redemption of Israel.

---

3. Rom 11:25–26a (RSV).
4. Acts 22:3.
5. Acts.9:1–30.
6. Gal 1:15–16.
7. Rom 9:2–3, (RSV).
8. Rom 10:1 (RSV).

PAUL'S PURPOSE IN WRITING ROMANS 11

It is evident that Paul wrote the eleventh chapter of Romans in order to counter the claim that the Gentile church (which at this time was just coming into its own) had replaced the Jews as God's chosen people. According to such erroneous thinking, since the Jews had rejected Yeshua, God had rejected them. Their usefulness to God and his purposes had been forfeited. The Jewish nation is thus thought to be forsaken by God[9] and replaced by those Gentiles who have believed in Yeshua.[10] This false doctrine of supersessionism or replacement theology, which sees the church as the true heir of all the promises and blessings of the Old Testament, was to develop and take hold in the ensuing years after Paul's death. But even in his own day Paul saw this error creeping in. Chapter 11 of his epistle was written, it seems, with the intention of nipping this false teaching in the bud. Paul emphasized, "God has not rejected his people whom he foreknew..."[11] and struck a blow at the arrogance of Gentiles who harbored this false doctrine by reminding them that "... it is not you that support the root, but the root that supports you."[12] Unfortunately Paul's warning has gone largely unheeded over the centuries. This is witnessed by a history of Christian persecution, pogrom, and inquisition against the Jewish people.

ISRAEL'S ONLY SALVATION

When Paul proclaimed, "and so all Israel will be saved," what exactly did he mean? Let us consider what sort of salvation Paul intended. First and foremost, he foresaw that Israel's future salvation would be through acceptance of Yeshua the Messiah. Some have suggested that Israel has a special covenant with God that provides salvation apart from Yeshua's atoning death and resurrection (so-called "Dual Covenant Theology"[13]). Paul clearly understood that Israel's hope of redemption is solely in the acceptance of Yeshua, the Lamb foreseen by Abraham.[14] The idea that because Israel is God's chosen covenant people they have some alternative means of salvation apart from Yeshua did not even enter Paul's mind. Considering the

---

9. Rom 11:1.
10. Rom 11:17–19.
11. Rom 11:2a (RSV).
12. Rom 11:18b (RSV).
13. Sigal, "Aspects of Dual Covenant Theology," 1–2.
14. Rom 4 (see chapter 1).

views that Paul expressed in his epistles generally,[15] and particularly in his Letter to the Romans,[16] it is inconceivable that the salvation he foresaw for the Jewish people could be apart from Yeshua. This is especially clear from Romans 11:26–27:

> *26:* and so all Israel will be saved; as it is written, "The Deliverer will come from Zion, he will banish ungodliness from Jacob";
> *27:* "and this will be my covenant with them when I take away their sins."[17]

Paul clearly understood this deliverer to be none other than Yeshua, who died to take away sin[18] and who will make a "new covenant" with the Jewish people.[19] This is consistent with the rest of Scripture as well.[20]

A NATIONAL REDEMPTION

The salvation of the Jewish people is first of all spiritual—the forgiveness of sin and rebirth through acceptance of Yeshua the Messiah—but it is of a national character as well. The Scriptures without fail perceive the Jewish people as an indivisible, corporate, national whole, the chosen people of God. The covenant that God contracted at Mount Sinai with the Israelites was made with the whole people.[21] A "new covenant" was envisioned by Jeremiah the prophet.[22] This new covenant is unquestionably that enacted by Yeshua.[23] Just as the covenant at Sinai was made with the entire people of Israel, the "new covenant" is to be made with the whole house of Israel and the whole house of Judah. An individual Jew, though he be a king, prophet, or judge, was seen significant primarily in that he was a member of *Bnêy Israel*, the "Sons of Israel."

This fundamental national perception persists to this day in Israel. It is unquestionably a major reason why the people of Israel were able to preserve their identity in the face of nearly two thousand years of dispersion. It miraculously gave them the strength to keep alive their hope of nationhood

---

15. Titus 2:11–14; Eph 1:19–20.
16. Rom 1:16; 10:9.
17. Rom 11:26–27 (RSV).
18. 1 Tim 1:15; Titus 2:14.
19. 1 Cor 11:25; cf. Jer 31:31–35 and Heb 8:6–8.
20. See for instance Mic 5:2–4; Isa 9:6–7; 11:1–16; Ezek 37:22–24.
21. Exod 34:10, 27.
22. Jer 31:31; Heb 8:6–8.
23. See Luke 22:20.

until they saw the rebirth of the Jewish state in its ancient homeland. In addition to this, B. D. Napier has described the phenomenon of

> . . . Israel's habitual identification of one and many, her sense of total participation as people in that which was in reality experienced by others of her number (e.g. "We were Pharaoh's slaves in Egypt," that ancient cultic phrase of Deuteronomy 6:21), whether the others were one, a few, or many, and whether in the past, present, or future. In the faith of Israel the glorious survival and reconstruction of a remnant is Israel's glory and Israel's reestablishment.[24]

Thus it need only be a single generation of the Jewish people that actually experience the future national salvation. In the redemption of that one generation "all Israel will be saved." This spirit of peoplehood and continuity with the Israel of ancient days is well expressed in a stirring popular Israeli folk song, "Od Avinu Chai," the lyrics of which are profoundly simple:

> *Am Israel chai*: The nation of Israel lives on!
> *'Od avinu chai*: Our forefathers live on![25]

This national spirit of "Am Israel" along with the "identification of one and many" are important keys to understanding Romans 11.

AN ESCHATOLOGICAL REDEMPTION

The salvation of Israel is also eschatological, that promised to Israel in the end of days. This is in fact the promise of salvation and peace declared by the prophets to the nation of Israel.[26] This is indeed the very salvation that the Jewish people had expected, and still expect, the Messiah to bring. Paul's thesis is logical: since God has promised the Jewish people salvation through Messiah, and since ". . . the gifts and the call of God are irrevocable,"[27] that salvation must inevitably occur in the future. This is how Paul can say with assurance that the day is coming when all Israel will be saved.

SALVATION FOR THE WORLD

In Romans 11:11 Paul contends:

24. Napier, "Prophet, Prophetism," 917.
25. Carlebach, "Od Avinu Chai."
26. E.g., Isa 11:1–16; 25:6–9; 60:1–22; Ezek 37.
27. Rom 11:29 (RSV).

> *11:* So I ask, have they stumbled so as to fall? By no means! But through their trespass salvation has come to the Gentiles . . .[28]

How has the rejection of Yeshua by the Jewish people brought salvation to the Gentiles, that is to say, the rest of the world? In considering this question, we might ask what would have happened if they had not rejected Yeshua as a nation.

In the opening chapter of Acts, the resurrected Yeshua meets with his disciples and is about to be taken up from them in his ascension:

> *6:* So when they had come together, they asked him, "Lord, will you at this time restore the kingdom to Israel?"[29]

The disciples' question seems reasonable. It had been difficult for them to grasp Yeshua's mission of death and resurrection for the redemption of the world, but now that it had been accomplished the apostles were understandably curious to know if Yeshua would finally get down to doing what the Messiah was expected to do. Would he reestablish the Davidic kingdom of Israel[30] along with all the ancient promises for its salvation and exaltation? Would he at that time take up rulership of the world and establish everlasting peace?

> *7:* He [Yeshua] said to them, "It is not for you to know times or seasons which the Father has fixed by his own authority. *8:* But you shall receive power when the Holy Spirit has come upon you; and you shall be my witnesses in Jerusalem and in all Judea and Sama'ria and to the end of the earth."[31]

NOT YET

Yeshua did not deny that the kingdom would someday be restored to Israel. Neither is there any intimation here that Yeshua's kingdom would be merely a spiritual one. Rather, it is understood that a literal kingdom of Israel in which he, the Messiah, will be physically present to rule and reign will indeed eventually be realized. The new creation free of sin and death will yet be. The problem was that Israel had rejected the king and so, for the time being, the kingdom could not be restored. In essence, Yeshua answered them, "not yet." The disciples could not comprehend the timing of God's

---

28. Rom 11:11 (RSV).
29. Acts 1:6–8 (RSV).
30. Ezek 37:24–28; 2 Sam 7:16; Amos 9:11.
31. Acts 1:7–8 (RSV).

plan. The next item on the itinerary was not the restoration of the kingdom to Israel, but rather the going forth of the good news—the proclamation of salvation—to the entire world.

The messianic promise of salvation extended to Israel by the prophets had been primarily national.[32] Nevertheless, it seems that the reception of the kingdom that Yeshua offered was conditional on its being accepted by the nation willingly.[33] Entrance into the kingdom of God and its blessings had been strictly the prerogative of the people of Israel. Consequently, it was restricted to members of the Jewish nation. Had the Jewish nation accepted Yeshua as king, he would presumably have at that time set up his kingdom. Then the wrath of God would have fallen upon the Gentiles who were separated from the knowledge and grace of the God of Israel.[34] But since the king had been rejected by the nation of Israel, so had the kingdom. As a result, the exclusive qualification of being Israelite was no longer prerequisite for having citizenship in the kingdom. Henceforth, anyone, Jewish or Gentile, who personally acknowledges Yeshua and submits to his rulership can have the assurance of salvation and entrance into the kingdom of God. This evidently reciprocal effect of Israel's rejection of Yeshua and the kingdom becoming accessible to the individual is proclaimed in John 1:11–12:

> *11:* He came to his own home, and his own people received him not. *12:* But to all who received him, who believed in his name, he gave power to become children of God; who were born, not of blood nor of the will of the flesh nor of the will of man, but of God.[35]

As a result, God's offer of salvation through Yeshua had, on one hand, narrowed from a national to an individual scale. Its availability, on the other hand, had widened from members of a single nation to those of all nations. Since the condition for coming into the kingdom was no longer national, but individual, members of all nations, both Jewish and Gentile, were granted entry into the kingdom on the basis of personal acceptance of Yeshua's kingship.[36] The restoration of the kingdom to Israel was deferred to a future date. Ironically, instead of wrath falling upon the Gentiles, blessing had come to them. Thus the rejection of Yeshua by the nation of Israel actually made salvation available to the entire world.

32. Ezek 37:26–28; Dan 12:1–2; Joel 3:16–31.
33. John 1:11–12.
34. Eph 2:12; Jer 10:25; Ps 2:1–9; Rom 1:19–32.
35. John 1:11–12 (RSV); see also Rom 10:9–13.
36. Rom 10:1–12.

GOD'S PURPOSE IN ISRAEL'S REJECTION OF YESHUA

The salvation of the nations by the Messiah is an important theme in the Scriptures.

> *7:* I will tell of the decree of the Lord: He said to me, "You are my son, today I have begotten you. *8:* Ask of me, and I will make the nations your heritage, and the ends of the earth your possession."[37]
>
> *10:* In that day the root of Jesse shall stand as an ensign to the peoples; him shall the nations seek, and his dwellings shall be glorious.[38]
>
> *6:* he [God] says: "It is too light a thing that you should be my servant to raise up the tribes of Jacob and to restore the preserved of Israel; I will give you as a light to the nations, that my salvation may reach to the end of the earth."[39]

Israel had not been created for the sake of its own redemption only, but in order that the whole world might know the salvation of God through Yeshua the Messiah. From the beginning, God promised that Israel would be a blessing to the nations. This was an important element in God's promise to Abraham.[40] Ironically, it was through Israel's rejection that this promise has been fulfilled. But this is only half of the story, and the best is yet to come!

THE REST OF THE STORY

Paul goes on to ask:

> *12:* Now if their trespass means riches for the world, and if their failure means riches for the Gentiles, how much more will their full inclusion mean![41]

The thinking here is that if the nation of Israel's having erred in the rejection of Yeshua has brought great good, how much more will their doing well by accepting him bring that which is better! Paul continues:

---

37. Ps 2:7–9 (RSV).
38. Isa 11:10 (RSV).
39. Isa 49:6 (RSV); see also Isa 42:6; Amos 9:11.
40. Gen 22:18.
41. Rom 11:12 (RSV).

> *15:* For if their rejection means the reconciliation of the world, what will their acceptance mean but life from the dead?[42]

This statement is so astonishing that few have grasped its true meaning! Often these words are taken metaphorically. It is thought that Paul was merely suggesting that Jews coming to Yeshua would stir believers in Yeshua to revival, or that Israel's acceptance of their Messiah would revitalize the Jewish nation with new spiritual life. But Paul had in mind something much, much greater. He was speaking of nothing less than the literal resurrection from the dead when Yeshua returns to the earth![43]

This is seen all the more clearly when we consider the meaning of "life from the dead" in Romans 11:15 in the light of Daniel 12:1b–2a. In this passage the angel addresses Daniel, describing the eschatological salvation of the Jewish people:

> *1b:* And there shall be a time of trouble, such as never has been since there was *a nation* till that time; but at that time *your people* shall be delivered, every one whose name shall be found written in the book. *2:* And many of those who sleep in the dust of the earth shall awake . . .[44]

The references to "nation" and "your people" again demonstrate the national character of the salvation. That the people at that time "shall be delivered" may be compared with Paul's proclamation in Romans 11:26 (evidently quoting Isaiah 59:20) that "The deliverer will come from Zion . . ."[45] The book mentioned in Daniel 12:1b here is surely the record of those who have accepted Yeshua and have found salvation in him.[46] It is clear that the resurrection in Daniel 12:2 is physical and not merely spiritual.

Paul thus proclaimed that a day is coming when the Jewish people will, as a nation, recognize Yeshua as king and Messiah and that as a result he will at that time return to restore the kingdom to Israel. At his appearance those who have died believing in him, throughout the ages, both Jewish and Gentile, shall be raised to eternal life even as he himself was resurrected. Scripture makes it clear that this national salvation of the Jewish people must take place in the land of Israel with Jerusalem as its capital.[47] This is

---

42. Rom 11:15 (RSV).
43. 1 Thess 4:13–18; 1 Cor 15:42–56.
44. Dan 12:1b–2a (RSV), emphasis added.
45. Rom 11:26 (RSV).
46. See Rev 3:5; 13:8; 20:12,15; 21:7.
47. Ezek 37; Isa 25:6–9; Zech 12.

moreover confirmed by the promise that Yeshua shall return to the Mount of Olives on the east of Jerusalem.

> *3:* Then the Lord will go forth and fight against those nations as when he fights on a day of battle. *4:* On that day his feet shall stand on the Mount of Olives which lies before Jerusalem on the east; and the Mount of Olives shall be split in two from east to west by a very wide valley; so that one half of the Mount shall withdraw northward, and the other half southward.[48]

That he will return as the result of his national acceptance by the Jewish people is attested to by a number of other passages in the New Testament. The best known is Matthew 23:37–39. Yeshua is addressing Jerusalem, the national, political capital of the Jewish people, when he proclaims:

> *37:* "O Jerusalem, Jerusalem, . . . How often would I have gathered your children together as a hen gathers her brood under her wings, and you would not! *38:* Behold, your house [the Temple] is forsaken and desolate. *39:* For I tell you, you will not see me again, until you say, 'Blessed is he who comes in the name of the Lord.'"[49]

The phrase translated "Blessed is he who comes" is the Hebraic expression *barûch ha ba*, which means "welcome."[50] Thus Yeshua will not return to Jerusalem until the city's inhabitants recognize him as Messiah and cry "welcome"!

Another example is found in Acts 3:13–26. Peter here addresses the Jewish nation from what was then its national spiritual center, the Temple of Jerusalem. He upbraids the people for their rejection of Yeshua.

> *17:* "Now I know, brothers, that neither you nor your leaders had any idea what you were really doing; *18:* this was the way God carried out what he had foretold when he said through all his prophets that his Messiah would suffer. *19:* Now you must repent and turn to God, so that your sins may be wiped out, *20:* and so that the Lord may send the time of comfort. Then he will send you the Messiah he has predestined, that is Yeshua, *21:* whom heaven must keep till the universal restoration comes which God proclaimed, speaking through his holy prophets.[51]

---

48. Zech 14:3–4 (RSV); see also Acts 1:9–12.
49. Matt 23:37–39 (RSV); cf. Luke 13:35; cf. Ps 18:26.
50. See Ps 118:26.
51. Acts 3:17–21 (Jerusalem Bible).

Peter declares here that when the Jewish people repent and turn to God, Yeshua the Messiah will be sent to them and that heaven must keep him until the time of the restoration. That which "God proclaimed, speaking through his holy prophets" in verse 21 of course refers to the messianic redemption, that is, the restoration of the kingdom to Israel. Its coming is evidently conditional upon the Jewish people accepting Yeshua. As in Acts 1:7–8 (see above), there is an emphasis on God's timing.

In Romans 11:15 Paul envisioned not only the restoration of the kingdom to Israel, but also the resurrection of all Jews and Gentiles who have individually accepted Yeshua during their lifetimes. He thus envisioned the final, total salvation in the Messiah. By their rejection the Jewish people opened the way of salvation for the world; by their acceptance they will bring the fullness of that salvation to the remnant of Israel and Gentile believers in Yeshua. By their acceptance of Yeshua, the Jewish people will fulfill the second half of their mandate to be a blessing to the nations!

HOLDING THE DOOR OPEN

Paul makes it clear that it was according to God's plan that Israel would reject the Messiah and so open the way for the salvation of the world. This is the subject of chapters 9 and 10 of Romans. Moreover, the hand of God can be seen in certain historical developments that have assured that this door of salvation remains open by, in effect, hindering the ability of the Jewish people to accept Yeshua as a unified nation in their own land.

The Destruction of Jerusalem

After the First Revolt of the Jews against Rome, in 70 CE, the Jewish national capital, Jerusalem, and its spiritual center, the Temple, were destroyed by the Romans, in fulfillment of Yeshua's word in Luke 21:24. Later, Jews were banned from living in Jerusalem by the decree of the emperor Hadrian following the Second Jewish Revolt against the Romans in 132–136 CE.

The Jewish Diaspora

For nearly two thousand years after the destruction, the Jewish people have been scattered throughout the nations of the world, again as prophesied by Yeshua in Luke 21: 24. Consequently, the Jewish nation has not been able to be united in its land to "repent and turn again."

Rabbinic Judaism

After the destruction of Jerusalem, a group of sages met in the academy at Yavneh in order to reconstitute Judaism without its Temple. The pluralism of Second Temple Period Judaism, which permitted a measure of liberty within Jewish practice and belief, was eliminated. On the one hand, this united the Jewish nation in the aftermath of the debacle of 70 CE; on the other hand, it resulted in Jewish Christianity being branded as heterodox. In effect, this assured that the Jewish nation would not accept Yeshua as Messiah (see chapter 10).

The Bar Kochba Revolt

The Jews of the land of Israel revolted against Rome a second time in the year 132 CE. The leader of the revolt, Shimon "Bar Kochba," was proclaimed the Messiah by Rabbi Akiba. Jewish believers in Yeshua of necessity withdrew their support of the revolt since they could not accept any messiah other than Yeshua. This drove an even deeper wedge between Jewish believers in Yeshua and their fellow Jewish countrymen.

Replacement Theology and the Gentilization of Yeshua

Towards the end of the first century AD, the good news of the Messiah had already reached the ends of the Roman Empire. By sheer numbers, the Gentiles grew to be predominant over the Jews within the body of believers in Yeshua. Because Gentile Christians did not understand Israel's unique role in the redemption of the world, they failed to recognize the Jewish nation's need to remain a distinct people faithful to the commandments of their covenant with God, the Torah. By the fourth century, Gentile Christians had succeeded in choking Jewish Christianity out of existence. The body of believers in Messiah being devoid of Jewish influence, Yeshua and the message of salvation were given a very Gentile appearance. Just as Joseph the patriarch in his Egyptian apparel[52] was not recognizable to his brothers, the sons of Israel, so the true identity of Yeshua the Messiah has been kept hidden from his Jewish brothers by the "attire" his Gentile followers have "clad" him in (see chapter 15).

---

52. Gen 42:8, 23.

Paul makes it clear that the time of rejection is divinely controlled and limited. It will end when the "full number of the Gentiles [who are to enter the kingdom] come in."[53]

THE TIME FOR ESTABLISHING ALL THINGS

A popular dispensationalist belief holds that God will one day turn away from the Gentiles and turn back to the Jews. According to this view, God revealed himself to Israel, his chosen people, in Old Testament times. But since the "birth of the church" we have been living in "the age of the Gentiles," a "dispensation" in which God is presently dealing exclusively with, and blessing only the predominantly Gentile church. The Jewish people are at this time far from his will and purposes. In the future, when "the age of the Gentiles" comes to an end, God will turn away from the Gentiles and will deal exclusively with the Jews. This thinking is closely akin to replacement theology. In order to turn back to the Jews, it is implied that God has turned away from them. But Romans 11:2 assures us that God has not rejected his people. He has always kept the Jewish people focused in the very center of his plan. Even at this time, through their rejection of Yeshua's messiahship, they are accomplishing God's purposes by holding open the door of salvation to the world.

The error in this thinking that God has turned away from Israel is partly the result of a confusion of two expressions found in the New Testament. The first is in Luke 21:24. Here Yeshua foresees a future when the Romans will besiege Jerusalem and the Jews will be dispersed throughout the nations:

> *23b:* "For there will be great distress in the land and wrath upon this people. *24:* And they will fall by the edge of the sword, and be led away captive into all nations. And Jerusalem will be trampled by Gentles until *the times of the Gentiles* are fulfilled."[54]

These "times of the Gentiles" thus represent the centuries during which the Gentiles ruled over Jerusalem. Since 70 CE, a long succession of nations has lorded over this city, from the Roman Empire to the British Empire and finally the Hashemite kingdom of Jordan. This period evidently came to an end in the 1967 Six-Day War, when Israel wrested control of East Jerusalem from the Jordanians. Since then, all of Jerusalem (with the possible exception of the Temple Mount[55]) has been in Jewish hands.

---

53. Rom 11:25 (RSV).
54. Luke 21:24b (NKJV), emphasis added.
55. The site of the ancient Temple, the spiritual center of the Jewish people, is the

The second expression is found in the passage that we have been discussing in Romans 11:25–26a. Paul writes:

> 25: For I do not desire, brethren, that you should be ignorant of this mystery, lest you should be wise in your own opinion, that blindness in part has happened to Israel until *the fullness of the Gentiles* has come in. 26: And so all Israel will be saved . . .[56]

The two expressions "the times of the Gentiles" and "the fullness of the Gentiles" sound somewhat alike (and thus the confusion), but they have two absolutely different meanings. The "times of the Gentiles" refers to the period that foreign nations occupied the land of Israel, evidently lasting until the year 1967; "the fullness of the Gentiles" refers to the full number of non-Jews who by faith in Yeshua enter into God's kingdom. The "times of the Gentiles" has, it seems, already passed, but "the fullness of the Gentiles" has not. In fact, Jewish and Gentile individuals shall continually come to faith in Yeshua right up to the moment of his return.

A LIGHT TO THE NATIONS—HAVE THE JEWISH PEOPLE FAILED?

It is often claimed that the Jewish people have failed their mandate to be a "light to the nations" and a blessing to the Gentiles. It is written, for instance:

> "Thus says the Lord of hosts: In those days ten men from the nations of every tongue shall take hold of the robe of a Jew, saying, 'Let us go with you, for we have heard that God is with you.'"[57]

The imagined scenario is that the Jewish people should have accepted Yeshua and all become believers in him. Then they would have become a nation of messengers sent out to the four corners of the earth to make known the good news to the Gentiles. But, because God's original plan had failed in that the Jewish people did not accept Yeshua, God had no choice but to go to a contingency "plan B." Thus God turned to the Gentiles instead, making them the primary agents in spreading the good news of Yeshua the Messiah to the world. As a result, the Jewish people have been left out of the picture at least until God "turns back to the Jews."

---

most important part of Jerusalem. The fact that it is legally in Jewish hands but under Muslim authority suggests that the "times of the Gentiles" may in fact not yet be completely over. In this regard, compare the language of Rev 11:2 with that of Luke. 21:24.

56. Rom 11:25–26a (NKJV), emphasis added.

57. Zech 8:23 (RSV).

However, as we have seen, the purpose of Romans 11 is to show that the Jewish people have not been left out in the cold and that God has not annulled his promises to them, including the promise that they would be a blessing to the Gentiles. Ironically, Paul tells us, that it is through their rejection that they have brought salvation to the world. This suggests that if the Jewish people had received Yeshua as Messiah, the world would not have had a chance to accept him! If after his death and resurrection the Jewish people had received him as Messiah, he would have begun his reign as king on this planet. Any door of opportunity for the Gentiles to accept him would have been shut forever. Rather, by Israel's rejection, salvation has come to the world. Their continuing rejection as a nation assures that the door remains open to all, both Jew and Gentile. God of course was hardly taken by surprise when Israel rejected the Messiah. That God foresaw that this would occur was prophesied, for instance, in Isaiah 53:3:

> He was despised and rejected by men; a man of sorrows, and acquainted with grief; and as one from whom men hide their faces he was despised, and we esteemed him not.[58]

And in Psalm 118:22–23:

> 22: The stone which the builders rejected has become the head of the corner. 23: This is the Lord's doing; it is marvelous in our eyes.[59]

Moreover, it is clear that, far from being a contingency plan, it was God's perfect will right from the beginning that the Jewish people would reject Yeshua. This is evident from reading the two chapters leading up to Romans 11, chapters 9 and 10. Moreover, the Jewish people will yet fulfill the second part of their mandate to be a blessing to the Gentiles through their acceptance as a nation of Yeshua as the Messiah.

There is nothing at all in Scripture to suggest that as Israel awakens to the true identity of her Messiah God will turn away from the Gentiles. Rather, he continues to extend his offer of grace to the world, ". . . to the Jew first and also to the Greek."[60] And he shall do so until he has reached everyone who will accept his offer. When the very last one has come in, God shall then respond to the unified cry of the Jewish people. He will send Yeshua, the long-promised Messiah, ". . .and so all Israel will be saved"!

---

58. Isa 53:3 (RSV).
59. Ps 118:22–23 (RSV); cf. 1 Pet 2:4–8.
60. Rom 1:16.

3

The Torah: A Schoolmaster to Lead Us to Messiah

God promised Abraham that he would make of him a great nation. However, with this assurance came bittersweet news:

> *13:* Then the Lord said to Abram, "Know of a surety that your descendants will be sojourners in a land that is not theirs, and will be slaves there, and they will be oppressed for four hundred years; *14:* but I will bring judgment on the nation which they serve, and afterward they shall come out with great possessions.[1]

Four hundred years later, when Abraham's descendants had indeed grown into a great and mighty people, God delivered them from the slavery of Egypt with an outstretched arm.

THE MOUNTAIN THAT BURNED WITH FIRE

En route to the promised land, under the leadership of Moses, God brought the people of Israel through the desert to Mount Sinai, also known as Mount Horeb. A terrifying sight greeted their eyes when they arose on the morning of the third day of their encampment there, described in Exodus 19–20. In the thick, gloomy darkness the mountain burned with fire. Thunderings and rumblings of an earthquake were accompanied by the frightful sounding of a trumpet that made all who heard it in the camp tremble. It was the

---

1. Gen 15:13–14 (RSV).

defining moment for the people of Israel as they stood, united as a single nation, and heard the voice of Almighty God speaking to them out of heaven. Such was the glory, the awe, and the terror that attended God's giving of the Torah, his Law, to Israel. In so doing, God established with the people of Israel his special covenant. The Torah was to be Israel's national constitution, code of laws, and spiritual guide of conduct for day to day living.

A SCHOOLMASTER

The Torah served yet another vital purpose. Paul wrote in Galatians 3:24, "Wherefore the law was our schoolmaster to bring us unto Messiah, that we might be justified by faith."[2] Paul called the Torah a "schoolmaster" to bring us to Messiah. The original Greek word he used that is translated as "schoolmaster" is *paidagogos*,[3] from the same root that we get our word "pedagogy," the art or profession of teaching. However, the *paidagogos* was not himself actually a teacher but was rather a servant who, in the aristocratic Roman family, was charged with the care of a child until he came of age.[4] One of the duties of this guardian was to conduct the juvenile to and from his lessons.

How is the Torah a "schoolmaster" to bring us to Messiah? In this chapter we will focus on how the Torah leads an individual to Messiah. In a later chapter we will extend the principles that we discuss here to see how they apply to the entire nation of Israel.

The Torah leads a person to the Messiah in two stages. In the first stage he becomes aware of his need for salvation. In the second stage, he recognizes that Yeshua the Messiah is the answer to that need.

STAGE 1: THE NEED FOR SALVATION

Paul asks, "Wherefore then serveth the law?"[5] If Abraham already had been given a sure promise by God that his descendants would be redeemed, why did God complicate matters by later giving the nation of Israel a rigorous system of commandments, the obedience to which was conditional for his blessing? Paul answers his own question by saying that the Law was added because of transgression, that is to say, the Law was added in order to deal with the problem of sin. In Romans 3:20 he says explicitly, ". . . through the

---

2. Gal 3:24 (KJV).
3. Vine, *Expository Dictionary*, 595.
4. Vine, *Expository Dictionary*, 595.
5. Gal 3:19 (KJV).

law comes knowledge of sin."[6] The Law was necessary in order to make sin visible and to show its true nature. It is the problem of sin that stands as the main obstacle to God's redeeming Israel.

The Way It Has Always Been

We have come to accept that pride dishonesty, greed, hate, lust, avarice, and violence are all normal components of human nature. We also acknowledge sickness, pain, and death as part of the natural cycle of life. When we see chaos and destruction in the world, we believe that this is how it has always been, but this is not so.

The Knowledge of Good and Evil

Scripture gives us a glimpse of a world created in perfect order and harmony without pain, sickness, or death.[7] It testifies to how God's creation originally demonstrated the perfection and order of the Creator; how it operated in flawless working order with God himself ruling it. Man was created as an eternal being intended to live forever in perfect health and peace. God delegated authority to man to rule over his own domain, that is to say, the earth and everything in it. Man was created in a totally sinless condition. As such, he was completely innocent.

By way of illustration, we may compare him with a small child who comes across a book for the first time in his life. The child of course does not understand its use or its value. When he starts tearing pages out of the book he has no inkling that he is doing anything at all wrong. He is simply exploring the book as a part of the world around him. The first time that it occurs to him that there may be something wrong is when his horrified mother comes rushing into the room angrily shouting at him to stop. It would be unjustified to punish the child, no matter how valuable the book is. He cannot be held responsible for knowing that what he is doing is not good. He simply does not know any better and his conscience remains completely clear of any wrongdoing. He has no knowledge of good and evil. The state of total innocence that man originally had in the garden is similar to that of the small child: whatever he did, he had no sense of wrongdoing or guilt.

---

6. Rom 3:20 (RSV); see also Rom 7:13.

7. Gen 1–2.

The Tree

There was nothing intrinsically bad about the Tree of the Knowledge of Good and Evil in the garden of Eden, that is to say, its fruit was not bitter or poisonous. In fact we are told that it was good for food.[8] The tree itself was neither good nor evil, but neutral. However, God had explicitly told the man that he was not to eat from it. By giving this single commandment that was neither difficult nor complex, God enabled the man to demonstrate his obedience and love toward him. As long as the man obeyed his Creator, the tree stood as a signpost, a symbol for the man's obedience and loyalty to his Maker. Up to the point that he ate the fruit, the man was totally innocent as the small child. Like the child without knowledge of good and evil, all was permitted to him. The man knew only good and had no sense of guilt. Satan entered the scene with the promise that by eating the fruit one would become like God, having the power of knowing good and evil. The thought of attaining equality with God greatly appealed to the man's pride.

The Rebellion

The rebellion against God's rule began with man's disobedience to God's commandment as a deliberate act of his will, made in the depths of his heart. Suddenly he experienced doing wrong. As a result, sin entered his heart and it became darkened, filled with every sort of evil. Well did Jeremiah the prophet say, "The heart is deceitful above all things, and desperately corrupt; who can understand it?"[9] Likewise, Yeshua declared:

> *21:* "For from within, out of the heart of man, come evil thoughts, fornication, theft, murder, adultery, *22:* coveting, wickedness, deceit, licentiousness, envy, slander, pride, foolishness. *23:* All these evil things come from within, and they defile a man."[10]

Man's Abdication of the Rule of the World

When he deliberately chose to disobey the single commandment that God had given him, man was introduced experientially to evil. Now, suddenly, he knew evil, not merely in theory, but through willful participation in it. By Satan's guile, he indeed gained knowledge of good and evil. Only

---

8. Gen 3:6.
9. Jer 17:9 (RSV).
10. Mark 7:21–23 (RSV).

when he had actually tasted of evil could he by contrast recognize what was truly good.

In obeying the voice of Satan rather than that of God, the man submitted to Satan's authority, trading the freedom he had in God's kingdom for servitude under Satan's rule. In doing so, he turned over all that God had delegated to his stewardship, the earth and everything in it, to the dominion of Satan. He abdicated not only his own right to rule but also that of his descendants. Thus, when Satan tempted Yeshua in the Judean wilderness he was rightfully able to claim ownership of all the kingdoms of the world.

> *5:* And the devil took him [Yeshua] up, and showed him all the kingdoms of the world in a moment of time, *6:* and said to him, "To you I will give all this authority and their glory; for it has been delivered to me, and I give it to whom I will. *7:* If you, then, will worship me, it shall all be yours." *8:* And Yeshua answered him, "It is written, 'You shall worship the Lord your God, and him only shall you serve.'"[11]

The one who had delivered this authority and the glory of the kingdoms to Satan was none other than Adam, the first man himself, by means of his obedience to Satan's voice. By changing his alliance from God to Satan, it was as if man had signed a legal contract giving power of attorney over all he had to Satan. Adam by his disobedience sold the entire human race into slavery to sin.[12]

A Chain Reaction

Man's rebellion against God's word created a chain reaction—". . . sin came into the world through one man . . ."[13]—opening a Pandora's box to all sorts of wrongdoing. Suddenly man's world was full of sin. The moment he chose to disobey God's single commandment, all other sins were already waiting at the door: lying, adultery, murder, etc. It was only a matter of time and opportunity for all these sins to be committed. Just as one lie naturally leads to a second in order to cover the first, so the initial transgression of man against God's command led to another and yet another wrong. Sin, like a cancer, had soon spread to every fiber of man's nature. Man's sin is the core reason for his lack of peace within and without and the root cause of war.

---

11. Luke 4:5–8 (RSV).
12. Rom 7:14.
13. Rom 5:12a (RSV).

1: What causes wars, and what causes fightings among you? Is it not your passions that are at war in your members? *2:* You desire and do not have; so you kill. And you covet and cannot obtain; so you fight and wage war. You do not have, because you do not ask. *3:* You ask and do not receive, because you ask wrongly, to spend it on your passions.[14]

The Broken Cog

Man's rebellion set him in conflict with his Creator. Since it is God's authority that runs every component of the universe that he created, and since man chose to rebel against him, man is at odds with his fellow human beings, and even with himself. Man became out of order in God's universe. Just as a single broken cog or a missing screw in a machine can cause the entire machine to break down, so man's sin has brought chaos to God's entire creation. In his rebellion man also dragged all that was under his care and authority into rebellion with him: his spouse, his offspring and even the very environment in which he lived. Romans 8:20 tells us that nature itself was made subject to the consequences of sin.

...for the creation was subjected to futility, not of its own will...[15]

The Obstacle to God's Establishing His Rule on Earth

Sin is what prevents God from establishing his kingdom on earth. God wants to restore his perfect order and peace to our world as it was in his original creation, and eventually someday he will. In order to do this he must reestablish his rulership over mankind, whom he had placed in charge of his creation. The obstacle to his doing so is man's continued rebellion against him. Man refuses to be ruled by God and there is no place in God's kingdom for one who will not submit to the authority of the king. The defiant mutineer, dissonant with his Maker, has become a liability to the world of which he had been placed at the helm.

---

14. Jas 4:1–3.
15. Rom 8:20 (RSV).

Consequences of Sin

The sentence for this high treason against God's rule is nothing less than death.

> 23: For the wages of sin is death . . .[16]
>
> 12: Therefore as sin came into the world through one man and death through sin, and so death spread to all men because all men sinned . . .[17]

Furthermore, the planet, which was placed in the charge of man, also came under the sentence of death.[18] So riddled is mankind with sin that he is no more able to rid himself of it by his own power than a terminal cancer patient can, by strength of his own will, heal himself of his disease. Sickness and pain are, after all, but minor facets of death.

Howbeit, a man is more than merely a physical body. His spirit remains eternal. Death is separation from life, and the ultimate source of all life is God. Because God is entirely holy, he cannot bear to look on iniquity.[19] The ultimate death is spiritual death, what the Scriptures call "the second death,"[20] which is eternal separation from God in hell.

When tempting Eve to eat the fruit, Satan assured her, "You will not die . . ."[21] This was partly true in that when she and Adam had eaten of the fruit they did not drop dead instantly. Rather, they died at once inwardly, spiritually, and at the same time began the process of dying physically. Although a cut flower may appear fresh for a time before it withers, it has nonetheless already begun to wilt the moment that its stem is severed. A terminal cancer patient is dying even though he may live for months or years after the disease has begun to affect him. Likewise, a person, because he is thoroughly affected by sin, has already begun to die from the moment he is born.

Death Reigned

To make matters worse, people are blithely unaware that the dilemma that besets them even exists or that there is anything that they can do about it. This ignorance does not, however, stay the execution of the sentence.

16. Rom 6:23a (RSV).
17. Rom 5:12 (RSV).
18. Rom 8:19–24.
19. Hab 1:13.
20. Rev 2:11; 20:6, 14.
21. Gen 3:4.

> *13:* To be sure, sin was in the world earlier than the law, but in absence of law, sin is not accounted. *14:* Death, however, held rule from Adam to Moses over those who sinned but did not transgress a command in the way Adam, who foreshadowed the Coming One, had done.[22]

Adam, by eating the fruit, transgressed the specific commandment that God had given him. It awakened within him the knowledge of good and evil, which he passed down to his descendants. From the time of Adam until the giving of the Torah at Mount Sinai, people continued to sin, although they did not transgressed any specific command, as had Adam. The knowledge of good and evil within their hearts condemned them. The awareness of sin was based on a person's conscience, which is quite malleable. What causes one man's conscience to accuse him allows another man's conscience to excuse him. In order to make sin visible, the commandments of the Torah set clear boundaries that were recognizable to everyone. These boundaries served as fences. Transgression is crossing the boundary. If the boundary or fence does not exist, it is impossible to transgress it. This is why Paul said, "in absence of law, sin is not accounted." This does not mean that the sin is not there, only that it cannot be recognized. The reason for the Law is to make sin visible in order that it can be dealt with.

Like the features of the body, sin is passed down from parent to child. Every person comes into this world with the inclination to sin. The moment he actually does sin, he must face sin's penalty, death. Between the time of Adam and the moment when the Torah was given to Moses, there was ignorance of sin and its consequences. Although Adam's descendants did not make the initial decision to rebel as he had, sin had nevertheless permeated every area of their existence and so had death. People over time came to accept that sickness and death were natural and inescapable. The first step to God establishing his kingdom and putting an end to the principles of sin and death was to make people aware of the problem and its cause. This is where the Torah came in.

God's Standard

How can a person be made aware of his sin if he has no means by which to judge it? The entire world around him is infected with the same disease. The world in which he lives is full of wrongdoing, and consequentially death. From cradle to coffin he knows nothing else. Only God, who is outside

---

22. Rom 5:14 (Revised Berkeley Version).

this sin-ridden world, is able set the sin-free standard of righteousness. His Torah, expressed mainly in the first five books of the Scriptures—Genesis, Exodus, Leviticus, Numbers, and Deuteronomy—is the perfect measure by which a man can judge himself and so recognize his sin. The Law acts as a mirror so that by looking into its perfection a man can see how extensive his own deformation is.

Each person tends to see himself as basically good. Only when he compares his life to the standard of the Torah does he immediately become aware of the flaw within himself. A sheep may appear absolutely white until it walks out onto a hillside covered with newly fallen snow.

All or Nothing

The Law promises that if a man is able to perfectly keep all of its demands he shall prove himself worthy of escaping death. The Torah, however, demands 100 percent compliance. With the first failure, all is lost. Hence, any attempt to keep God's commandments perfectly as described in the Law quickly ends in frustration.

The people of Israel, at Mount Sinai, obliged themselves before God to keep the entire Law.

> 8: And all the people answered together and said, "All that the Lord has spoken we will do.: And Moses reported the words of the people to the Lord."[23]

However, as much as they wished to keep the Law perfectly, they were unable to do so. Paul, quoting Deuteronomy 27:26, tells us:

> 10: For all who rely on works of the law are under a curse; for it is written, "Cursed be every one who does not abide by *all things* written in the book of the law, and do them."[24]

James, the half-brother of Yeshua, also spoke absolutely clearly about this matter:

> 10: For whoever keeps the whole law but fails in one point has become guilty of all of it.[25]

An interesting account in the New Testament tells how Yeshua was teaching when a rich young ruler approached him:

---

23. Exod 19:8 (RSV).
24. Gal 3:10 (RSV), emphasis added.
25. Jas 2:10 (RSV).

16: And behold, one came up to him, saying, "Teacher, what good deed must I do, to have eternal life?" *17:* And he said to him, "Why do you ask me about what is good? One there is who is good. If you would enter life, keep the commandments." *18:* He said to him, "Which?" And Yeshua said, "You shall not kill, You shall not commit adultery, You shall not steal, You shall not bear false witness, *19:* Honor your father and mother, and, You shall love your neighbor as yourself." *20:* The young man said to him, "All these I have observed; what do I still lack?" *21:* Yeshua said to him, "If you would be perfect, go, sell what you possess and give to the poor, and you will have treasure in heaven; and come, follow me." *22:* When the young man heard this he went away sorrowful; for he had great possessions.[26]

Note that when the young man asks Yeshua what needs to be done to obtain eternal life, Yeshua responds by listing specific commandments of the Torah. If it were possible for a man to keep all the commandments of the Torah perfectly from cradle to grave, he would be free from sin and consequently also free from the penalty of death. Apparently, the young man was convinced in his own mind that he had succeeded in keeping all the commandments. However, Yeshua targeted the area in his life that made it evident to him that he had failed to meet the mark. His love of money prevented him from loving God with all his heart, soul, and strength, and his neighbor as himself.

The Spiritual Depth of the Law

Yeshua, in his Sermon on the Mount, emphasized that the spirit of the Law goes much deeper than the mere mechanical observance of the Law's commands outwardly. True obedience to the Law begins within a person's heart. We have seen that the source of the rebellion is man's heart. Therefore, it is important that the Torah, in its role of pointing out sin, thoroughly exposes the true intention of every heart. Yeshua made it clear that being angry with one's fellow is tantamount to murder[27] and that looking lustfully upon a woman is synonymous with adultery.[28] In this light it quickly becomes evident that the evil of sin has so penetrated the heart of every man that it is irreparable and that a person is entirely powerless to save himself. Thus he becomes aware of his total dependence on God to provide the solution for his sinfulness.

26. Matt 19:16–22 (RSV).
27. Matt 5:21–22.
28. Matt 5:27–28.

Why is it so impossible for a person to faithfully keep the commandments, not only for a lifetime, but even for a few moments? We might conclude that the problem is in the Torah itself, that somehow it is defective, but this is not so. "The law of the Lord is perfect, reviving the soul . . ."[29] Likewise, Paul proclaimed that the "Law is holy and good." There is no defect at all in the Torah. Rather, the reason that we find it impossible to keep its precepts is that the defect is within us; it is our sin. It is only through the Torah that we are made fully aware of it. Paul sums up in Romans 7:10–15:

> *10:* the very commandment which promised life proved to be death to me. *11:* For sin, finding opportunity in the commandment, deceived me and by it killed me. *12:* So the law is holy, and the commandment is holy and just and good. *13:* Did that which is good, then, bring death to me? By no means! It was sin, working death in me through what is good, in order that sin might be shown to be sin, and through the commandment might become sinful beyond measure. *14:* We know that the law is spiritual; but I am carnal, sold under sin. *15:* I do not understand my own actions. For I do not do what I want, but I do the very thing I hate.[30]

Looking for a Loophole

My father loved sports of all kinds. He was even invited as a young man to a try out for professional baseball with the St. Louis Cardinals. He enjoyed playing all sorts of ball games. His meager stature did not prevent him from competing wholeheartedly in basketball. When we moved into a new home, he had the cement laid for a half-court in the backyard. The day we went out to play on it for the first time, we realized that there was something different about this court. The basket was somewhat lower than regulation height! Not only did this even the odds considerably in my dad's favor, but it also made it possible for him to fulfill his lifetime dream to be able to slam-dunk the ball.

Lowering the Hoop

Such is human nature. We are always looking to bend the rules of the game to our advantage. In fact, this is what all human religions do. They present a set of rules of dos and don'ts that a person must keep for his justification, based on a balance-scales system in which if the good in a person's life

---

29. Ps 19:7a (RSV).
30. Rom 7:10–15 (RSV).

outweighs the bad, then he has earned his just reward: Paradise, Nirvana, or the like. But this is merely lowering the hoop to one's own height The problem is that every religion of mankind has been made up by sinful men who live in a sin-riddled world. Again, only God, who is himself outside of his creation and entirely sinless, can set the measure of righteousness. God's standard is infinitely higher than ours. He demands nothing less than absolute holiness and perfection.

The people of Israel were instructed to keep the Torah before them at all times:

> *4:* "Hear, O Israel: The Lord our God is one Lord; *5:* and you shall love the Lord your God with all your heart, and with all your soul, and with all your might. *6:* And these words which I command you this day shall be upon your heart; *7:* and you shall teach them diligently to your children, and shall talk of them when you sit in your house, and when you walk by the way, and when you lie down, and when you rise. *8:* And you shall bind them as a sign upon your hand, and they shall be as frontlets between your eyes. *9:* And you shall write them on the doorposts of your house and on your gates."[31]
>
> *46:* he [Moses] said to them, "Lay to heart all the words which I enjoin upon you this day, that you may command them to your children, that they may be careful to do all the words of this law. *47:* For it is no trifle for you, but it is your life, and thereby you shall live long in the land which you are going over the Jordan to possess."[32]

A person constantly looking into the perfection of the Torah recognizes his total inability to meet God's standard. The defect within himself, sin, suddenly becomes clearly visible.

The religions of the world make all sorts of claims to bring peace and happiness, but as they say, "the proof is in the pudding"! The penalty for sin is death. Any philosophy or religion that claims to justify a man before God must provide a solution that will completely put an end to death, both spiritually and physically. None of the world's religions has ever done so. Sin has infected every person on the planet and so has death! All are guilty.

> *10:* as it is written: "None is righteous, no, not one; *11:* no one understands, no one seeks for God. *12:* All have turned aside, together they have gone wrong; no one does good, not even one."[33]

---

31. Deut 6:4 (RSV).
32. Deut 32:46–47 (RSV).
33. Rom 3:10–12, (RSV); cf. Ps 14:1–3.

Because of the extent of sin, no person is capable of escaping the punishment of death. Scripture tells us that the Law is intended to convict us and to shut us up in jail.

> 23 Now before faith came, we were imprisoned and guarded under the law until faith would be revealed.[34]

The intent is to show that no man can justify himself by his own efforts before God.

> *19:* Now we know that whatever the law says it speaks to those who are under the law, so that every mouth may be stopped, and the whole world may be held accountable to God. *20:* For no human being will be justified in his sight by works of the law, since through the law comes knowledge of sin.[35]

Thus the Torah makes us aware that we are caught in a cage with steel bars on every side, a prison cell on death row from which there is no escape except through a single narrow door. That door is Yeshua the Messiah.[36]

STAGE 2: POINTING THE WAY TO REDEMPTION

The fact that the Law makes us aware of our sin does not provide a solution to our dilemma. M. R. DeHann uses the illustration of how a mirror is useful to show a man that he has a dirty face, but makes a poor implement to clean it.

> The law then became like a mirror to reveal the true condition of the sinner as he is. Without the mirror man did not see himself as he really is. But that is all a mirror can do—show the filthiness of the face, and the need for cleansing. It cannot do the washing. To take the mirror and try to use it for a washcloth will only smear the dirt and spread it all over your face. To rub the mirror over your soiled complexion will only make matters worse. We must turn from the mirror to soap and water. So, too, with the ministry of the law—it was given to show man his true condition and his need for cleansing, but beyond this it cannot go.[37]

The Law in and of itself cannot provide a solution to the principle of sin and death. Trying harder to keep the Torah will never save a man from death.

---

34. Gal 3:23 (RSV).
35. Rom 3:19–20 (RSV).
36. John 10:7–9.
37. DeHann *Law or Grace*, 47.

THE TORAH: A SCHOOLMASTER TO LEAD US TO MESSIAH   37

In fact it has never in the history of mankind ever saved a single person. In the second stage of the Torah's being a schoolmaster, it points to the way of salvation, which is Yeshua the Messiah. It does so by painting an accurate, detailed portrait of Yeshua. As we have already seen, the Scriptures prophesied with amazing accuracy details about Yeshua's life and what he would accomplish. This depiction began in the Pentateuch; for example, foreshadowing Yeshua's coming, God told Moses in Deuteronomy 18:18–19:

> *18:* I will raise up for them a prophet like you from among their brethren; and I will put my words in his mouth, and he shall speak to them all that I command him. *19:* And whoever will not give heed to my words which he shall speak in my name, I myself will require it of him.[38]

This portrayal continued throughout the pages of the *Tanakh* (the Old Testament scriptures), gradually adding more and more details, like pixels to a photo, bringing into focus the identity of the Messiah with ever-increasing clarity. They foretold about Yeshua's birthplace,[39] his birth,[40] how his sacrifice would save many from their sins,[41] the means by which he would die,[42] his death and resurrection,[43] the precise time and place in history when and where he would appear,[44] and his future reign as king over all the earth.[45] The Torah also pointed to Yeshua and the redemption he would bring through yearly calendar of appointed feasts. Passover, for example, when the Paschal lamb was to be sacrificed,[46] celebrated yearly on the eve of the fifteenth of the first month, was the very day that Yeshua himself was put to death. The Scriptures assure us that this was no coincidence. "Cleanse out the old leaven that you may be a new lump, as you really are unleavened. For Messiah, our paschal lamb, has been sacrificed."[47] Likewise, the day he rose from the dead was another biblical holiday, *Yom ha-Nafah*, when the priest waved the first fruits of the barley harvest in the Temple.[48] "But

---

38. Deut 18:18–19 (RSV); cf. Acts 3:23.
39. Mic 5:2.
40. Isa 7:14.
41. Isa 53:11–12.
42. Ps 22.
43. Ps 116.
44. Dan 9:25–26.
45. Ps 2:6–9.
46. Exod 12; Lev 23:5.
47. 1 Cor 5:7 (RSV).
48. Lev 23:10–14.

in fact Messiah has been raised from the dead, the first fruits of those who have fallen asleep."[49]

Yet another way that the Law pointed to Messiah was through the intricate system of ordinances and sacrifices offered in the Tabernacle and later in the Temple in Jerusalem. These foreshadowed the eternal sacrifice that Yeshua would one day accomplish, by which he would destroy sin and death forever!

---

49. 1 Cor 15:20 (RSV).

4

From the Foundation of the World: The Meaning of Sacrifice

A MODERN SACRIFICE FROM THE DAYS OF THE BIBLE

ONE OF THE MOST exciting events of the year in Israel is the Samaritan Passover. Few people realize that the Samaritans continue to exist and, moreover, since the founding of the state of Israel, are in fact growing in number. Amazingly, this ancient people still celebrates the Passover very much the way that they did in biblical times. Every spring, the Israeli government Ministry of Religion provides each Samaritan family with a lamb. On Passover eve, late in the day, the Samaritans gather into a very large field on the top of their sacred Mount Gerizim, the same mountain where Joshua son of Nun was commanded to bless the people of Israel.[1] Many people from all different walks of life attend this annual happening. One can see Orthodox Jewish rabbis, Catholic priests, some rather odd-looking sectarians, and many onlookers from Israel and from all over the world. These have come to watch and take notes on how a biblical sacrifice is performed.

Precisely at sundown on the appointed day,[2] the head of each family takes his lamb. At a signal from the Samaritan high priest, each man draws a knife across his lamb's throat. An indescribable feeling of alarm and dread,

---

1. Josh 8:31–34.
2. Exod 12:6.

bordering on panic, surges through the air, with the knowledge that at that very moment innocent blood is being spilt. This sense is heightened by the chilling, warbling trill that spontaneously rises in the throats of the Samaritan women, causing the hair to stand on the back of one's neck. This is immediately followed by frenzied preparation. In the dwindling twilight, the lambs are cleaned and the wool is taken off. The entrails, prescribed inward parts,[3] and the right shoulder for the priest[4] are removed. Otherwise, the lambs remain whole, as stipulated by Exodus 12:8–9, 46b.

> 8: They shall eat the flesh that night, roasted; with unleavened bread and bitter herbs they shall eat it. 9: Do not eat any of it raw or boiled with water, but roasted, its head with its legs and its inner parts.[5]
>
> 46: . . . and you shall not break a bone of it.[6]

A long stake is passed through the length of each lamb's body. Several deep pits have been dug in the ground in preparation. Tongues of flame leap from the mouths of these pits, giving light to an infernal landscape. Beside each pit awaits a pile of leaves and a heap of earth. The men take their lambs and stand holding the stakes upright, that is to say vertically, in circles surrounding the pits. For a moment, the sacrificed lamb stands on its pole, hanging from the wood of the sacrifice. Then suddenly the men plunge the stakes into the pits. Quickly, the piles of leaves are dumped on top of the pits and the soil is shoveled over the leaves. The lambs are buried, the flame goes out, but the heat remains. When we think of roasting a lamb we usually imagine it being cooked on a horizontal spit, but at the Samaritan Passover the lambs remain standing vertically within the deep narrow pit. The lambs stay buried in the pits for three full hours. When the pits are finally opened, the lambs that have gone into the pit as dead bodies are taken out, and become sustenance for an entire family.

There is little doubt that the Samaritans keep the Passover in very much the same way Jews did in the first century. The Mishnah,[7] for instance, stipulates that the stake used be made of pomegranate.

---

3. Exod 29:1.
4. Deut 18:3.
5. Exod 12:8–9 (RSV).
6. Exod 12:46b RSV.
7. M. Pesahim 7:1. The Mishnah, an encyclopedia of Jewish tradition and Oral Law, was compiled and organized in about 300 CE, however, it contains much material from earlier periods. This particular mishnah tells of Jewish practices regarding the Passover as they were kept before the destruction of the Temple.

> How do they roast the Passover-offering? They bring a skewer of pomegranate-wood and thrust it through from its mouth to its buttocks, laying its legs and its entrails inside it.[8]

The imagery is striking. The sacrificed Passover lamb hangs from the wooden stave even as Yeshua, the Passover Lamb who was slain to take away the sin of the world,[9] hung from the wooden pole that was the cross. Just as the lamb is buried for three hours, Yeshua remained in the tomb for three days and three nights.[10] Like the lamb, he went into the tomb a corpse, but when his body came forth from the grave, it had become spiritual sustenance for the family of his followers.

> *53:* So Yeshua said to them, "Truly, truly, I say to you, unless you eat the flesh of the Son of man and drink his blood, you have no life in you; *54:* he who eats my flesh and drinks my blood has eternal life, and I will raise him up at the last day. *55:* For my flesh is food indeed, and my blood is drink indeed. *56:* He who eats my flesh and drinks my blood abides in me, and I in him. *57:* As the living Father sent me, and I live because of the Father, so he who eats me will live because of me.[11]

Some years ago I heard an intriguing story, the veracity of which I can neither confirm nor deny: A young Jewish man who was watching the proceedings of the Samaritan Passover was overheard remarking to himself, ". . . then he really was the Messiah!"

THE TEMPLE SACRIFICE

One of the most important ways that the Torah points to Messiah is through the Temple sacrifice. God demanded that the people of Israel bring before him at the Tabernacle in the wilderness and later in the Temple at Jerusalem offerings twice daily and at various times during the month and the year. There were besides these offerings that every individual was to bring before God. The complex order of sacrifices and their appointed times are outlined in Numbers 28–29.

---

8. M. Pesahim 7:1; Danby, *Mishnah*, 143.
9. 1 Cor 5:7–8; John 1:29.
10. Matt 12:40.
11. John 5:53–57 (RSV).

THE PRINCIPLE OF SACRIFICE

We have seen how sin separated man from God, how sin had crept into every area of human existence, and how the penalty for sin is death. In order to atone for his sin, a man brought an innocent animal as a substitute to the priest in the Temple, who put it to death, on his behalf, before the Lord. The idea behind the sacrifice was that an innocent paid the penalty for the guilty. Because the demanded payment of death for his sin was met, the worshipper by this act was set free and brought near God. However, the life of an animal is hardly equal to that of a man. It could never in reality pay for him.

> *4:* For it is impossible that the blood of bulls and goats should take away sins.[12]

Only the death of another man, one who is himself totally sinless in heart and deed could pay his price. The Temple sacrifice was in reality intended to prefigure the true sacrifice of Yeshua the Messiah.

> *11:* And every priest stands daily at his service, offering repeatedly the same sacrifices, which can never take away sins. *12:* But when Messiah had offered for all time a single sacrifice for sins, he sat down at the right hand of God . . .[13]

BREAKING THE CYCLE OF SIN

In order for Yeshua to be the promised "Lamb who takes away the sin of the world," he himself had to be entirely without sin. As we have seen, sin is passed down from parent to child. Although Eve first partook of the fruit, it was Adam whom God held accountable for bringing death into the world.

> *12:* Therefore as sin came into the world through one man and death through sin, and so death spread to all men because all men sinned—[14]

Evidently, the responsibility for sin is passed down from one's father. In order to interrupt the cycle of sin being handed down from father to child, God created Yeshua in the womb of Mary, a virgin, bypassing the role of a natural biological father. In place of a natural father, he imprinted upon him his own characteristics.

---

12. Heb 10:4–8 (RSV).
13. Heb 10:11–12 (RSV).
14. Rom 5:12 (RSV).

> *34:* And Mary said to the angel, "How shall this be, since I have no husband?" *35:* And the angel said to her, "The Holy Spirit will come upon you, and the power of the Most High will overshadow you; therefore the child to be born will be called holy, the Son of God.[15]

Already about seven hundred years before Yeshua's coming, Isaiah prophesied how Messiah would be born of a virgin:

> *14:* Therefore the Lord Himself will give you a sign: Behold, the virgin shall conceive and bear a Son, and shall call his name Immanuel.[16]

Because Yeshua was conceived without a human father, he was born entirely without sin. As the blameless lamb of God, he was able to bear in himself the sin of mankind.

THE LOGOS

The Gospel of John (1:1) describes Yeshua as the "Word," in the original Greek, *Logos*. The *Logos* in the Hellenistic Jewish thought of Yeshua's time was a supernatural agent through whom God created the heavens and the earth.[17] God is a spirit.[18] As such, he is invisible and without form:

> *17:* To the King of the ages, immortal, invisible, the only God, be honor and glory forever and ever. Amen.[19]

As such, he is outside of his creation. In order to create the physical universe, God spoke the Word (*Logos*) and his Word took form. Within the *Logos* is the logic and pattern of the entire creation:

> *1:* In the beginning was the Word [*Logos*], and the Word [*Logos*] was with God, and the Word [*Logos*] was God. *2:* He was in the beginning with God; *3:* all things were made through him, and without him was not anything made that was made.[20]

---

15. Luke 1:34–35 (RSV).
16. Isa 7:14 New KJV.
17. Philo, *Her.* 205.
18. John 2:24.
19. 1 Tim 1:17 (RSV).
20. John 1:1–3 RSV).

> *9:* and to make all see what is the fellowship of the mystery, which from the beginning of the ages has been hidden in God who created all things through Yeshua the Messiah.[21]
>
> *15:* He is the image of the invisible God, the first-born of all creation; *16:* for in him all things were created, in heaven and on earth, visible and invisible, whether thrones or dominions or principalities or authorities—all things were created through him and for him. *17:* He is before all things, and in him all things hold together.[22]

The *Logos* is the personified interface between God and his creation. Every time Scripture speaks of God as having anthropomorphic features, that is to say, a head, eyes, arms, hands, and feet, etc., it is describing him in terms of the *Logos*. It was these very characteristics of God as the *Logos* that the Spirit of God impressed upon Yeshua's DNA at the moment of his conception.

Yeshua, born in the image of God, was entirely free of sin, and lived completely obedient to the commandments of the Law in heart, mind, and action. He was uniquely capable of reversing man's act of rebellion.

REVERSING THE REBELLION

From the moment man succumbed to the temptation of Satan in the garden, he has aspired to be like God. When Satan tempted Eve to eat the fruit he told her,

> *4:* . . . "You will not die. *5:* For God knows that when you eat of it your eyes will be opened, and you will be like God, knowing good and evil."[23]

The thought of achieving equality with God greatly appealed to man's sense of pride. Throughout history man has continued his audacious quest to exalt himself to the status of his creator.

Yeshua, however, conceived by God's Spirit and impressed with God's characteristics, was himself in the very form of God.

> *15:* He [Yeshua] is the image of the invisible God, the first-born of all creation.[24]

---

21 Eph 3:9 (New KJV).
22. Col 1:15–17 (RSV).
23. Gen 3:4–5 (RSV).
24. Col 1:15 (RSV).

Whereas man sought to be like God, Yeshua, having the form of God, humbled himself, being born as a man and lowering himself to the depths of becoming as a servant of men.[25] By emptying himself, he reversed man's impudent pride in aspiring to be like God. Yeshua became completely submissive to his father's will.

Man sought to be completely independent from his Creator, thinking that he would be his own master, when he rejected God's commandment. Man's rebellion began with disobedience to a single commandment that was neither difficult nor complicated. That initial disobedience, however, led to sin permeating every area of man's life. In order for Yeshua to reverse man's rebellion, it was no longer a matter of obeying a single commandment. Now, Yeshua had to keep commandments upon commandments.

> *4:* But when the time had fully come, God sent forth his Son, born of woman, born under the law . . .[26]

In order to reverse man's rebellion, Yeshua had to be obedient to his Father's will in every single area of life according to the standard of the Torah, both in letter and in spirit.

> *5:* Have this mind among yourselves, which is yours in Messiah Yeshua, *6:* who, though he was in the form of God, did not count equality with God a thing to be grasped, *7:* but emptied himself, taking the form of a servant, being born in the likeness of men. *8:* And being found in human form he humbled himself and became obedient unto death, even death on a cross.[27]

The final and ultimate act of Yeshua's obedience was his death upon the cross. This was a death that was not merely from the physical effects of crucifixion. He submitted to being thoroughly crushed to death by his Father.

> *5:* But he was wounded for our transgressions, he was bruised for our iniquities; upon him was the chastisement that made us whole, and with his stripes we are healed.[28]
> *10:* Yet it was the will of the Lord to bruise him; he has put him to grief . . .[29]

---

25. Luke 22:27; Phil 2:7.
26. Gal 4:4 (RSV).
27. Phil 2:5–8 (RSV).
28. Isa 53:5 (RSV).
29. Isa 53:10a (RSV).

12: . . . he poured out his soul to death, and was numbered with the transgressors; yet he bore the sin of many, and made intercession for the transgressors.[30]

Yeshua's submission involved his mind, heart, and will. By fully submitting to his Father's will to the bitter end, he succeeded in completely undoing man's rebellion.

THE NEW CREATION

God has promised that a future day is coming when he will make a new heaven and a new earth. This new creation will be perfect, devoid of sin and its consequence, death. Neither will there be found in it any pain or sickness. In this flawless world, all nature shall be restored to its original perfection.[31] In it God will be king and ever present with his people.[32] Those who will inherit this new creation will live eternally in peace and exceeding joy. It is intended for the remnant of Israel that shall be saved and will also include the redeemed from all mankind, those who have trusted in Yeshua throughout the ages, and who will be resurrected at his appearing.

Yeshua completely destroyed sin and death in his body by giving his life in submission to his Father's will. Yeshua's entire being was thoroughly crushed to lifelessness. he emptied himself entirely. As in the beginning when God created the universe out of nothing, he began a new act of creation out of the void of Yeshua's death. In raising Yeshua from death to life, God began to lay the foundation of the new heaven and new earth, based on the unwavering obedience of Yeshua. In fact, the new creation began within the very cells of Yeshua's body in the tomb at the moment of his resurrection. The substance of his resurrected body will serve as the very blueprint from which the new heaven and the new earth of the future will be formed.

THE KINGDOM

God desires to reestablish his perfect order in the world. As we have seen, man's rebellion destroyed this perfect order and his continuing rebellion prevents God from restoring it even now. By rejecting God's commandment and listening to Satan's voice and submitting to Satan's authority, man

---

30. Isa 53:12b (RSV).
31. Isa 11:6–9; 25:7–8; Rom 8:19–22.
32. Ezek 43:7; 48:15.

abdicated his rule of the earth, which had been delegated to him by God, signing it over, as it were, to the devil.

By reversing man's rebellion through total submission to his Father, Yeshua won back the right to rule. That Yeshua, the "Lion of Judah," is destined to rule Israel was already foreseen in Genesis 49:9–10:

> *9:* Judah is a lion's whelp; from the prey, my son, you have gone up. He stooped down, he couched as a lion, and as a lioness; who dares rouse him up? *10:* The scepter shall not depart from Judah, nor the ruler's staff from between his feet, until he comes to whom it belongs; and to him shall be the obedience of the peoples.[33]

The book of Revelation envisions the king of this kingdom of Israel as Yeshua the Lion of Judah, worthy to reign:

> *4:* and I wept much that no one was found worthy to open the scroll or to look into it. *5:* Then one of the elders said to me, "Weep not; lo, the Lion of the tribe of Judah, the Root of David, has conquered, so that he can open the scroll and its seven seals."[34]

The prophet Nathan prophesied to David that the kingdom of his descendant would be established forever.[35] Isaiah also prophesied:

> *6:* For to us a child is born, to us a son is given; and the government will be upon his shoulder, and his name will be called "Wonderful Counselor, Mighty God, Everlasting Father, Prince of Peace." *7:* Of the increase of his government and of peace there will be no end, upon the throne of David, and over his kingdom, to establish it, and to uphold it with justice and with righteousness from this time forth and for evermore. The zeal of the Lord of hosts will do this.[36]

Yeshua fulfilled all these messianic prophecies, being from the tribe of Judah and the line of King David.[37]

The angel Gabriel, who appeared to Mary, foretold of Yeshua,

> *32:* He will be great, and will be called the Son of the Most High; and the Lord God will give to him the throne of his father David,

---

33. Gen 49:9–10 (RSV).
34. Rev 5:4–5.
35. 2 Sam 7:16.
36. Isa 9:6–7 (RSV).
37. Luke 1:27, 32; Rev 22:16.

> 33: and he will reign over the house of Jacob for ever; and of his kingdom there will be no end."[38]

It was prophesied that when God restores the Jewish people to the land of Israel, David will rule over the nation:

> 24: "My servant David shall be king over them; and they shall all have one shepherd. They shall follow my ordinances and be careful to observe my statutes. 25: They shall dwell in the land where your fathers dwelt that I gave to my servant Jacob; they and their children and their children's children shall dwell there forever; and David my servant shall be their prince for ever."[39]

This obviously speaks not of David himself but rather his promised descendant, the Messiah.

Simon Peter, addressing the crowd on the morning of Shavuot (Pentecost), told them:

> 29: "Brethren, I may say to you confidently of the patriarch David that he both died and was buried, and his tomb is with us to this day. 30: Being therefore a prophet, and knowing that God had sworn with an oath to him that he would set one of his descendants upon his throne, 31: he foresaw and spoke of the resurrection of the Messiah, that he was not abandoned to Hades, nor did his flesh see corruption. 32: This Yeshua God raised up, and of that we all are witnesses."[40]

Yeshua was at times called by his messianic title, Son of David. On one occasion when Yeshua entered Jericho, he was met by a blind man calling out to him from the crowd.

> 38: And he cried, "Yeshua, Son of David, have mercy on me!" 39: And those who were in front rebuked him, telling him to be silent; but he cried out all the more, "Son of David, have mercy on me!"[41]

On another occasion Yeshua was addressing some scribes:

> 41: But he said to them, "How can they say that the Messiah is David's son? 42: For David himself says in the Book of Psalms, 'The Lord said to my Lord, Sit at my right hand, 43: till I make

---

38. Luke 1:32–33 (RSV).
39. Ezek 37:24–25 (RSV).
40. Acts 2:29–32 (RSV).
41. Luke 18:38–39 (RSV).

thy enemies a stool for thy feet.' *44:* David thus calls him Lord; so how is he his son?"[42]

When God establishes his kingdom on earth, Yeshua, his Messiah, the son of David, will reign over it as king.

The capital of this future kingdom of Israel will be Jerusalem; however, the kingdom will not be confined to the borders of the land of Israel. Rather it is destined to be a global kingdom. Daniel was shown a vision of four great empires that will dominate the world. In the end a final kingdom that is God's kingdom will supersede all the others.

> *44:* And in the days of those kings the God of heaven will set up a kingdom which shall never be destroyed, nor shall its sovereignty be left to another people. It shall break in pieces all these kingdoms and bring them to an end, and it shall stand for ever . . .[43]

The place where Yeshua's throne will be established is Mount Zion (that is, the Temple Mount in Jerusalem).

> *6:* Yet have I set my King upon my holy hill of Zion. *7:* I will declare the decree: the Lord hath said unto me, Thou art my Son; this day have I begotten thee. *8:* Ask of me, and I shall give thee the heathen for thine inheritance, and the uttermost parts of the earth for thy possession. *9:* Thou shalt break them with a rod of iron; thou shalt dash them in pieces like a potter's vessel. *10:* Be wise now therefore, O ye kings: be instructed, ye judges of the earth. *11:* Serve the Lord with fear and rejoice with trembling. *12:* Kiss the Son, lest he be angry, and ye perish from the way when his wrath is kindled but a little. Blessed are all they that put their trust in him.[44]

Revelation 11:15 envisions the day when Yeshua, born of the tribe of Judah and of the lineage of David, will begin to reign.

> *15:* Then the seventh angel blew his trumpet, and there were loud voices in heaven, saying, "The kingdom of the world has become the kingdom of our Lord and of his Messiah, and he shall reign for ever and ever."[45]

---

42. Luke 20:41–44 (RSV).
43. Dan 2:44 (RSV).
44. Ps 2:6–12 (KJV).
45. Rev 11:15 (RSV).

THE TITLE DEED OF EARTH

Yeshua's death and resurrection has immense power to bring forgiveness and undo the effects of sin, that is, death with its lesser facets, sickness and pain. Furthermore by reversing the rebellion and reestablishing God's rule, he cancelled the legal right of Satan's authority over mankind and the earth. In the first century, a title deed in the form of a scroll was tied shut and sealed with seals. Only the rightful owner was legally permitted to break these seals. The book of Revelation envisions Yeshua as the Lamb that was slain, recalling the power of his sacrifice. As the rightful owner of the title deed to the earth, he takes the scroll and breaks the seals:

> 6: And between the throne and the four living creatures and among the elders, I saw a Lamb standing, as though it had been slain, with seven horns and with seven eyes, which are the seven spirits of God sent out into all the earth; 7: and he went and took the scroll from the right hand of him who was seated on the throne. 8: And when he had taken the scroll, the four living creatures and the twenty-four elders fell down before the Lamb, each holding a harp, and with golden bowls full of incense, which are the prayers of the saints; 9: and they sang a new song, saying, "Worthy art thou to take the scroll and to open its seals, for thou wast slain and by thy blood didst ransom men for God from every tribe and tongue and people and nation, 10: and hast made them a kingdom and priests to our God, and they shall reign on earth."[46]

The Lamb of God alone is worthy to take the title deed of the earth and open its seals.

ONCE FOR ALL TIME

Yeshua died at a specific moment in history:

> 27: He has no need, like those high priests, to offer sacrifices daily, first for his own sins and then for those of the people; he did this once for all when he offered up himself.[47]

It was already a sure fact that from before the foundation of the world that Yeshua would pay for the sins of mankind and rise again.

---

46. Rev 5:6–10(RSV).
47. Heb 7:27 (RSV).

Revelation 13:8 speaks of those who will be deceived into worshiping the evil one known as the "beast":

> 8: All who dwell on the earth will worship him, whose names have not been written in the Book of Life of the Lamb slain from the foundation of the world.[48]

Whether this passage is saying that Yeshua, the Lamb of God, was sacrificed from the foundation of the world, or rather that those who are written in it were chosen from the foundation of the world, it is clear that salvation through Yeshua's atoning death was available right from the very beginning to all who would trust in him.

> 3: Blessed be the God and Father of our Lord Yeshua Messiah, who has blessed us in Messiah with every spiritual blessing in the heavenly places, 4: even as he chose us in him before the foundation of the world, that we should be holy and blameless before him.[49]
>
> 24: For Messiah has entered, not into a sanctuary made with hands, a copy of the true one, but into heaven itself, now to appear in the presence of God on our behalf. 25: Nor was it to offer himself repeatedly, as the high priest enters the Holy Place yearly with blood not his own; 26: for then he would have had to suffer repeatedly since the foundation of the world. But as it is, he has appeared once for all at the end of the age to put away sin by the sacrifice of himself.[50]

THE TIMELESS POWER OF YESHUA'S ATONEMENT

The power of Yeshua's sacrifice is effective throughout time, past, present, and future. In his own day, Yeshua himself was able to call upon the power of his death and resurrection to heal the sick, raise the dead, and cast out demons, even before he had actually gone to the cross.

When Yeshua cast out demons and healed many people at one time, the writer of the Gospel of Matthew commented,

> 16: That evening they brought to him many who were possessed with demons; and he cast out the spirits with a word, and healed

---

48. Rev 13:8 (NKJV); cf. 1 Pet 1:19–20.
49. Eph 1:3–4 (RSV).
50. Heb 9:26 (RSV).

all who were sick. *17:* This was to fulfill what was spoken by the prophet Isaiah, 'He took our infirmities and bore our diseases.'[51]

Each time that Yeshua used the power of his death and resurrection to heal a person, a measure of the kingdom of God was established in that person's life. In doing so, he dispossessed Satan of his authority in the lives he touched and so restored a degree of God's perfect order in them.[52] This is especially clear in Yeshua's declaration to the people of his day,

> *20:* But if it is by the finger of God that I cast out demons, then the kingdom of God has come upon you. *21:* When a strong man, fully armed, guards his own palace, his goods are in peace; *22:* but when one stronger than he assails him and overcomes him, he takes away his armor in which he trusted, and divides his spoil.[53]

Thus Yeshua dispossessed Satan of his authority over man.[54] As Yeshua walked through the land of Israel, he went about reestablishing the kingdom of God with the timeless power of his sacrifice, which he was then yet to accomplish by his death and resurrection. In every case, the one receiving forgiveness, healing, and deliverance did so through faith. Faith is the ingredient that enables the power of Yeshua's sacrifice to operate in one's life. This power is made available today to those who trust in Yeshua and put their faith in his death and resurrection.

In the thinking of Robert Lindsey, author of *Jesus, Rabbi and Lord*, Yeshua spoke of the kingdom, meaning people, the body of his followers.[55] They were the kingdom of God on earth since Yeshua the king was present with them and ruling them. In this regard, Lindsey found very significant Luke 17:20–21:

> *20:* Being asked by the Pharisees when the kingdom of God was coming, he [Yeshua] answered them, "The kingdom of God is not coming with signs to be observed; *21:* nor will they say, 'Lo, here it is!' or 'There!' for behold, the kingdom of God is in the midst of you."[56]

---

51. Matt 8:16–17 (RSV).
52. Lindsey, *Jesus, Rabbi and Lord*, 57–58.
53. Luke 11:20–22 (RSV).
54. Lindsey, *Jesus, Rabbi and Lord*, 57–58.
55. Lindsey *Jesus, Rabbi and Lord*, 58.
56. Luke 17:20–21 (RSV).

FROM THE FOUNDATION OF THE WORLD: THE MEANING OF SACRIFICE

Lindsey understood by this that Yeshua meant to say that his own followers who were there at that moment present with him were the kingdom of God in the midst of the people of Israel.[57] Moreover, even after Yeshua had departed from them and left the world, he would continue to reign over them through the power of God's Spirit, who dwelt within them. Yeshua exhorted them, "For where two or three are gathered in my name, there am I in the midst of them."[58]

The kingdom of God began with Yeshua's first coming when he first began calling disciples, and it continues today.[59] Yeshua's followers thus continue to make up his kingdom on earth until now, and will carry on doing so until his return to this earth. It would of course be wrong, however, to see this as the end of the story. There is coming a day in the future when Yeshua himself will physically return to restore the kingdom to Israel and reign not only over his disciples, but over *all* the people of the earth.

THE KINGDOM OF HEAVEN OR THE KINGDOM OF GOD

There have been many ideas about what Yeshua meant when he spoke of the "kingdom of heaven." Some people believe that it has to do with heaven's rule coming to earth or that it speaks of those who go to heaven when they die. A comparison of the passages mentioning the "kingdom of heaven" in Matthew and the "kingdom of God" in Luke demonstrates that they are one and the same.

As a Child

> *3:* and said, "Truly, I say to you, unless you turn and become like children, you will never enter the kingdom of heaven."[60]
> *17:* "Truly, I say to you, whoever does not receive the kingdom of God like a child shall not enter it."[61]

---

57. Lindsey *Jesus, Rabbi and Lord*, 58.
58. Matt 18:20 (RSV).
59. Lindsey, *Jesus, Rabbi and Lord*, 112.
60. Matt 18:3 (RSV).
61. Luke 18:17 (RSV).

The Rich

> *23:* And Jesus said to his disciples, "Truly, I say to you, it will be hard for a rich man to enter the kingdom of heaven. *24:* Again I tell you, it is easier for a camel to go through the eye of a needle than for a rich man to enter the kingdom of God."[62]
>
> *24:* Jesus looking at him said, "How hard it is for those who have riches to enter the kingdom of God! *25:* For it is easier for a camel to go through the eye of a needle than for a rich man to enter the kingdom of God."[63]

Poor in Spirit

> *3:* "Blessed are the poor in spirit, for theirs is the kingdom of heaven.[64]
>
> *20:* And he lifted up his eyes on his disciples, and said: "Blessed are you poor, for yours is the kingdom of God.[65]

"Heaven" in the phrase "kingdom of heaven" was employed as a circumlocution of God's name. In order to avoid even getting close to breaking the first commandment by using God's name in vain, observant Jews are careful not to refer directly to God by name. Today an observant Jew will speak in Hebrew of *Adonai* ("Lord"), *Elokim* (substituting a k for an h in *Elohim*, so as not to pronounce God's name), or simply refer to God as *ha Shem* (that is, "the Name"). In English he writes "G-d," leaving out the o in God's name, or "L-rd," leaving out the o in "Lord." In Yeshua's day, one way Jews referenced God without mentioning his name directly was by calling him "Heaven," evidently since he is ruler of heaven. In the apocryphal First Book of Maccabees, written in the intertestamental period[66] some years before the birth of Yeshua, we see an example of "Heaven" used in place of God's name:

> *21:* Heaven preserve us from forsaking the Law and its observances.[67]

---

62. Matt 19:23–24 (RSV).
63. Luke 18:24–25 (RSV).
64. Matt 5:3 (RSV).
65. Luke 6:20 (RSV).
66. About 100 BCE.
67. 1 Macc 2:21 (Jerusalem Bible).

It may well have been that Yeshua, not wishing to offend his listeners, referred to the "kingdom of heaven." Alternatively, it may be that it was the author of the synoptic Gospel of Matthew who employed the phrase "kingdom of heaven" so as not to offend the sensitive ears of some of his readers with the phrase "kingdom of God."

THE FAITH EQUATION

The timeless power of Yeshua's sacrifice to save people from their sins was available long before Yeshua was even born. We observed in the opening chapter how Abraham "saw Yeshua's day," how he grasped the promise by faith and it was counted to him by God as righteousness. It was thus possible, even in ancient times, before Yeshua's birth, to receive the promise of salvation through the power of Yeshua's sacrifice. What was required was a means by which a person might focus his faith on God's promise the same way that Abraham did.

This was the purpose for which God gave the people of Israel Temple sacrifices. God made the power of Yeshua's sacrifice accessible by means of a two-sided equation. On the one side of the equation, God commanded animal sacrifices be brought to the Temple, fully aware that they symbolized the sacrifice that Yeshua, his Son, would one day accomplish. On the other side of the equation, a man brought a perfect, unblemished animal in faith and obedience to God's commandment to be slain as an atonement for his sin. It was not necessary that the worshiper bringing the sacrifice entirely understood the meaning of his symbolic act. It was enough that God knew that it represented Yeshua's sacrifice and that the worshipper acted in faith. Thus a man was able to find a measure of forgiveness for his sins and draw near to God through performing the Temple sacrifices. Likewise, the entire nation of Israel as a whole found atonement in the sacrifice of Yeshua.

ABUSE OF THE SACRIFICE

An important prerequisite in offering the Temple sacrifice was the right condition of the heart of the one bringing the offering. He was to present his sacrifice before the Lord with a humble and contrite spirit. We have observed how the source of man's rebellion was his heart. The ultimate purpose in providing the Temple sacrifice was to redeem the hearts of men. After all, the Temple sacrifice represented the total submission of Yeshua's mind and heart to his Father's will.

At one point in the history of Israel, the people began to offer the Temple sacrifices merely as a matter of mechanical ritual. They continued to practice terrible social injustice, believing that they could appease God by simply bringing more animals for slaughter in the Temple. In response to this God protested:

> *11:* "What to me is the multitude of your sacrifices? says the Lord; I have had enough of burnt offerings of rams and the fat of fed beasts; I do not delight in the blood of bulls, or of lambs, or of he-goats. *12:* "When you come to appear before me, who requires of you this trampling of my courts? *13:* Bring no more vain offerings; incense is an abomination to me. New moon and sabbath and the calling of assemblies—I cannot endure iniquity and solemn assembly. *14:* Your new moons and your appointed feasts my soul hates; they have become a burden to me, I am weary of bearing them. *15:* When you spread forth your hands, I will hide my eyes from you; even though you make many prayers, I will not listen; your hands are full of blood. *16:* Wash yourselves; make yourselves clean; remove the evil of your doings from before my eyes; cease to do evil, *17:* learn to do good; seek justice, correct oppression; defend the fatherless, plead for the widow."[68]

Some have misunderstood this to mean that God is opposed the bringing of sacrifices altogether. There was, however, of course nothing inherently wrong with the sacrifices themselves. Rather, what God hated was bringing a sacrifice without a right heart before him!

> *17:* The sacrifice acceptable to God is a broken spirit; a broken and contrite heart, O God, thou wilt not despise.[69]

Likewise, Yeshua enjoined his listeners,

> *23:* "So if you are offering your gift at the altar, and there remember that your brother has something against you, *24:* leave your gift there before the altar and go; first be reconciled to your brother, and then come and offer your gift."[70]

What is important to remember is that it was not the slaughtering of an animal or faith itself that brought forgiveness and blessing. Rather, it was

---

68. Isa 1:11–17 (RSV).
69. Ps 51:17 (RSV).
70. Matt 5:23–24 (RSV).

the timeless power of Yeshua's sacrifice of perfect obedience to the will of his Father, by which he reversed the rebellion and did away with sin and death.

> *4:* For it is impossible that the blood of bulls and goats should take away sins. *5:* Consequently, when Messiah came into the world, he said, "Sacrifices and offerings thou hast not desired, but a body hast thou prepared for me; *6:* in burnt offerings and sin offerings thou hast taken no pleasure. *7:* Then I said, 'Lo, I have come to do thy will, O God,' as it is written of me in the roll of the book."[71]

By his submission to his father's will, Yeshua indeed did away with sin in his body, dying on the cross. The Temple sacrifice looked forward to the true sacrifice of Yeshua. God's purpose was to make available the immense power of Yeshua's death and resurrection to transform the hearts of those who would enter into his kingdom.

---

71. Heb 10:4–8 (RSV), evidently quoting Ps 40:6–8.

5

The Two Realms

A NEW CREATION

A NEW WORLD IS coming! It is a world of perfect peace and order, where there will be no death, sickness, or tears and where God will be king and ever present with his people. It is the inheritance of the redeemed remnant of Israel and those called out from every nation who have put their trust in Messiah.

> *9:* But as it is written, Eye hath not seen, nor ear heard, neither have entered into the heart of man, the things which God hath prepared for them that love him.[1]

We have observed how the new creation began within the very cells of Yeshua's body in the tomb, at the moment of his resurrection, and that the substance of his resurrected body will serve as the very blueprint from which the new creation will be formed.

THE GREAT TRANSFORMATION

At the moment a person puts his trust in Yeshua and accepts his sacrifice by faith, a major change occurs within him. The enmity between him and God because of his sin is taken away by the timeless and transcending power

---

1. 1 Cor 2:9 (KJV).

of Yeshua's atonement. Thus God reconciles the believer to himself. A miraculous exchange takes place in the believer's heart: his sinfulness is traded for Yeshua's righteousness. At that moment God's Spirit enters the believer's body and bonds with his human spirit, effecting his transformation into a new creature.

> *17:* Therefore, if anyone is in Messiah, he is a new creation; the old has passed away, behold, the new has come.[2]

In that instant, he becomes part of that new and eternal heaven and earth that will be fully manifested in the future.

IN MESSIAH

Scripture tells us that the believer who by faith accepts Yeshua and puts his trust in him shares in his destiny. The believer partakes in Yeshua's death and resurrection. He enters the new creation with Yeshua and spiritually becomes part of it. Paul speaks of the believer being "in Messiah" using the original Greek term *eis Christos*, which means "in Messiah."

A marvelous type of the Messiah in Scripture is Noah's ark.[3] The few who heeded Noah's warning and came inside the ark were saved. Everyone outside the ark was doomed and drowned in the waters of the flood. When the door closed on the ark, those who were sealed within it, though tossed about by waves, were safe from harm until dry ground once again appeared. Similarly, when a passenger boards an airliner, he puts his faith in it to take him to his destiny and to keep him safe during the flight. The fate of the airplane becomes *his* fate. When it takes off, he flies with it wherever it goes. In whatever airport the plane lands, he lands with it. So it is in Messiah. When one chooses to put his trust in him, that person commits his fate to him, and travels with him wherever he goes.

THE PORT OF DEATH

Scripture tells us that those who are in Messiah have died with him.

> *3:* Do you not know that all of us who have been baptized into Messiah Yeshua were baptized into his death?[4]

---

2. 2 Cor 5:17 (RSV).
3. Gen 6:1—9:19.
4. Rom 6:3 (RSV).

> *14:* . . . we are convinced that one has died for all; therefore all have died.[5]

We have seen that the penalty for sin is death. Death is the most severe punishment that the Torah can possibly inflict. Once the death penalty has been carried out on someone, it cannot be imposed again. It is futile to attempt to execute a dead man. Thus, those who are in Messiah, having died with Yeshua, are beyond being punished again by the Law. They are no longer under the jurisdiction of the Law.

> *1:* There is therefore now no condemnation to those who are in Messiah Yeshua. *2:* for the life-giving principles of the Spirit have freed you in Messiah Yeshua from the control of the principles sin and death.[6]

Furthermore, a dead person is no longer enslaved by sin:

> *6:* We know that our old self was crucified with him so that the sinful body might be destroyed, and we might no longer be enslaved to sin. *7:* For he who has died is freed from sin.[7]

THE PORT OF RESURRECTION

Those who are "in Messiah" not only have died with Yeshua but are also resurrected with him. When he was raised from the dead, all those who are in him received newness of life.

> *4:* We were buried therefore with him by baptism into death, so that as Messiah was raised from the dead by the glory of the Father, we too might walk in newness of life. *5:* For if we have been united with him in a death like his, we shall certainly be united with him in a resurrection like his.[8]
>
> *11:* If the Spirit of him who raised Yeshua from the dead dwells in you, he who raised Messiah Yeshua from the dead will give life to your mortal bodies also through his Spirit which dwells in you.[9]

---

5. 2 Cor 5:14 (RSV).
6. Rom 8:1–2 (Berkley Version).
7. Rom 6:6–7 (RSV).
8. Rom 6:4–5 (RSV).
9. Rom 8:11 (RSV).

Just as Yeshua was resurrected as the foundation of the new creation, so the believer who is in Messiah becomes a new creature, part of the new heaven and new earth.

> *17:* Therefore, if any one is in Messiah, he is a new creation; the old has passed away, behold, the new has come.[10]

HIDDEN WITH MESSIAH

Forty days after his resurrection, Yeshua was taken up into heaven. Acts 3:21 tells us that heaven must hold him until the "time for the restoration of all things." We have seen how, when the Jewish people accept him as a nation, he will return to this earth and his feet will stand upon the Mount of Olives[11] and every eye will see him.[12] Until now, he remains in heaven, hidden from the eyes of the world. Likewise, those who have trusted in Yeshua and have been transformed by the power of his resurrection into new creatures are hidden with him. They have risen with him and have been transformed inwardly with him by the power of God's Spirit. The physical manifestation of this transformation, however, will not be made visible to the world until Yeshua himself returns.

> *1:* If then you have been raised with Messiah, seek the things that are above, where Messiah is seated at the right hand of God. *2:* Set your minds on things that are above, not on things that are on earth. *3:* For you have died and your life is hid with Messiah in God. When Messiah who is our life appears then you also will appear with him in glory.[13]

When Yeshua appears, those who have died believing in him will be resurrected first. Then those who are still alive at his coming will be transformed physically:

> *13:* But we would not have you ignorant, brethren, concerning those who are asleep, that you may not grieve as others do who have no hope. *14:* For since we believe that Yeshua died and rose again, even so, through Yeshua, God will bring with him those who have fallen asleep. *15:* For this we declare to you by the word of the Lord, that we who are alive, who are left until

---

10. 2 Cor 5:17 (RSV).
11. Zech 14:4.
12. Rev 1:7 (RSV).
13. Col 3:1–4 (RSV).

> the coming of the Lord, shall not precede those who have fallen asleep. *16:* For the Lord himself will descend from heaven with a cry of command, with the archangel's call, and with the sound of the trumpet of God. And the dead in Messiah will rise first; *17:* then we who are alive, who are left, shall be caught up together with them in the clouds to meet the Lord in the air; and so we shall always be with the Lord.[14]

Both those who have been raised and those who are transformed will have eternal, incorruptible bodies like that of Yeshua.

> *20:* But our commonwealth is in heaven, and from it we await a Savior, the Lord Yeshua the Messiah, *21:* who will change our lowly body to be like his glorious body, by the power which enables him even to subject all things to himself.[15]

These will then return with him as he touches down on earth to reign with him in his kingdom. A friend of mine, Kevin Gyllenberg compared Yeshua's followers going out to meet him at his appearing with the return of King Hussein in 1995. At that time the monarch, who had undergone treatment for cancer in the United States, returned home to Aman, the capital of Jordan. Nearly the entire populace of the city came out to greet him at the airport to escort him back to the royal palace. So it will be when Yeshua returns to this earth. The redeemed believers from throughout the ages will go up to meet him and escort him back to this earth. In the end, nature itself will be restored as well.

> *19:* For the creation waits with eager longing for the revealing of the sons of God; *20:* for the creation was subjected to futility, not of its own will but by the will of him who subjected it in hope; *21:* because the creation itself will be set free from its bondage to decay and obtain the glorious liberty of the children of God. *22:* We know that the whole creation has been groaning in travail together until now; *23:* and not only the creation, but we ourselves, who have the first fruits of the Spirit, groan inwardly as we wait for adoption as sons, the redemption of our bodies.[16]

---

14. 1 Thess 4:14–17 (RSV).
15. Phil 3:17–21 (RSV).
16. Rom 8:19–23 (RSV).

REIGNING WITH MESSIAH—THE INHERITANCE

We have seen how Yeshua, through his total obedience to his Father's will, succeeded in reversing man's rebellion and so won the right to rule the earth. At his return Yeshua shall restore the kingdom to Israel. Then the kingdom of the world will become the "'kingdom of our Lord and of his Messiah, and he shall reign for ever and ever.'"[17] God will establish Yeshua's throne on Mount Zion, the Temple Mount in Jerusalem,[18] and from there he will rule the world with perfect justice and peace.

THE ADOPTION OF SONS

God intended that the people of Israel should become his sons and that as such they should receive an inheritance:

> *18:* In those days the house of Judah shall walk with the house of Israel, and they shall come together out of the land of the north to the land that I have given for an inheritance unto your fathers. *19:* But I said, How shall I put thee among the children, and give thee a pleasant land, a goodly heritage of the hosts of nations? and I said, Thou shalt call me, My father; and shalt not turn away from me.[19]

Indeed, the Scripture speaks of the "adoption of sons" in the day when Yeshua will return to restore the kingdom to Israel. God will restore all creation and resurrect and redeem the bodies those who have been made righteous through the atonement of Yeshua's sacrifice.

> *19:* For the creation waits with eager longing for the *revealing of the sons of God; 20:* for the creation was subjected to futility, not of its own will but by the will of him who subjected it in hope; *21:* because the creation itself will be set free from its bondage to decay and obtain the glorious liberty of *the children of God. 22:* We know that the whole creation has been groaning in travail together until now; *23:* and not only the creation, but we ourselves, who have the first fruits of the Spirit, groan inwardly *as we wait for adoption as sons*, the redemption of our bodies. *24:* For in this hope we were saved . . .[20]

17. Rev 11:15 (RSV).
18. Ps 2:6.
19. Jer 3:19 (KJV).
20. Rom 8:22–24 (RSV), emphasis added.

15: For ye have not received the spirit of bondage again to fear; but ye have received the Spirit of adoption, whereby we cry, Abba, Father. *16:* The Spirit itself beareth witness with our spirit, that we are the children of God: *17:* And if children, then heirs; heirs of God, and joint-heirs with Messiah; if so be that we suffer with him, that we may be also glorified together.[21]

TO ISRAEL BELONGS THE ADOPTION

This adoption of sons was specially intended for the people of Israel:

4: Who are Israelites; *to whom pertaineth the adoption,* and the glory, and the covenants, and the giving of the law, and the service of God, and the promises; *5:* Whose are the fathers, and of whom as concerning the flesh Messiah came, who is over all, God blessed for ever. Amen.[22]

INCLUSION OF THOSE FROM AMONG THE NATIONS

We have seen, that when the Jewish people rejected Yeshua as Messiah and king, the door to salvation was thrown open to whoever by faith would accept Yeshua. Anyone who receives him, Jew or Gentile, becomes a child of God.

10: He was in the world, and the world was made through him, yet the world knew him not. *11:* He came to his own home, and his own people received him not. *12:* But to all who received him, who believed in his name, he gave power to become children of God; *13:* who were born, not of blood nor of the will of the flesh nor of the will of man, but of God.[23]

Kyu Seop Kim pointed out that Paul's metaphor of adoption based on Greco-Roman practices is unusual. Rarely would a man choose an outsider to be his adopted son. Usually he would choose someone from among his close relatives. Neither was a slave normally adopted in the presence of legitimate heirs. He suggested that Paul used this metaphor in order to

---

21. Rom 8:15–17 (KJV).
22. Rom 9:4–5 (KJV), emphasis added.
23. John 1:10–13 (RSV).

emphasize the magnanimous grace of God toward the believer.[24] This is particularly relevant when we consider Paul's words that the adoption of sons belongs to Israel. It was expected that God would choose his adopted sons from those of his own household. But now God, in his great mercy, has extended his offer of adoption and redemption to include all who come to him through Yeshua by faith.

> *13:* The promise to Abraham and his descendants, that they should inherit the world, did not come through the law but through the righteousness of faith.[25]

This of course means through faith in the atonement of Yeshua. Thus, because of the nation of Israel's rejection of Yeshua, Gentiles who personally put their faith in Yeshua also have a part in the adoption as sons and the inheritance. Paul, addressing the Ephesians, admonished them:

> *12:* remember that you were at that time separated from Messiah, alienated from the commonwealth of Israel, and strangers to the covenants of promise, having no hope and without God in the world. *13:* But now in Messiah Yeshua you who once were far off have been brought near in the blood of Messiah . . . *18:* for through him we both have access in one Spirit to the Father. *19:* So then you are no longer strangers and sojourners, but you are fellow citizens with the saints *and members of the household of God* . . .[26]

HEIRS OF ALL THINGS

Those who are adopted sons of God and are willing to suffer with Yeshua become joint heirs with him.

> *17:* And if children, then heirs; heirs of God, and joint-heirs with Messiah; if so be that we suffer with him, that we may be also glorified together.[27]

So what, exactly, do they stand to inherit? We have already seen that they shall inherit redeemed, immortal bodies impervious to sickness or aging. They will also receive a new, recreated, and perfect world. Even more than

---

24. Kim, "Another Look at Adoption."
25. Rom 4:13 (RSV).
26. Eph 2:12–13, 18–19 (RSV), emphasis added.
27. Rom 8:17 (KJV).

this, they will inherit rulership in the kingdom of God. Yeshua encouraged his disciples:

> "Fear not, little flock, for it is your Father's good pleasure to give you the kingdom."[28]

The prophet Daniel was given a vision of the future:

> *21:* I watched, and that horn made war with the holy ones and was winning, *22:* until the Ancient One came, judgment was given in favor of the holy ones of the Most High, and the time came for the holy ones to take over the kingdom.[29]

Likewise, John, in the book of Revelation, envisioned the time when:

> *3:* There shall no more be anything accursed, but the throne of God and of the Lamb shall be in it, and his servants shall worship him; *4:* they shall see his face, and his name shall be on their foreheads. *5:* And night shall be no more; they need no light of lamp or sun, for the Lord God will be their light, and they shall reign for ever and ever.[30]

In the Sermon on the Mount, Yeshua proclaimed:

> *5:* "Blessed are the meek, for they shall inherit the earth."[31]

This oft-quoted verse is usually viewed as a metaphor. It is used to admonish Sunday school children to be polite and wait their turn. No one, however, really believes that mild-mannered people will ever succeed in triumphing over this earth. After all, everything we learn about our world tells us that survival belongs to the fittest, that only the aggressive get ahead, and that "nice guys don't win ball games." Yeshua was of course actually referring here to his followers inheriting the earth not in this age, but in the age to come. Yeshua, by his total obedience, reversed man's rebellion. Those who follow him must scorn pride and in meekness yield their will to the Father even as Yeshua himself did.

> *21:* He who conquers, I will grant him to sit with me on my throne, as I myself conquered and sat down with my Father on his throne.[32]

---

28. Luke 12:32 (RSV).
29. Daniel 7:21–22 (Complete Jewish Bible).
30. Rev 22:3–5 RSV).
31. Matt 5:5 (RSV).
32. Rev 3:21 (RSV).

Those who are in Messiah will coinherit with him the rulership of the world. All that belongs to him will be theirs as well!

> *17:* And if children, then heirs; heirs of God, and joint-heirs with Messiah; if so be that we suffer with him, that we may be also glorified together.[33]

In short, the redeemed remnant of Israel, along with those individuals from among the nations who have put their faith in Yeshua throughout the ages, will literally inherit the fullness of the earth of the new creation to rule and reign over it together with him. The Lord promises, "He that overcometh shall inherit all things; and I will be his God, and he shall be my son."[34]

DOWN PAYMENT

According to the Scriptures, the presence of God's Spirit within a person's body is his assurance that he will be raised from death or, if he is alive at Yeshua's coming, transformed physically at the moment of Yeshua's return, to share in the inheritance of the new creation.

> *11:* If the Spirit of him who raised Yeshua from the dead dwells in you, he who raised Messiah Yeshua from the dead will give life to your mortal bodies also through his Spirit which dwells in you.[35]

Since Yeshua has already paid the price in full, this inheritance *already* belongs to the one who accepts him. According to 2 Corinthians 5:17, the believer in Yeshua is *already* a new creature, that is to say, part of the new creation of the age to come.

> *17:* Therefore, if any one is in Messiah, he is a new creation; the old has passed away, behold, the new has come.[36]

In knowing the joy of the indwelling of the God's Spirit, the believer has indeed already tasted of the powers of the age to come.[37]

> *13:* In him you also, who have heard the word of truth, the gospel of your salvation, and have believed in him, were sealed

---

33. Rom 8:17 (KJV).
34. Rev 21:7 (KJV).
35. (Rom 8:11 RSV).
36. 2 Cor 5:17 (RSV).
37. Heb 6:4–5.

> with the promised Holy Spirit, *14: which is the guarantee of our inheritance until we acquire possession of it,* to the praise of his glory.[38]

That is to say that those who have the Spirit of God resident within their bodies already now have the absolute assurance that they will be raised from the dead to be joint heirs with Yeshua in the future when he inherits the rulership of the earth.

THE TWO REALMS

One who is in Messiah is currently living in two realms at the same time: the present creation and the new creation. He is *already* seated with Messiah, ruling and reigning with him in heavenly places.

> 4: But God, who is rich in mercy, out of the great love with which he loved us, 5: even when we were dead through our trespasses, made us alive together with Messiah (by grace you have been saved), 6: and raised us up with him, and made us sit with him in the heavenly places in Messiah Yeshua . . .[39]

However, paradoxically, the believer in Yeshua is called to share in the sufferings of Messiah here in this world.

> 17: And if children, then heirs; heirs of God, and joint-heirs with Messiah; if so be that we suffer with him, that we may be also glorified together.[40]

RENEWING OF THE MIND

The action of God's Spirit upon a person who puts his trust in Yeshua is in his spirit. Although the believer's spirit is transformed instantly, his body will not be changed until the return of Yeshua. This is because the body remains a part of the realm of this present creation and is consequently still subject to sin and death.

> 10: But if Messiah is in you, although your bodies are dead because of sin, your spirits are alive because of righteousness.[41]

---

38. Eph 1:13–14 (RSV), emphasis added.
39. Eph 2:4–6 (RSV).
40. Rom 8:17 (KJV).
41. Rom 8:10 (RSV).

The believer in Yeshua must still struggle with the sinful urges of the flesh on the one hand and the effects of aging and sickness on the other.

> *22:* For I delight in the law of God, in my inmost self, *23:* but I see in my members another law at war with the law of my mind and making me captive to the law of sin which dwells in my members. *24:* Wretched man that I am! Who will deliver me from this body of death? *25:* Thanks be to God through Yeshua Messiah our Lord! So then, I of myself serve the law of God with my mind, but with my flesh I serve the law of sin.[42]

The believer's mind is not transformed instantly either. It can be enticed by the desires of the body, which is still subject to sin and death, or it can rather be influenced by his spirit, which is already transformed, joined to God's Spirit and part of the new creation. Thus Paul admonishes believers in Yeshua,

> *2:* Do not be conformed to this world but be transformed by the renewal of your mind, that you may prove what is the will of God, what is good and acceptable and perfect.[43]

In order to demonstrate how this works, Bob George, in his book *Growing in Grace*, gives a very useful illustration:

> It reminds me of an AM/FM radio. I can switch to AM and listen to AM programming if I choose, or I can switch to FM and listen to FM programming. AM stations do not play on FM, nor do FM stations play on AM. I can't determine the programming that is being broadcast, but I can choose which one I will tune in.[44]

George goes on to say that in a similar way a believer in Yeshua can give his mind to the influences and philosophies of this world.

> His emotions and desires will predictably respond to that programming, and his actions will be characterized as the "works of the flesh." However having been born again by the Holy Spirit, he can present himself to God for the "renewing of the mind" through the word of God. Then he can choose to walk in that truth—that is, step out by dependent faith in God as his total sufficiency. He will then be walking by the Spirit.[45]

---

42. Rom 7:22–25 (RSV).
43. Rom 12:2 (RSV).
44. George, *Growing in Grace*, 114.
45. George, *Growing in Grace*, 114–15.

The renewal of the mind is an ongoing process that continues throughout the lifetime of a believer. It is the training ground for life in the coming new creation, of which he will have a part. Through this struggle he learns to overcome by relying on the power of God's Spirit dwelling within him, which is the power of Yeshua's resurrection and the assurance that his sins have already been forgiven in this present world by means of Yeshua's sacrifice.

THE REALM OF THE PRESENT CREATION

The contrast between the two realms is evident in the occasions when Paul spoke of the present age in distinction to the age to come.

> *20:* which he accomplished in Messiah when he raised him from the dead and made him sit at his right hand in the heavenly places, *21:* far above all rule and authority and power and dominion, and above every name that is named, not only *in this age but also in that which is to come* . . .[46]
>
> *8:* for while bodily training is of some value, godliness is of value in every way as it holds promise *for the present life and also for the age to come.*[47]

The believer in Yeshua and unbeliever both live in the present creation. It is important to remember that this present creation was originally formed by God in absolute perfection but was spoiled by its permeation by man's sin.

THE REALM OF THE NEW CREATION

We have seen that in the moment a believer accepts Yeshua he spiritually becomes a new creature. It is critical that we recognize when Scripture is speaking of the status that the believer already now has in the realm of the new creation, especially in the writings of Paul. These instances are easy to identify because Paul without fail includes the phrase in the Greek *eis Christos*, that is, "in Messiah," or a similar expression having the equivalent meaning. We have in fact seen a number of these already. In these Scripture passages below (many of which have been used in this chapter), pay close attention to the included phrase, which is in each case emphasized.

---

46. Eph 1:20–21 (RSV), emphasis added.
47. 1 Tim 4:8 (RSV), emphasis added; see also 1 Tim 6:17 and Heb 9:9.

3: Do you not know that all of us who have been baptized *into Messiah Yeshua* were baptized into his death?[48]

10: But *if Messiah is in you*, although your bodies are dead because of sin, your spirits are alive because of righteousness.[49]

3: For you have died and your life is hid *with Messiah in God*. When Messiah who is our life appears then you also will appear with him in glory.[50]

1: There is therefore now no condemnation to those who are *in Messiah Yeshua*. *2:* for the life-giving principles of the Spirit have freed you *in Messiah Yeshua* from the control of the principles sin and death.[51]

6: and [he] raised us up with him, and made us sit with him in the heavenly places *in Messiah Yeshua* . . .[52]

13: But now *in Messiah Yeshua* you who once were far off have been brought near in the blood of Messiah.[53]

26: for *in Messiah Yeshua* you are all sons of God, through faith.[54]

17: And if children, then heirs; heirs of God, and joint-heirs *with Messiah*; if so be that we suffer with him, that we may be also glorified together.[55]

3: Blessed be the God and Father of our Lord Jesus Christ, who has blessed us *in Messiah* with every spiritual blessing in the heavenly places . . .[56]

13: In him you also, who have heard the word of truth, the gospel of your salvation, and have believed in him, were sealed with the promised Holy Spirit, *14:* which is the guarantee of our inheritance until we acquire possession of it, to the praise of his glory.[57]

16: For the Lord himself will descend from heaven with a cry of command, with the archangel's call, and with the sound of the trumpet of God. And the dead *in Messiah* will rise first . . .[58]

---

48. Rom 6:3 (RSV).
49. Rom 8:10 (RSV).
50. Col 3:3 (RSV).
51. Rom 8:1–2 (Berkley Version).
52. Eph 2:4–6 (RSV).
53. Eph 2:13(RSV).
54. Gal 3:26 (RSV).
55. Rom 8:15–17 (KJV).
56. Eph 1:3 (RSV).
57. Eph 1:13–14 (RSV).
58. 1 Thess 4:16 (RSV).

> *11: If the Spirit of him who raised Yeshua from the dead dwells in you*, he who raised Messiah Yeshua from the dead will give life to your mortal bodies also through his Spirit which dwells in you.[59]
>
> *5:* For if we have been *united with him* in a death like his, we shall certainly be united with him in a resurrection like his.[60]
>
> *17:* Therefore, if any one is *in Messiah*, he is a new creation; the old has passed away, behold, the new has come.[61]

To sum up this chapter, the believer in Yeshua, being "in Messiah," has died with him, is raised with him, and is hidden with him. He awaits the return of Yeshua and the "adoption of sons," when he will receive a new, imperishable body and inherit the fullness of the earth of the new creation to rule and reign over it together with Yeshua. In the meantime, the believer lives in two realms simultaneously, that of the present creation and that of the new creation, the Spirit of God within his body assuring him of his future joint inheritance with Messiah.

---

59. Rom 8:11 (RSV).
60. Rom 6:5 (RSV).
61. 2 Cor 5:17 (RSV).

6

The Covenant

IN CHAPTER 3 WE examined how the Torah as a "schoolmaster" serves to lead an individual to Messiah. It is clear, however, that the Torah was not given to individuals. Rather, it was delivered by God at Mount Sinai to the entire nation of Israel as a special covenant with them.[1] The Torah was meant to be kept within the framework of an complete society. The Law was designed in such a way that it could only be observed by a community as a whole. The complex economic and social demands of the Law alone require its maintenance by no less than an entire society. Moreover, it is only in the context of a society whose administration was based on the Law that the Messiah and his role could be fully recognized and understood. As such, many of the commandments cannot be kept outside the context of a community and often commandments are directed toward the nation as a whole.

THE EXAMPLE NATION

When God set in motion his plan for the redemption of mankind, he required a people who would be completely devoted to his purposes, a nation that was holy and separate. No existing nation was found entirely fitting. Thus, beginning with Abraham, he created Israel, a nation unlike any other, to be his tool for redemption.

> 5: "Now therefore, if you will obey my voice and keep my covenant, you shall be my own possession among all peoples; for all

---

1. Exod 19:11; 20:1–26; 24:3.

> the earth is mine, *6:* and you shall be to me a kingdom of priests and a holy nation. These are the words which you shall speak to the children of Israel."[2]
>
> *1:* But now thus says the Lord, he who created you, O Jacob, he who formed you, O Israel: "Fear not, for I have redeemed you; I have called you by name, you are mine. *2:* When you pass through the waters I will be with you; and through the rivers, they shall not overwhelm you; when you walk through fire you shall not be burned, and the flame shall not consume you.[3]

Israel was intended to serve through its successes and failures as an example nation to mankind.

> *11:* Now all these things happened to them as examples, and they were written for our admonition, upon whom the ends of the ages have come.[4]

Just as the Law points an individual to Yeshua (see chapter 3), the Torah was ultimately intended to point Israel as a nation to Yeshua as the Messiah. As we have seen, the Torah leads a person to the Messiah in two stages. In the first stage it makes him conscious of his need for salvation by making him aware of his sin. In the second stage the Torah, in tandem with the writings of the prophets, points him to Yeshua the Messiah as the answer to that need. Moreover, God wanted to show the entire world through Israel that man, because of the sin resident within him, is, by his own means, incapable of meeting God's righteous requirements and so needs a savior.

> *19:* Now we know that whatever the law says it speaks to those who are under the law, so that every mouth may be stopped, and the whole world may be held accountable to God. *20:* For no human being will be justified in his sight by works of the law, since through the law comes knowledge of sin.[5]

In order to do this, God set up laboratory conditions in which all the circumstances were completely controlled and in which every irrelevant factor was, in effect, eliminated. He called Israel as a special nation to himself. He placed Israel in its own land, isolating it from the influence of the heathen nations surrounding it. He gave Israel his perfect laws and statutes, which were enumerated in detail and with absolute clarity, as the basis of his covenant with them. He moreover laid out the blueprint for a unique society

2. Exod 19:5–6 (RSV); cf. Deut 4:34–38.
3. Isa 43:1–2 (RSV).
4. 1 Cor 10:11 (NKJV).
5. Rom 3:19–20 (RSV).

in which his commandments could be kept without hindrance and in which he himself would even be present and available for consultation. All this was to make it crystal clear that even under the best possible conditions man is unable to meet God's demands and thus incapable of saving himself.

NO BANANAS!

In this regard, M. R. DeHann offers this amusing allegory[6]:

> To illustrate the giving of the law to Israel in order to prove to the whole world that it could not save anyone, imagine a farmer from Central America moving to northern Canada. He rents a 640-acre farm and tells the owner of the farm he plans to raise bananas. However, the landlord objects and tells him that it cannot be done. Neither the soil nor the climate is adapted to producing bananas. But the man insists, saying he has had years of experience raising bananas in the tropics, while the Canadian farmer says he has had years of experience farming in Canada and *knows* it cannot be done. But the banana man insists, and so to prove its impossibility and to convince the tenant of his folly, the owner gives his consent. He decides to set aside just one acre of the best-suited ground of the entire farm. No use planting the whole 640 acres in bananas unless it is first tested and proven on the most likely place. A spot is chosen in the lee of the mountain, with south exposure. Here the soil is the best and the temperature the highest. The ground is thoroughly worked, liberally fertilized, and the best of plants are procured, and all summer the best care in cultivating the plants is given. But in August there is a frost and the crop fails. No bananas!
>
> Not discouraged, the man tries it again the next year, for after all, you can't judge by one season. The second year it is the same early frost, and then the third year and the frost comes in July. They try another year—same result. No bananas! And then another and another. Now suppose they try it for fifteen hundred years, and yet no bananas. Finally the boss says, "Now are you convinced you cannot raise bananas on this farm in Canada?" But the man says, "Let's try it out on the rest of the farm." This would be folly, for if it cannot be done on the most likely and advantageous spot, it certainly cannot succeed under less favorable circumstances.

---

6. Dehann, *Law or Grace*, 60–61.

The prophet Isaiah, in a similar way, allegorized Israel as the vineyard of God:

> *1:* Let me sing for my beloved a love song concerning his vineyard: My beloved had a vineyard on a very fertile hill. *2:* He digged it and cleared it of stones, and planted it with choice vines; he built a watchtower in the midst of it, and hewed out a wine vat in it; and he looked for it to yield grapes, but it yielded wild grapes. *3:* And now, O inhabitants of Jerusalem and men of Judah, judge, I pray you, between me and my vineyard. *4:* What more was there to do for my vineyard, that I have not done in it? When I looked for it to yield grapes, why did it yield wild grapes?[7]

Thus, as the example nation, Israel showed the entire world how impossible it is to produce righteousness through works of the Law. Israel served as an example nation not only with regard to keeping the Torah, but in other capacities as well. By their reception of the Torah, they revealed God's perfect Law to all mankind. By their failure to observe the Torah entirely, they demonstrated to all mankind the utter futility of seeking salvation through works. It was in the context of Jewish society that the Messiah came into the world. By their rejection of Messiah, Israel opened the door for men of all nations to enter into the kingdom of God. By their eventual acceptance of him, they will bring Yeshua's return, the resurrection of the dead, and the new creation.

BETWEEN WE AND YE

Even when we take a closer look at Galatians 3:24–26 regarding the Law as a schoolmaster, here too we find that the Torah was not given to all individuals, but specifically to the Jewish people.[8]

> *24:* Wherefore the law was *our* schoolmaster to bring *us* unto Messiah, that *we* might be justified by faith. *25:* But after that faith is come, *we* are no longer under a schoolmaster. *26:* For *ye* are all children of God by faith in Messiah Yeshua.[9]

The difference between "we" in verses 24–25 and "ye" in verse 26 implies the distinction between Jewish and Gentile believers. When Paul says "we" in

---

7. Isa 5:1–4 (RSV).
8. Dehann, *Law or Grace*, 97–98.
9. Gal 3:24–26 (KJV), emphasis added.

verses 24–25 he is speaking as a member of the Jewish people. The Torah, given to the nation of Israel, was a schoolmaster to bring Jewish people to Messiah. The "ye" in verse 26 refers to the Gentile believers in Yeshua in Galatia to whom Paul is writing. These have become children of God by faith in Yeshua The implication is that while the Jewish believers are guided to the Messiah by the Torah, the Gentile believers come to be children of God by faith, entirely apart from the Torah.[10]

". . . THAT I MIGHT DWELL AMONG THEM . . ."

At the very heart of the covenant was God's promise to dwell among his people.

> 45: And I will dwell among the people of Israel, and will be their God. 46: And they shall know that I am the Lord their God, who brought them forth out of the land of Egypt that I might dwell among them; I am the Lord their God.[11]

He accomplished this through his Spirit inhabiting the Tabernacle, and later the Temple at Jerusalem.

THE CENTER OF JEWISH LIFE

During the second Jewish commonwealth, the Temple at Jerusalem was the center of everything for the people of Israel. It served as the national and international forum, the national bank, the supreme court, and the seat of the rulers of the people. The archives, where all the genealogical records of the people were kept, were located nearby. In short, it was the center of social and political Jewish life. But far above and beyond this, the Temple was the place where the Jewish people met with God! It was there where they found forgiveness for their sins through the sacrifice; it was the one and only place on the face of the earth where they could worship him fully.

Today, Jews gather in synagogues for worship. But it is important to realize that a synagogue is altogether different from what the Temple had been. The synagogue is a place of prayer and study of Torah, but within the Temple the very presence of God dwelt, his glory at times appearing in

---

10 Rom 3:28–29; Dehann, *Law or Grace*.
11. Exod 29:45–46 (RSV).

the visible form of smoke or a cloud.[12] When the Jewish people met at the Temple of Jerusalem, they literally stood before the Almighty!

A TOUR OF THE TEMPLE

We read that Yeshua's disciples marveled at the visage of the Temple buildings.[13] We know what the Temple looked like in the first century mainly from the descriptions of Josephus Flavius and the Mishnah.[14] The Temple of Jerusalem was reputed to be the grandest temple of the entire Roman Empire. It was admired as the object of no little pride by the Jewish people. The Temple in the time of Yeshua was truly a magnificent edifice of incredible splendor, spreading over the entire summit of Mount Moriah. In order to expand the Temple, King Herod the Great had created a spacious platform over the top of the hill, supported on its four sides by massive retaining walls constructed of gigantic ashlars.

THE COURT OF THE GENTILES

Within these retaining walls was a spacious courtyard known as the Court of the Gentiles since Gentiles were admitted into the courtyard, but no further. The Court of the Gentiles was surrounded on all four sides by magnificent porticoes. The oldest portico, located on the eastern side, Solomon's Porch, was frequented by Yeshua and his disciples.[15] At the southern side of the Court of the Gentiles was built the Royal Stoa, a magnificent colonnaded hall, similar to a basilica. A low balustrade ran around the space, separating the courtyard from the inner buildings of the Temple. All along the length of the balustrade there were fixed signs etched in limestone in Greek and Latin warning Gentiles not to enter further beyond that point under penalty of death. This is likely "the wall of partition" mentioned by Paul in Ephesians 2:11–22 (see chapter 9).

The outer retaining walls were pierced with magnificent portals. At the southeastern corner a monumental staircase climbed several stories to a glorious gate situated above it. Farther north, a bridge linked the Temple complex to the high-priestly quarter in the upper city.

---

12. Exod 40:35; 2 Chr 5:13–14; Isa 6:4; Ezek 10:3–4.
13. Matt 24:1–2.
14. Josephus, *War* 5.5 136–247; m. Middot.
15. John 10:23; Acts 3:11; 5:12.

The inner buildings of the Temple included chambers for storage and preparation of wood, oil purification for the completion of Nazirite vows,[16] and priestly garments. The Women's Court was called such because women were permitted to enter into it, but were allowed to proceed no farther. On the western side of the Woman's Court was an ascent of fifteen steps rising to Nicanor's Gate. Upon these steps the Levites sung the Songs of Ascent.[17] Nicanor's Gate was adorned with bronze doors that, according to legend, miraculously floated upon the sea when the ship transporting them was wrecked in a storm. Inside Nicanor's Gate was a courtyard that was broad from north to south but narrow from east to west. It was known as the Court of Israel, where a man of Israel could come watch while his sacrifice was being offered on his behalf. Beyond this point only the priests were allowed.

In the spacious courtyard between the Court of Israel and the main Temple building was an altar. With it were tables and hooks used in the preparation of the sacrifices. Also in the courtyard stood the laver[18] where the high priest washed his hands and feet when they approached the altar or entered the sanctuary.

Beyond these towered the sanctuary itself, standing fifteen stories high, 60 meters (200 feet) long, and 32.4 meters (108 feet) wide, and topped by a golden parapet.[19] It was oriented east to west with its facade facing the Mount of Olives. Constructed of gleaming white stone, the sanctuary with its facade and porch was wider at the front and narrower at the rear, like a crouching lion.[20] The overall impression was that of a glistening mountain of snow.[21] This building was entirely the realm of the priests. It was comprised of three parts: the *Ulam*, the porch; the *Hechal*, the hall; and the *Debir*, the holy of holies.

ULAM, THE PORCH

The "porch" ran along the width of the eastern side of the temple building. An enormous portal, 20 meters (66 feet) tall and 10 meters (33 feet) wide, gave entrance into the building. It was flanked by a gigantic column on either side, possibly reminiscent of Yachin and Boaz, the two bronze monumental columns that stood in front of the Temple in King Solomon's

16. Num 6:21.
17. Pss 120–134.
18. Exod 30:17–21.
19. See Deut 22:8.
20. M. Middot 4:6.
21. Josephus, *War* 5, 5:7.

day.[22] Inside the entrance spread an enormous votive golden grapevine. The people of Israel would donate leaves and branches to be added to it.

HECHAL, THE HALL (THE HOLY PLACE)

The *Hechal* was a long magnificent hall six meters (20 feet) long east to west with a tall ceiling. On the north and south of the *Hechal* were staircases ascending to chambers built into the walls. At the western end of the hall in front of the *Parochet*, the veil that divided the *Hechal* from the *Debir*, stood three objects associated with the maintenance and ministry of the Temple: On the north was the table of the bread of the presence.[23] The bread on the table was replaced weekly on the Sabbath. On the south was the seven-branched lampstand, the *menorah*.[24] Between the table of the bread of the presence and the *menorah*, facing the veil, was the bronze altar, upon which incense was burned every day.[25] The *Parochet*, the veil,[26] measured a full handbreadth thick.[27] Presumably it was embroidered, like the veil of the Tabernacle, with cherubim.[28]

DEBIR, THE HOLY OF HOLIES

Within the veil, the *Debir*, the holy of holies, was the place where the presence of the Almighty resided. It measured 12 meters (40 feet) long and, like the *Ulam*, it had a very high ceiling. The room was not furnished with any form of lighting. The only person allowed into this room was the high priest, and only on Yom Kippur, the Day of Atonement.[29] He was required to enter the holy of holies on that day with the blood of a bull,[30] a type of the blood of Yeshua's atonement, and a cloud of incense that served as a screen, blocking direct contact with the presence of the Almighty.

22. 1 Kgs 7:5–21.
23. Exod 25:23–30.
24. Exod 25:31–40..
25. Exod 30:1–10; Luke 1:9.
26. Exod 26:31–33 ; Matt 27:51.
27. M. Shekalim 8:5.
28. Exod 26:31–33.
29. Lev 16:1–2.
30. Heb 9:7.

THE ARK OF THE COVENANT

Within the holy of holies is in the Tabernacle and the Temple of Solomon rested the ark of the covenant. This receptacle was a chest measuring 115 centimeters (45 inches) long, 70 centimeters (27 inches) wide, and 70 centimeters (27 inches) high, made of acacia wood and plated with gold.[31] It contained the two tablets of the Ten Commandments, which were the summary of the Torah. It also contained, at one time, Aaron's rod that budded, and the golden pot of manna that God fed Israel with during their wanderings in the wilderness. The ark was topped by a lid upon which two golden cherubim[32] spread their wings.[33] There, between the cherubim, the Almighty was enthroned in the midst of the people of Israel.[34] Besides the cherubim on the cover of the ark, in Solomon's Temple, the ark itself was flanked by two gigantic cherubim, one on either side of it.[35] The ark, then, was a representation of God's covenant with Israel and his promise to dwell among them.

In the time of Yeshua, the ark of the covenant was absent.[36] Within the holy of holies there was only the "rock," the *Even Shita*, the foundation stone. This was evidently the exposed bedrock of the hill upon which the Temple was built. The sanctuary was originally built on the threshing floor of Ornan the Jebusite (see below). The main feature of an ancient threshing floor was an exposed, smoothed patch of bedrock. John the Baptist warned that God was about to purge his threshing floor, obviously foreshadowing the destruction of the Second Temple (see chapter 10).

A MODEL OF HEAVENLY THINGS

The writer of the book of Hebrews tells us that when Moses ascended Mount Sinai he was shown the ground plan for the Tabernacle, the portable "tent of meeting" after which the Jerusalem Temple would eventually be designed. He was told to be careful, in constructing the Tabernacle, to pay

---

31. Exod 25:10–22.

32. A cherub (pl. cherubim) is a winged supernatural spirit being usually serving in a guardian and or heraldic role. In Scripture, cherubim display the attributes of oxen, lions, eagles, and humans (Ezek 1:5–7; Rev 4:6–8). They express God's glory and power. In ancient Near Eastern iconography, a cherub is a composite creature usually depicted as a winged lion or an ox having a human head.

33. Exod 25:18–20.

34. Exod 25:22, Pss 80:1; 90:1.

35. 2 Chr 3:10–13.

36. M. Yoma 5:2.

close attention to the pattern that he saw on the mount.[37] Now, if the Tabernacle and the Temple after it were "shadows of heavenly things," models only, what is the substance?

THE ABODE OF GOD

In attempting to perceive the substance, it helps to see that the Temple represents three things: firstly, it represents heaven, the abode of God; secondly, it represents the way into heaven; thirdly, it represents the body of Yeshua. In the book of Revelation, it seems that heaven is set up very similarly to the Temple. At the very core of the Temple was the holy of holies, where the Almighty dwelt. The mercy seat, the cover over the ark of the covenant within the holy of holies, was the throne of God.[38] Likewise in the book of Revelation, the throne of God is in the center of heaven. The Letter to the Hebrews tells us,

> *24:* For Messiah has entered, not into a sanctuary made with hands, a copy of the true one, but into heaven itself, now to appear in the presence of God on our behalf.[39]

The Temple, then, represents heaven.

THE WAY INTO HEAVEN

Secondly, the Temple stands for the way into heaven, that is to say, into the presence of God. When the priest entered into the Temple, he brought his sacrifice to the altar of burnt offering, which speaks of the cross. He bathed in the laver,[40] which speaks of baptism. Psalm 100 admonishes, "Enter into his gates with thanksgiving, and into his courts with praise!"[41] When the priest entered into the holy place, he saw to his right the table of the bread of the presence, signifying the "Bread of Life."[42] On the opposite side, he saw the *menorah*, the candelabra, representing the "Light of the World."[43] In front of him was the altar of incense. In Revelation 5:8 incense represents

---

37. Heb 8:5; see Exod 25:40.
38. Pss 80:1; 99:1–2.
39. Heb 9:24 (RSV).
40. Exod 30:18–21.
41. Ps 100:4 (RSV).
42. John 6:35.
43. John 8:12.

the prayers of the saints (believers in Yeshua). Before the priest could come into the presence of God, he had to pass through the veil, which Hebrews 10:20 tells us represented the flesh of Yeshua. Thus, the Temple stood for the sacrificial death of Yeshua, the true way into heaven and the presence of God.

THE BODY OF YESHUA

Finally, the Temple represents the body of Yeshua. While a number of New Testament passages allude to this, probably the passage that makes this point most clear is found in the second chapter of the Gospel According to John. Here Yeshua cleanses the Temple of the money-changers. "His disciples remembered that it was written, 'Zeal for thy house will consume me.'"[44] The Jewish authorities approached him and asked, "'What sign have you to show us for doing this?'"[45] "Yeshua answered them, 'Destroy this temple, and in three days I will raise it up.'"[46] The leaders thought that he spoke of the building; later his disciples understood that he spoke rather of his body, in which the whole fulness of deity dwells bodily[47] and which was resurrected on the third day. Mention has already been made of how the veil was equated with his flesh.

REJECTED CORNERSTONE

In Acts 4:11, Peter relates what is written in Psalm 118:22 to Yeshua. "The stone which the builders rejected Has become the chief cornerstone."[48] The question is, of what building is he the cornerstone? When a person accepts Yeshua and is born anew, God's spirit comes to dwell in his heart and in that sense the believer literally becomes God's Temple.

> *19:* Do you not know that your body is a temple of the Holy Spirit within you, which you have from God? You are not your own; *20:* you were bought with a price. So glorify God in your body.[49]

---

44. John 2:17 (RSV).
45. John 2:18 RSV).
46. John 2:19 (RSV).
47. Col 2:9.
48. Ps 118:22 (NKJV).
49. 1 Cor 6:19 (RSV).

Each believer is, however, only a small portion of the complete Temple of God's Spirit on earth represented by the collective body of believers in Yeshua. Peter admonishes, "Ye also, as lively stones, are built up a spiritual house..."[50] Likewise, Paul exhorts the believers in Yeshua at Ephesus,

> *19:* So then you are no longer strangers and sojourners, but you are fellow citizens with the saints and members of the household of God, *20:* built upon the foundation of the apostles and prophets, Messiah Yeshua himself being the cornerstone, *21:* in whom the whole structure is joined together and grows into a holy temple in the Lord; *22:* in whom you also are built into it for a dwelling place of God in the Spirit.[51]

The Temple, then, represents both the single and corporate body of Yeshua.

A PARALLEL GOSPEL IN STONE

In addition to the Jewish longing to see the Temple rebuilt, a number of scriptural passages seem to predict that the Temple will indeed one day stand again on its ancient site in Jerusalem.[52]

Some believers in Yeshua see the effectuality of the Temple as having ended with the death and resurrection of Yeshua. The thinking goes that since the primary activity carried out in the Temple was sacrifice, which was only a shadow of the true sacrifice of Yeshua, the Temple and the Temple sacrifice are of no more use. The destruction of the Temple in 70 CE is offered as proof that God is no longer interested in sacrifice or Temple service. Moreover, those who hold such views see a return to the Temple sacrifices as devaluing Yeshua's sacrifice, treating it as less than all-sufficient and thus an offense to God's offer of grace to mankind. The Temple, however, is not in competition with the Gospel but rather parallel to it! Just as the Temple sacrifice helped the people of Israel to look forward to the atonement of Yeshua, the Temple sacrifice in the future Temple will help them look back to remember the cross and comprehend its significance. In representing heaven, the way to heaven through Yeshua's sacrificial death, and the body of Yeshua, the future Temple will act as a kind of living Gospel. But the question that must be asked is: if we have the reality, why then should we return to the model? The answer is that, as the jewel of the Torah in its role as a schoolmaster, the Temple in the most vivid way points to the Messiah and his atonement. It

---

50. 1 Pet 2:5–8 (RSV).
51. Eph 2:19–22 (RSV).
52. E.g., Mic 4:2; 2 Thess 2:4; Rev 11:1–2.

must be remembered that the Torah was primarily given not to individuals, and neither was it given to all mankind, but rather to the "house of Judah and the house of Israel." The Temple then has yet a glorious role to fulfill in leading the Jewish people as a nation to its Messiah. Rabbinic Judaism teaches that the way to God is through prayer, good works, and the giving of charity, but where is the atonement for sin; where in the observance of these things is there power to resurrect the dead? One day Israel will indeed accept its Messiah, but before the Jewish people will be ready to recognize him and comprehend what he has done for them, they must first understand that the way to God is by means of the altar of sacrifice and that ". . . without the shedding of blood there is no forgiveness of sins."[53]

THE MESSAGE OF THE TEMPLE

According to Genesis 2:8-9, a prominent feature in the garden of Eden was the tree of life growing in its midst. There it nourished man with the sustenance of eternal life. However, through transgression of God's commandment and rebellion against his rule, man was expelled from the garden and was consequently denied the tree's life-giving fruit.[54]

Using the image of the tree of life, the ornamentation employed in Solomon's Temple was carefully devised to convey a powerful message.

RECEPTACLE OF THE COVENANT

As the throne of God, the ark represented the tangible sign of his presence. As the receptacle of the Torah, it contained the two tablets of the Ten Commandments,[55] which were the summary of the Torah. At one point it also contained a golden pot filled with manna that God fed Israel with during their wanderings in the wilderness,[56] and Aaron's rod that budded.[57] The ark held the stated terms of the covenant between God and his people Israel.[58] The covenant was ratified when all the tribes of Israel stood together beneath Mount Sinai and corporately heard the voice of God.[59] As such, it represented

---

53. Heb 9:22 (RSV); see also Lev 17:11.
54. Gen 3.
55. Deut 10:4-5.
56. Exod 16:33-34.
57. Num 17:10.
58. Exod 25:21.
59. Exod 19; Deut 5.

the embodiment of the covenant, the symbol of Israel's choseness. This iconography within the Temple of Solomon is detailed in 1 Kings 6:29, 32:

> *29:* He carved all the walls of the house round about with carved figures of cherubim and palm trees and open flowers, in the inner and outer rooms.[60]
>
> *32:* He covered the two doors of olivewood with carvings of cherubim, palm trees and open flowers; he overlaid them with gold, and spread gold upon the cherubim and the palm trees.[61]

AN ANCIENT ARTISTIC MOTIF

These verses describe a very ancient motif found throughout the ancient Near East, beginning in the Bronze and Iron Ages.[62] It featured naturalistic figures of animals, often ibexes, posed antithetically (that is standing opposite each other) on either side of a palm tree .

The late Yigal Shiloh pointed out the extensive influence that this iconography had on Israelite art and architecture, particularly how the palm inspired the so-called Proto-Aeolic capital, which he demonstrated was also employed in Solomon's Temple.[63] It is evident, then, that the palmettes together with cherubim mentioned in 1 Kings 6:29, 32, 35 represented an expression of this ancient motif. This being so, they must have been arranged as a palmette flanked on either side by a cherub. In Ezekiel's vision of the Temple, which he saw in the interim period between the destruction of the First Temple in 586 BCE and before the construction of the Second Temple in 515 BCE, the prophet described the inner walls of the *Hechal*, the main hall, as having been carved with precisely this scheme:

> And on all the walls round about the inner room and the nave were carved likenesses *18:* of cherubim and palm trees, a palm tree between cherub and cherub.[64]

The tree guarded on either side by cherubim recalls Genesis 3:22–24:

---

60. I Kgs 6:29 (RSV).

61. I Kgs 6:29, 32 (RSV).

62. The palm tree and ibex motif was popular in the Levant and much of the rest of the ancient world for many centuries. The name given this motif is derived from the decoration of a class of a Late Bronze Age and Early Iron Age pottery described by Ruth Amiran in Amiran, *Ancient Pottery*, 161–65.

63. Shiloh, *Proto-Aeolic Capital*, 90.

64. Ezek 41:17b–18a (RSV).

> *22:* Then the Lord God said, "Behold, the man has become like one of us, knowing good and evil; and now, lest he put forth his hand and take also of the tree of life, and eat, and live for ever" *23:* therefore the Lord God sent him forth from the garden of Eden, to till the ground from which he was taken. *24:* He drove out the man; and at the east of the garden of Eden he placed the cherubim, and a flaming sword which turned every way, to guard the way to the tree of life.[65]

The palm flanked by cherubim carved into the walls of the inner room of the Temple, then, evidently represented the tree of life. The pattern of the cherubim standing on either side of the tree of life was carved repeatedly into the walls of the *Hechal* of Solomon's Temple.[66] However, within the *Debir* (the holy of holies), gilded cherubim stood on either side, not of the tree of life, but of the ark of the covenant.

> *23:* In the inner sanctuary he made two cherubim of olivewood, each ten cubits high. *24:* Five cubits was the length of one wing of the cherub, and five cubits the length of the other wing of the cherub; it was ten cubits from the tip of one wing to the tip of the other. *25:* The other cherub also measured ten cubits; both cherubim had the same measure and the same form. *26:* The height of one cherub was ten cubits, and so was that of the other cherub. *27:* He put the cherubim in the innermost part of the house; and the wings of the cherubim were spread out so that a wing of one touched the one wall, and a wing of the other cherub touched the other wall; their other wings touched each other in the middle of the house. *28:* And he overlaid the cherubim with gold.[67]
>
> *6:* Then the priests brought the ark of the covenant of the Lord to its place, in the inner sanctuary of the house, in the most holy place, underneath the wings of the cherubim. *7:* For the cherubim spread out their wings over the place of the ark, so that the cherubim made a covering above the ark and its poles.[68]

The sight of two golden fifteen-foot cherubim with a combined wing-span of thirty feet filling the holy of holies must have been truly awe-inspiring.[69]

65. Gen 3:22–24 (RSV).
66. 1 Kgs 6:29; cf. Ezek 41:18–20.
67. 1 Kgs 6:23–28 (RSV).
68. 1 Kgs 8:6–7 (RSV).

69. This is based on the reckoning that the standard cubit equals 18 inches. A cubit was the distance between the middle finger and the elbow and as a measurement varied from about 17.7 to 20.5 inches. Gower, *New Manners and Customs*, 147. With regard to

(These are of course not to be confused with the two smaller cherubim fashioned on the lid of the ark, the so-called mercy seat.[70]) The supreme holiness that prevented the common man of Israel from seeing within the *Debir* and relegated the sight of the ark and its guardians to the eye of his imagination surely added to his sense of wonder and mystery. That he was banished from seeing behind the veil into this hallowed place reminded him of his expulsion from the delights of Eden. The extensive repetition of the tree of life and cherubim carved into the walls of the *Hechal* of the Temple served to emphasize the point: *the ark of the covenant within the holy of holies replaced the tree of life.* Here in the holy of holies, in the heart of the Temple, God's covenant stood in place of the tree of life. A careful reading of Genesis 3:24 reveals the fine point that the cherubim guarded not the tree of life itself but rather the *way* to the tree of life. God's covenant with the people of Israel was not the tree of life, but only the *way* to the tree of life. This really makes sense when we remember that the Torah, God's covenant, was intended to lead the Jewish people as a nation to Yeshua and his atonement. The cherubim were set as guardians of the way to life as a result of sin. Their task was to assure that access to eternal life was only by authorized means. Yeshua proclaimed:

> *14:* For the gate is narrow and the way is hard, that leads to life, and those who find it are few.[71]

The way is narrow to the point of its being exclusive. There is but one way to eternal life. Yeshua declared, "I am the way, and the truth, and the life; no one comes to the Father, but by me."[72]

The message of the Temple, then, is that Yeshua is the one and only means into the presence of God and the eternal life that only he can give. It is only through Yeshua's atonement that we can have fellowship with God.

It is important to realize that all of this imagery was in Solomon's Temple. In the Second Temple, when Yeshua arrived on the scene, the ark of the covenant and the cherubim were absent.

THE RISE AND FALL OF THE TEMPLE

In order to better understand the significance of the Temple and the role it must yet play in God's plan for the redemption of Israel, it is worthwhile

---

measurements used in Solomon's Temple, see Paul and Dever, *Biblical Archaeology*, 173–74.

70. Exod 25:17–21.
71. Matt 7:14 (RSV).
72. John 14:6 (RSV).

to review a brief history of the Temple. The redemption of Israel is tied to specific dates and events in history.

THE TABERNACLE

At Mt. Sinai Israel was given the Tabernacle, a portable form of the Temple.[73] This they carried throughout their desert wanderings and the first generations of their settlement in the land of Canaan. The Tabernacle served as a blueprint for the Temple that would be built on Mount Zion (Temple Mount) in Jerusalem.

". . . THE PLACE WHICH THE LORD YOUR GOD WILL CHOOSE . . ."

While still in the Sinai Desert, God spoke to the people of Israel,

> *5:* But you shall seek the place which the Lord your God will choose out of all your tribes to put his name and make his habitation there; thither you shall go, *6:* and thither you shall bring your burnt offerings and your sacrifices, your tithes and the offering that you present, your votive offerings, your freewill offerings, and the firstlings of your herd and of your flock; *7:* and there you shall eat before the Lord your God, and you shall rejoice, you and your households, in all that you undertake, in which the Lord your God has blessed you.[74]

It was only after they had entered the land of Israel that they found out where "the place" was. Its location was revealed by a miracle. The background of the story is found in the book of 1 Chronicles 21:1–8:

> *1:* Satan stood up against Israel, and incited David to number Israel. *2:* So David said to Jo'ab and the commanders of the army, "Go, number Israel, from Beer-sheba to Dan, and bring me a report, that I may know their number." *3:* But Jo'ab said, "May the Lord add to his people a hundred times as many as they are! Are they not, my lord the king, all of them my lord's servants? Why then should my lord require this? Why should he bring guilt upon Israel?" *4:* But the king's word prevailed against Jo'ab. So Jo'ab departed and went throughout all Israel, and came back to Jerusalem. *5:* And Jo'ab gave the sum of the

---

73. Exod 25—27.
74. Deut 12:5–7 (RSV).

> numbering of the people to David. In all Israel there were one million one hundred thousand men who drew the sword, and in Judah four hundred and seventy thousand who drew the sword. 6: But he did not include Levi and Benjamin in the numbering, for the king's command was abhorrent to Jo'ab. 7: But God was displeased with this thing, and he smote Israel. 8: And David said to God, "I have sinned greatly in that I have done this thing. But now, I pray thee, take away the iniquity of thy servant; for I have done very foolishly."[75]

David had sinned by taking a census of the people of Israel. Exodus 30:12 states that if a census of the people of Israel is taken a ransom must be paid so that no plague falls upon them. As a punishment for his transgression, God presented David with a choice of options. He chose a plague upon the nation by the hand of God.

> 9: And the Lord spoke to Gad, David's seer, saying, 10: "Go and say to David, 'Thus says the Lord, Three things I offer you; choose one of them, that I may do it to you.'" 11: So Gad came to David and said to him, "Thus says the Lord, 'Take which you will: 12: either three years of famine; or three months of devastation by your foes, while the sword of your enemies overtakes you; or else three days of the sword of the Lord, pestilence upon the land, and the angel of the Lord destroying throughout all the territory of Israel.' Now decide what answer I shall return to him who sent me." 13: Then David said to Gad, "I am in great distress; let me fall into the hand of the Lord, for his mercy is very great; but let me not fall into the hand of man." 14: So the Lord sent a pestilence upon Israel; and there fell seventy thousand men of Israel. 15: And God sent the angel to Jerusalem to destroy it; but when he was about to destroy it, the Lord saw, and he repented of the evil; and he said to the destroying angel, "It is enough; now stay your hand." And the angel of the Lord was standing by the threshing floor of Ornan the Jeb'usite. 16: And David lifted his eyes and saw the angel of the Lord standing between earth and heaven, and in his hand a drawn sword stretched out over Jerusalem. Then David and the elders, clothed in sackcloth, fell upon their faces. 17: And David said to God, "Was it not I who gave command to number the people? It is I who have sinned and done very wickedly. But these sheep, what have they done? Let thy hand, I pray thee, O Lord my God, be against me and against my father's house; but let not the plague be upon thy people." 18: Then the angel of the Lord commanded Gad to say

---

75. 1 Chr 21:1–8 (RSV).

to David that David should go up and rear an altar to the Lord on the threshing floor of Ornan the Jeb'usite. *19:* So David went up at Gad's word, which he had spoken in the name of the Lord. *20:* Now Ornan was threshing wheat; he turned and saw the angel, and his four sons who were with him hid themselves. *21:* As David came to Ornan, Ornan looked and saw David and went forth from the threshing floor, and did obeisance to David with his face to the ground. *22:* And David said to Ornan, "Give me the site of the threshing floor that I may build on it an altar to the Lord —give it to me at its full price—that the plague may be averted from the people." *23:* Then Ornan said to David, "Take it; and let my lord the king do what seems good to him; see, I give the oxen for burnt offerings, and the threshing sledges for the wood, and the wheat for a cereal offering. I give it all." *24:* But King David said to Ornan, "No, but I will buy it for the full price; I will not take for the Lord what is yours, nor offer burnt offerings which cost me nothing."[76]

It is no coincidence that the place where God heard David's entreaty and stayed the plague was also the place of Abraham's intended sacrifice of Isaac, Mount Moriah, known in the Scripture as Mount Zion.[77] This was the very place that Abraham had called "the Lord will provide."

> *14:* So Abraham called the name of that place The Lord will provide; as it is said to this day, "On the mount of the Lord it shall be provided."[78]

THE TABERNACLE OF DAVID

God promised that he would bring them to the place that he would choose. In the time of King David (about 1000 BCE) it was determined that this place was at Mount Moriah, in Jerusalem, the very place of Isaac's near-sacrifice. King David's revelation led him to purchase the mount for 600 shekels

---

76. 1 Chr 21:9–24 (RSV).

77. Visitors to modern Jerusalem may find this somewhat confusing since today Mount Moriah (the Temple Mount) and Mount Zion are two different hills. Mount Moriah is located on the eastern side of the Old City of Jerusalem, while modern Mount Zion is to the southwestern side of it. How this came to be is a long and fascinating story. Let it suffice here that Mount Moriah and Mount Zion in the Scriptures refer to the very same hill on the eastern side of the city, at the northern end of which the Temple was constructed.

78. Gen 22:14 (RSV).

of gold from Ornan the Jebusite.[79] David built a tabernacle (evidently after the manner of the Tabernacle of the desert wanderings[80]). When James in Acts 15:16–17, quoting Amos 9:11, says that God will raise up the Tabernacle of David, this refers to a restoration of Davidic rule in the messianic kingdom (see chapter 4). David wished to build the Temple itself but he was prevented from doing so because he was a man of war. Rather, the task was passed down to his son, Solomon.[81]

The essential thing about the Tabernacle, and later the Temple, was that within it the very presence of God dwelt in a tangible way. God's promise that he would dwell with the people of Israel was not merely allegorical or poetic. The God of Israel was actually present with his people in the Tabernacle as they traveled to and settled in the land. Once the place that God had chosen was determined, the place where he would meet with his people became established and permanently fixed in the Temple. At the dedication of the Temple, Solomon asked,

> *27:* "But will God indeed dwell on the earth? Behold, heaven and the highest heaven cannot contain thee; how much less this house which I have built!"[82]

Solomon prayed,

> *38:* whatever prayer, whatever supplication is made by any man or by all thy people Israel, each knowing the affliction of his own heart and stretching out his hands toward this house; *39:* then hear thou in heaven thy dwelling place, and forgive, and act, and render to each whose heart thou knowest, according to all his ways (for thou, thou only, knowest the hearts of all the children of men); *40:* that they may fear thee all the days that they live in the land which thou gavest to our fathers. *41:* "Likewise when a foreigner, who is not of thy people Israel, comes from a far country for thy name's sake *42:* (for they shall hear of thy great name, and thy mighty hand, and of thy outstretched arm), when he comes and prays toward this house, *43:* hear thou in heaven thy dwelling place, and do according to all for which the foreigner calls to thee; in order that all the peoples of the earth may know thy name and fear thee, as do thy people Israel, and that they may know that this house which I have built is called by thy name.[83]

---

79. 1 Chr 21:25; cf. 2 Sam 24:24.
80. 2 Sam 6:17; 1 Chr 15:1; 16:1,4–38; 17:1.
81. 2 Sam 7:4–17; 1 Kgs 5–6.
82. 1 Kgs 8:27 (RSV).
83. 1 Kgs 8:38–43 (RSV).

EVICTED!

As time passed, Israel became overconfident of the continued presence of God in their midst and the continuance of the Temple was taken for granted. Their hearts were not right before the Lord when they brought the sacrifice.[84] To carry out his purposes, God had no choice but to start over. The Temple was destroyed and the Jewish people were evicted from Jerusalem and the land of Israel twice in their history. The first diaspora began in the year 586 BCE. The people until that time had been living continually on the land of Israel. That they could be uprooted from their place or that the Temple could be destroyed was unthinkable. The prophets warned time and again that a day of judgment was coming. It came as a great shock when the Babylonians, led by Nebuchadnezzar, king of Babylon, destroyed the Temple and laid the city waste,[85] and the people of Israel found themselves led away captive to Babylon. The first exile was of comparatively short duration. At the outset, the prophet Jeremiah warned that the first diaspora would continue seventy years, after which time the Jews would return to their land.[86]

EZEKIEL'S VISION OF THE TEMPLE

During the intervening years between the destruction of Jerusalem in 586 BCE and the rebuilding of Jerusalem and the construction of the Second Temple in 515 BCE, the prophet Ezekiel, residing in Babylon, was carried away by the Spirit of God to the land of Israel and given a detailed vision of Jerusalem and the Temple.

> *1:* In the twenty-fifth year of our exile, at the beginning of the year, on the tenth day of the month, in the fourteenth year after the city was conquered, on that very day, the hand of the Lord was upon me, *2:* and brought me in the visions of God into the land of Israel, and set me down upon a very high mountain, on which was a structure like a city opposite me. *3:* When he brought me there, behold, there was a man, whose appearance was like bronze, with a line of flax and a measuring reed in his hand; and he was standing in the gateway. *4:* And the man said to me, "Son of man, look with your eyes, and hear with your ears, and set your mind upon all that I shall show you, for you

---

84. See for example Isa 1:2–31.
85. 2 Kgs 25:1–21; 2 Chr 36:15–20.
86. Jer 25:11–12; 29:10, 2 Chr 36:20–21.

were brought here in order that I might show it to you; declare all that you see to the house of Israel."[87]

It is important to remember that at the time that the vision was given Jerusalem and the Temple lay in ruins and the Jewish people were for the most part living in exile in Babylon. A number of details here of the Temple are unlike those of the either the First or Second Temple. This has led some to conclude that it is a vision of the future Temple that will be standing when Messiah will be reigning in Jerusalem. We will return to Ezekiel's vision of the Temple in chapter 11.

REBUILDING THE TEMPLE

Babylon passed through the vicissitudes of political change. The land of the Chaldeans changed hands when the Babylonians lost out to the Medes and the Persians. King Cyrus of the Persians gave a command permitting the Jews to return to their ancient homeland and rebuild the Temple.[88] The exile in Babylon, among other things, served to purify Israel from idolatrous practices and put them back on the track of God's plan. In the year 515 BCE, the Temple was rebuilt at the hands of the governor of Judea, Zerababel, son of Shaltiel, and Jeshua, son of Jozadak, the high priest.[89] These two men faced many great and difficult obstacles in completing their mission of restoring the house of God. After the disappearance of the ark of the covenant, the high priest would place the incense censor on the rock known in Hebrew as the *Even Shytia* on the day of Yom Kippur.[90]

The Second Temple stood for a total of 585 years. In the year 167 BCE, the Temple was defiled by the invading Syrian Seleucid monarch, Antiochus IV Epiphanes. The Syrians were driven out and the Temple cleansed and rededicated in the year 164 BCE. This is commemorated every year in the holiday Chanukah, meaning "dedication."

King Herod the Great (who reigned 37–4 BCE), renovated the Temple from the ground up. (This was the same king who, hoping to kill Yeshua, ordered the slaughter of all male children under two years of age in Bethlehem.[91]) It is important to realize that, though the building was reconstructed from top to bottom and is called "Herod's Temple," it was nonetheless

---

87. Ezek 40:1–4 (RSV).
88. 2 Chr 36:22–23; Ezra 1:1–4.
89. Ezra 3:7–12; Zech 4:16–19.
90. M. Yoma 5:2.
91. Matt 1:16–18.

considered to be a continuation of the same Temple originally built by Jeshua and Zerubbabel. The reconstructed Temple was that to which Yeshua the Messiah came, according to the promise of Malachi 3:1–4.

> *1:* "Behold, I send my messenger to prepare the way before me, and the Lord whom you seek will suddenly come to his temple; the messenger of the covenant in whom you delight, behold, he is coming, says the Lord of hosts. *2:* But who can endure the day of his coming, and who can stand when he appears? "For he is like a refiner's fire and like fullers' soap; *3:* he will sit as a refiner and purifier of silver, and he will purify the sons of Levi and refine them like gold and silver, till they present right offerings to the Lord. *4:* Then the offering of Judah and Jerusalem will be pleasing to the Lord as in the days of old and as in former years.[92]

The city of Jerusalem and the Temple were destroyed a second time in the year 70 CE, this time at the hands of the Romans. The first, seventy-year-long diaspora had served as a dry run for the later, two-thousand-year-long exile that followed the destruction of the Second Temple. The seventy years of the first diaspora allowed the people of Israel to form a plan by which Israel could exist for a long period of time without a Temple.

MADE INTO A DUNG HEAP

Sixty-two years later, the Jews rebelled again against Roman rule in the Second (so-called Bar-Kochba) Revolt, resulting in their being permanently banned from Jerusalem.

In the years that followed the expulsion of the Jews from Jerusalem after the Bar-Kochba Revolt, the Temple Mount was a less important quarter of the city. The Roman emperor Hadrian (who reigned 117–138 CE) occupied the area and is believed to have built a pagan temple or at least placed pagan statues on the mount.[93] The Byzantines (Christianized Romans), who ruled the land of Israel from 324 to 636, made the Temple Mount into a huge garbage dump in order to emphasize Yeshua's words in Matthew 24:2 that the Temple would lay in ruins.

---

92. Mal 3:1–4 (RSV).
93. Mazar, "Hadrian's Legion," 53–58, 82–82.

THE DOME OF THE ROCK

The fortunes of the Temple Mount began to change when the Arabs conquered Jerusalem in the year 638.[94] The Umayyad dynasty rulers, hoping to legitimize Islam and at the same time attract Jews to the fledgling religion, built the Dome of the Rock over the former place of the holy of holies. Constructed in 692 by Abd al-Malik[95] and inspired from octagonal commemorative churches, the building evidently marked the rock upon which the most holy place of the Temple had stood. The patch of bedrock upon which it is built is reportedly the rock that is known in Hebrew as the *Even Shytia*, the foundation stone. Al-Aqsa Mosque was built in the early eighth century, shortly after the Dome of the Rock, as a place of Islamic prayer,[96] on the southern end of the Temple Mount, where the Royal Stoa had once stood in the days of Herod's Temple. The Jews did not convert in droves to Islam as it had been expected. Much later, a legend grew up that the Dome of the Rock was the place where Mohamed had leaped into heaven in his night vision on his mythical steed, Barak.

THE INDELIBLE JEWISH MEMORY OF THE TEMPLE

Although it was destroyed two thousand years ago, the memory of the Temple remains firm in Jewish consciousness. In every observant Jewish household, the wall facing Jerusalem and the Temple is left unadorned. At the height of every Jewish wedding, the couple shares a cup of wine symbolizing their joy. Immediately afterward, the groom takes this same cup, places it on the floor, and smashes it with his foot, lest in the midst of their gladness they not forget that the Temple lies in ruins. In the Amidah, the daily prayer, the petition is made that the Temple be built "speedily in our day."[97]

THE WESTERN WALL

On June 7 of 1967 the nation of Israel was stunned by the announcement of General Mordechai Gur, "The Temple Mount is in our hands."[98] However, immediately after the Six-Day War was over General Chief of Staff Moshe

---

94. Avigad, *Discovering Jerusalem*, 247.
95. Anwarul and Islam, "Dome of the Rock," 109.
96. Avigad, *Discovering Jerusalem*, 247.
97. The *Amidah* (*Eighteen Benedictions*).
98. "Six-Day War."

Dayan returned the operation of the Temple Mount to the Waqf, Muslim authorities.[99] The Western Wall of the Temple, also known as the "Wailing Wall," or in Hebrew *ha Kotel ha Maaravi*, is a massive wall built of huge blocks of limestone. The average-sized stones weigh two tons a piece. Its construction was begun by King Herod the Great over two thousand years ago. It was spared by the Romans in the destruction of Jerusalem and the Temple in 70 CE.[100] It is an outer retaining wall supporting the platform upon which he expanded the Temple courtyard. It is one of the few structures of the Temple yet remaining. The Midrash claims that the Shekina (the residing presence and glory of God) remains in the west.[101] While this probably referred to the western wall of the sanctuary that was destroyed by the Romans, it is today applied to the present so-called Western Wall, the outer retaining wall, in order to give it sanctity. For many hundreds of years Jews were denied access to the wall by the Muslim authorities except on the ninth of the Jewish month of Av, the day that commemorated the destruction of the Temple. On that day Jews would gather before the wall to mourn the loss of the Temple; hence it became known as the Wailing Wall. In June of 1967, with the liberation of East Jerusalem, the Jewish people gathered and rejoiced under the wall. Shortly afterward a large plaza in front of the wall was cleared and the area just below it was divided into men's and women's prayer courts. The Western Wall is ironically a most appropriate symbol of rabbinical Judaism. The Western Wall was the outer retaining wall of the Temple and those who worship there have settled for a place outside the Temple, the true place of worship. As such, they have made themselves outsiders, foreigners to the courts of the Lord, which were located on the other side of the wall. For the time being, political considerations, not the least of which is the Dome of the Rock standing over the holy of holies, do not permit the Temple to be rebuilt. This is important because until the Temple is rebuilt the Jewish people will not be prepared to accept Yeshua as a nation. This in turn holds open the door of salvation to both individual Jews and Gentiles who will trust in him.

THE LEGAL SITUATION OF THE TEMPLE MOUNT

In 1976 a group of observant Jews were arrested for attempting to pray publicly on the Temple Mount. As a result of this bold attempt, massive Arab

---

99. Dunetz, "Moshe Dayan."
100. Midrash Lamentations Raba 1:31.
101. Bamidbar Rabba 11:63.

riots broke out in Jerusalem and all across the country. Eventually, the high court of Israel ruled that

> ... in view of the sensitive and dangerous situation prevailing against the international background, the exercise of the Jewish right of prayer on the Temple Mount is charged with grave danger to public order as long as no regulations are adopted.[102]

Virtually nothing has changed regarding the status of the Temple Mount since this ruling.

The services of the Temple, especially the sacrifices, foreshadowed the eternal sacrifice of the Messiah. The sign of the continuous operation of the Temple was the continual sacrifice (called the *tamid* in Hebrew, meaning "constant" or "continuous"), offered without fail every morning and evening, as long as the Temple stood.

> *38:* "Now this is what you shall offer upon the altar: two lambs a year old day by day continually. *39:* One lamb you shall offer in the morning, and the other lamb you shall offer in the evening; *40:* and with the first lamb a tenth measure of fine flour mingled with a fourth of a hin of beaten oil, and a fourth of a hin of wine for a libation. *41:* And the other lamb you shall offer in the evening, and shall offer with it a cereal offering and its libation, as in the morning, for a pleasing odor, an offering by fire to the Lord. *42:* It shall be a continual burnt offering throughout your generations at the door of the tent of meeting before the Lord, where I will meet with you, to speak there to you."[103]

The ultimate purpose of the Mosaic Law, with the Temple at it center, is to serve as a schoolmaster to lead Israel as a nation to Yeshua the Messiah. The precise steps by which this will occur are laid out in Scripture with amazing detail, as we shall see.

---

102. Rabinovich, "No Temple Mount Prayers."
103. Exod 29:38–42 (RSV).

7

Until Heaven and Earth Pass Away

DESPITE THE FACT THAT the Temple was destroyed nearly two thousand years ago, the Torah continues to exist. How long will the Law continue? In Matthew 5:17–19, Yeshua makes it clear that he has not come to take away the Torah, and that it will endure as long as heaven and earth continue to exist.

> *17:* "Think not that I have come to abolish the law and the prophets; I have come not to abolish them but to fulfil them. *18:* For truly, I say to you, till heaven and earth pass away, not an iota, not a dot, will pass from the law until all is accomplished. *19:* Whoever then relaxes one of the least of these commandments and teaches men so, shall be called least in the kingdom of heaven; but he who does them and teaches them shall be called great in the kingdom of heaven.[1]

Ironically, some have mistakenly understood that this passage teaches that the Law has in fact already passed away. This error may be due largely to the wording of this passage in the King James Version:

> *17:* Think not that I am come to destroy the law, or the prophets: I am not come to destroy, but to fulfil. *18:* For verily I say unto you, Till heaven and earth pass, one jot or one tittle shall in no wise pass from the law, till all be fulfilled.[2]

---

1. Matt 5:17–19 (RSV).
2. Matt 5:17–18 (KJV).

The thinking goes that the Law and the Prophets would not pass away until all be fulfilled. Yeshua by his obedience and death on the cross completely fulfilled the Law, and since all has been fulfilled, the Law has already passed away. If so, what then does Yeshua mean when he says "till heaven and earth pass away"? It is important from the outset to realize that the words translated in the King James Version as "fulfil" in verse 17 and "fulfilled" in verse 18 in the original Greek have two completely different meanings. The first, "fulfil" in verse 17, is in the Greek *pleyrousai*, which means "fill up" or "complete." The phrase "till all be fulfilled" in verse 18 is in Greek *heos an panta geneytai*. *Heos an* means "until"; *panta*, "all"; *geneytai*, "happens" or "come to pass." It is interesting to see how other versions translate this expression: "until all is accomplished" (Revised Standard Version and New American Standard Bible); "until everything is accomplished" (New International Version); "until its [the Law's and the Prophets'] purpose is achieved" (Jerusalem Bible).

A very similar expression to *heos an panta geneytai* is found in the same book of the New Testament, in Matthew 24:34: *heos an panta tauta geneytai*, translated in the Revised Standard Version as "till all these things take place," the additional word *tauta* meaning "these." In this passage Yeshua is speaking of the signs that will accompany his return to earth.

> *32:* "From the fig tree learn its lesson: as soon as its branch becomes tender and puts forth its leaves, you know that summer is near. *33:* So also, when you see all these things, you know that he is near, at the very gates. *34:* Truly, I say to you, this generation will not pass away till all these things take place [*heos an panta tauta geneytai*]."[3]

It is quite possible that Yeshua borrowed this expression from Daniel 12:7. In this rather strange passage, Daniel is speaking to an angel who is showing him what will happen in the end times.

> *6:* And I said to the man clothed in linen, who was above the waters of the stream, "How long shall it be till the end of these wonders?" *7:* The man clothed in linen, who was above the waters of the stream, raised his right hand and his left hand toward heaven; and I heard him swear by him who lives for ever that it would be for a time, two times, and half a time; and that when the shattering of the power of the holy people comes to an end *all these things would be accomplished*. *8:* I heard, but I did not understand. Then I said, "O my lord, what shall be the issue of

---

3. Matt 24:32–34 (RSV).

these things?" *9:* He said, "Go your way, Daniel, for the words are shut up and sealed until the time of the end."[4]

The expression in Daniel 12:7 "all these things would be accomplished' is in the Hebrew of the *Tanakh* (Old Testament) *cal tichlena eleh: cal* means "all"; *tichlena*, "completely come to an end"; *eleh*, "these." It is very similar to *panta tauta geneytai* in Greek and both expressions refer to the same thing, the events that will accompany Yeshua's return at the end of days. That the expression used by Yeshua in Matthew 24 may have been borrowed from Daniel 12 finds support in that Yeshua specifically mentions the prophet Daniel by name in Matthew 24 with regard to the abomination of desolation, which is a central topic mentioned in the twelfth chapter of Daniel:

> *15:* "So when you see the desolating sacrilege spoken of by the prophet Daniel, standing in the holy place (let the reader understand), *16:* then let those who are in Judea flee to the mountains; *17:* let him who is on the housetop not go down to take what is in his house; *18:* and let him who is in the field not turn back to take his mantle.[5]

Returning to Matthew 5:18, it is possible that *heos an panta geneytai* is an abbreviated form of *heos an panta tauta geneytai*,[6] again referring to the events that will occur when Yeshua returns and establishes the new creation, thus bringing to an end the present heaven and earth. If this is so, then *heos an panta geneytai* is actually parallel to "till heaven and earth pass away."[7] Parallelism is a literary device often used in the Hebrew poetry of the *Tanakh*, in which phrase is restated in other words that serve to both emphasize and clarify its meaning. If it this read as an example of parallelism, then suddenly the passage makes perfect sense: The expression "till heaven and earth pass away" is further explained by *heos an panta geneytai*, meaning the events that will accompany Yeshua's return.

---

4. Dan 12:6–9 RSV), emphasis added.
5. Matt 24:15–18 (RSV).
6. This finds support in Luke's parallel version of Matthew 24:32–34, the budding of the fig tree: "*29:* And he told them a parable: 'Look at the fig tree, and all the trees; *30:* as soon as they come out in leaf, you see for yourselves and know that the summer is already near. *31:* So also, when you see these things taking place, you know that the kingdom of God is near. *32:* Truly, I say to you, this generation will not pass away till all has taken place'" (Luke 21:29–32 [RSV]). The phrase rendered "till all has taken place" is *heos an panta geneytai*, leaving out the word *tauta*, which is in Matthew's account.
7. Viljoen, "Foundational Statement in Matthew 5:17–20," 396.

> *18:* "For truly, I say to you, till heaven and earth pass away, not an iota, not a dot, will pass from the law [*heos an panta geneytai*] until all is accomplished."[8]

Thus the Torah is to continue until heaven and earth pass away, that is to say, until the new heaven and the new earth replace this present creation. It is no coincidence that the existence of Israel, whose constitution is the Torah, is also associated with the heavens and earth of this present creation. A number of passages of Scripture demonstrate the essential link between Israel with its national constitution the Torah and the terrestrial and cosmological elements of the present creation:

We have already seen how the final disclosure of the promise was given to Abraham when he had faithfully carried out preparations to offer up Isaac as a sacrifice.

> *17:* "I will indeed bless you, and I will multiply your descendants as the *stars of heaven* and as the *sand which is on the seashore*. And your descendants shall possess the gate of their enemies . . ."[9]

The association of Abraham's descendants with the stars of heaven and the sand of the seashore is more than mere poetry. This theme of Israel connected with the celestial bodies and the land often in conjunction with the sea persists throughout the Scriptures. Later in the book of Genesis, we read the tale of Joseph's dreams:

> *5:* Now Joseph had a dream, and when he told it to his brothers they only hated him the more. *6:* He said to them, "Hear this dream which I have dreamed: *7:* behold, we were *binding sheaves in the field*, and lo, my sheaf arose and stood upright; and behold, your sheaves gathered round it, and bowed down to my sheaf." *8:* His brothers said to him, "Are you indeed to reign over us? Or are you indeed to have dominion over us?" So they hated him yet more for his dreams and for his words. *9:* Then he dreamed another dream, and told it to his brothers, and said, "Behold, I have dreamed another dream; and behold, *the sun, the moon, and eleven stars* were bowing down to me." *10:* But when he told it to his father and to his brothers, his father rebuked him, and said to him, "What is this dream that you have dreamed? Shall I and your mother and your brothers indeed come to bow ourselves to the ground before you?"[10]

8. Matt 5:18 (RSV).
9. Gen 22:17 (RSV), emphasis added.
10. Gen 37:9–10 (RSV), emphasis added.

In Joseph's first dream, the sheaves, the produce of the earth, represent Joseph and his brothers, the sons of Israel. In his second dream, Joseph's family is symbolized by the bodies of heaven. Israel, his father, is depicted as the sun, Leah the matriarch as the moon, and Joseph and his brothers as the twelve stars.

Moses, speaking to the sons of Israel, admonished them regarding the Torah:

> *18:* "You shall therefore lay up these words of mine in your heart and in your soul; and you shall bind them as a sign upon your hand, and they shall be as frontlets between your eyes. *19:* And you shall teach them to your children, talking of them when you are sitting in your house, and when you are walking by the way, and when you lie down, and when you rise. *20:* And you shall write them upon the doorposts of your house and upon your gates, *21:* that your days and the days of your children may be multiplied *in the land which the* Lord *swore to your fathers to give them, as long as the heavens are above the earth.*"[11]

In Revelation 12 Israel is described in allegorical terms that are reminiscent of Joseph's dreams:

> *1:* And a great portent appeared in heaven, a woman clothed with the sun, with the moon under her feet, and on her head a crown of twelve stars . . .[12]

When Satan, represented by a red dragon, pursues the woman, she is not in heaven, but rather upon earth.

> *12b:* But woe to you, *O earth and sea,* for the devil has come down to you in great wrath, because he knows that his time is short!" *13:* And when the dragon saw that he had been thrown down to the earth, he pursued the woman . . .[13]

Furthermore, in her persecution by the dragon, the earth comes to the woman's aid:

> *16:* But the earth came to the help of the woman, and the earth opened its mouth and swallowed the river which the dragon had poured from his mouth.[14]

---

11. Deut 11:18–21 (RSV), emphasis added.
12. Rev 12:1 (RSV).
13. Rev 12:12b–13a (RSV), emphasis added.
14. Rev 12:16 (RSV).

This link between Israel and the established order of the present creation, described in terms of the powers of heaven and earth, is explicitly stated in Jeremiah 31:35-37.

> *35:* Thus says the Lord, who gives the *sun for light by day and the fixed order of the moon and the stars* for light by night, who stirs up *the sea so that its waves roar*—the Lord of hosts is his name; *36:* "If this fixed order departs from before me, says the Lord, then shall the descendants of Israel cease from being a nation before me for ever." *37:* Thus says the Lord: "If the *heavens above* can be measured, and the foundations of the *earth below* can be explored, then I will cast off all the descendants of Israel for all that they have done, says the Lord."[15]

Even more relevant are Moses words to the people of Israel after he had presented God's covenant with them:

> *19:* "I call heaven and earth to witness against you this day, that I have set before you life and death, blessing and curse; therefore choose life, that you and your descendants may live, *20:* loving the Lord your God, obeying his voice, and cleaving to him; for that means life to you and length of days, that you may dwell in the land which the Lord swore to your fathers, to Abraham, to Isaac, and to Jacob, to give them."[16]

The writer of the book of Hebrews, speaking of the Torah as types and shadows, makes clear the connection between the Torah and the present age.

> *6:* These preparations having thus been made, the priests go continually into the outer tent, performing their ritual duties; *7:* but into the second only the high priest goes, and he but once a year, and not without taking blood which he offers for himself and for the errors of the people. *8:* By this the Holy Spirit indicates that the way into the sanctuary is not yet opened as long as the outer tent is still standing *9: (which is symbolic for the present age).* According to this arrangement, gifts and sacrifices are offered which cannot perfect the conscience of the worshiper, *10:* but deal only with food and drink and various ablutions, regulations for the body imposed *until the time of reformation.*[17]

---

15. Jer 31:35-37 (RSV), emphasis added.
16. Deut 30:19-20.
17. Heb 9:6-10 (RSV), emphasis added.

What is being described here are the daily functions of the priests in the tabernacle. We have seen that the pattern of the Tabernacle was the blueprint for the Temple when Israel had settled into the land. The writer uses the tabernacle here as an idealized form of the Temple, emphasizing its temporality and its being a mere copy of heavenly realities.[18] The most important functions of the priests were carried out within the *Ulam*, or hall, the "holy place," which accommodated the seven-branched lampstand, the menorah, the table of the bread of the presence, and the altar of incense. These stood before the veil that led into the holy of holies, where the very presence of the Almighty himself dwelt. The King James Version and the Revised Standard Version refer to the "holy place" outside the veil as the "outer tent" and the holy of holies inside the veil as the "inner tent." The New International Version may be clearer, referring to them as the "outer room" and "inner room," respectively. Because of God's holiness, it would have been dangerous for the people of Israel to come into direct contact with him. The Tabernacle and later the Temple were constructed in such a way as to allow the Almighty to dwell in the midst of the people of Israel and that they would be shielded from God's wrath against sin. The writer of Hebrews claims that the "way into the sanctuary . . . ," that is, the part of the Tabernacle where the presence of God was actually resident, ". . . is not yet opened as long as the outer tent is still standing . . ."[19] Even the priests themselves were not allowed beyond the veil (with the exception of the high priest on Yom Kippur, and only with the blood of the sacrifice representing Yeshua's atonement). Thus, as long as the practices and precepts of the Torah remain in force, access into the true heavenly temple and the presence of the Almighty is denied. As such, the practices, precepts, commandments, and statutes of the Torah, embodied in the Tabernacle and later the Temple and its services, are symbolic for the present age.[20] These will remain in force ". . . until the time of reformation."[21] The term "reformation" is employed by both the King James Version and the Revised Standard Version. The New International Version makes this more clear: "applying until the time of the new order." What is meant here is unquestionably the new creation.

The believer, however, having put his trust in Yeshua and having already become part of the new creation (and this is the real point of the writer of Hebrews), already has access to the very presence of God through God's Spirit. We have seen how Israel, inseparable from the Torah, will endure as

---

18. see Heb 8:5.
19. Heb 9:8 (RSV).
20. Heb 9:9 (RSV).
21. Heb 9:10 (RSV).

long as the heaven and the earth of this present creation exist. The Torah must yet fulfill its role as a schoolmaster to lead Israel as a nation to Yeshua the Messiah. The day is coming when an entire generation of Israel will accept Yeshua. In the end this will result in the coming of the new creation.

> *19:* For the creation waits with eager longing for the revealing of the sons of God; *20:* for the creation was subjected to futility, not of its own will but by the will of him who subjected it in hope; *21:* because the creation itself will be set free from its bondage to decay and obtain the glorious liberty of the children of God. *22:* We know that the whole creation has been groaning in travail together until now; *23:* and not only the creation, but we ourselves, who have the first fruits of the Spirit, groan inwardly as we wait for adoption as sons, the redemption of our bodies.[22]

When the new creation has fully come, the Torah will have then, at last, served its purpose.

---

22. Rom 8:19–23 (RSV).

8

Free From the Law

THE BELIEVER IN YESHUA is free from the Law! This is the unequivocal conclusion of Scripture. We have seen that every person who, whether he be Jewish or Gentile, puts his trust in Messiah, dies in him, and is raised with him is a new creature, that is to say, he becomes part of the new creation. The most severe punishment that the Torah can impose on a person for his sin is that of death. If he has died in Messiah, then his sentence has already been served. He cannot be tried or convicted for his crimes, which have already been paid for by Yeshua. He cannot be put to death again. He has already died in Messiah; it is impossible to execute a dead man! He is thus no longer under the jurisdiction of the Torah and thus free from obligations to the Law.

> *1:* There is therefore now no condemnation to those who are in Messiah Yeshua. *2:* for the life-giving principles of the Spirit have freed you in Messiah Yeshua from the control of the principles sin and death.[1]

THE TORAH HAS NOT PASSED AWAY

This does not mean, however, that the Law has passed away. As we have seen in the previous chapter, the Torah is still in full force and will be as long as heaven and earth exist, that is to say, as long as this present creation lasts. This is because the Torah still has an important role to fulfill in convicting

---

1. Rom 8:1–2 (Berkley Version).

people of sin and serving as a schoolmaster to lead the Jewish people to Messiah. The Law has not passed away or changed one iota. Rather, it is the believer in Yeshua who changes. Since he has already become part of the new creation, he is totally free from the Law.

We have seen in chapter 7 that in Matthew 5:17–19 Yeshua himself taught that the Law has not passed away. Some nonetheless claim that Paul, and with him other writers of the New Testament, taught that the Law has come to an end. A careful study of the New Testament scriptures, however, clearly shows that this is not the case. For instance, in Romans 10:4 Paul asserts:

> 4: For Messiah is the end of the law for righteousness to everyone that believeth.[2]

This verse is very much like those in the writings of Paul that we looked at in chapter 5, which speak of the status that the believer already now has in the realm of the new creation as a result of his trusting in Yeshua. We have seen that these instances are easy to identify because Paul without fail includes the phrase "in Messiah" or a similar expression with the equivalent meaning. The phase that is used in this verse with the equivalent meaning to "in Messiah" is "to everyone that believeth." Paul does not say that the Law has come to an end, period. Rather, he says that Messiah is the end of the Law for righteousness *for everyone who believes*, that is to say, everyone who has put his faith and trust in Yeshua. The believer in Yeshua no longer relies on keeping the commandments of the Law for his righteousness (which, as we have seen, could never make him righteous before God anyway). The believer, rather, puts his trust in Messiah, the sacrifice and resurrection of Yeshua. In doing so, the believer receives the righteousness of Messiah himself. Again, it is not the Torah that has changed but rather the believer.

THE END OF THE LAW

The Torah did not come to an end on the date when Yeshua died on the cross, as some believe. As we have seen in chapter 4, Yeshua's sacrifice is timeless, that is to say, it is effective throughout time, past, present, and future. Thus, Abraham was able by faith to put his trust in Yeshua and it was counted to him as righteousness, thousands of years before Yeshua's birth. In the same way, we are able to look back to the moment of Yeshua's sacrifice and receive atonement. The date that the Law comes to an end for

---

2. Rom 10:4 (KJV).

righteousness is different for each person who accepts Messiah. It ends the moment he comes to faith in Yeshua and becomes part of the new creation.

> *4:* For Messiah is the end of the law for righteousness *to everyone that believeth.*[3]

The Torah will finally come to an end altogether when Israel welcomes Yeshua back, heaven and earth pass away and the new creation comes.

There are other scriptural passages that are mistakenly thought to teach that the Law has come to an end, such as:

> *1:* For freedom Messiah has set us free; stand fast therefore, and do not submit again to a yoke of slavery.[4]

Once again, this scripture is saying that those who are in Messiah are made free by his atonement. This does not mean that the Law has passed away.

The superiority of the new covenant over the Mosaic covenant is expressed in the book of Hebrews:

> *6:* But as it is, Messiah has obtained a ministry which is as much more excellent than the old as the covenant he mediates is better, since it is enacted on better promises.[5]
>
> *13:* In speaking of a new covenant he treats the first as obsolete. And what is becoming obsolete and growing old is ready to vanish away.[6]

Yeshua, through his death and resurrection has effected a new covenant that supersedes that of the Torah, which only foreshadowed it. Unlike the Torah, this new covenant makes a person righteous and has the power to deliver him from death, physically and spiritually. Moreover, the new covenant does no rely on human fallibility as does the Torah, whose blessings are conditional on a person obeying all the commandments. However, the writer of Hebrews does not say that the old covenant, the Torah, has passed away yet. Rather, he says that it is growing old and is *"ready to vanish away."* He is proclaiming that Yeshua has died and is risen. Entrance into the kingdom is available to everyone who comes to faith in Yeshua. He is obviously anticipating with excitement the coming of the new creation (when the Torah has fulfilled its purpose), however, he dares not say that the Torah has already passed away. The most that he can possibly say is that it is getting *ready* to pass away. The New Testament scriptures are entirely consistent. Whenever

---

3. Rom 10:4 (KJV), emphasis added.
4. Gal 5:1 (RSV).
5. Heb 8:6 (RSV).
6. Heb 8:13 (RSV).

they speak of the Torah having been in any way annulled, superseded, or ended, it is only with regard to the believer in Yeshua, who has been transformed and is already part of the new creation. At some point the Law will indeed pass away; the question is, when? As we have seen in the previous chapter, it is when the present heaven and earth pass away and the new creation is made manifest.

Let us examine some other instances in Scripture that seem to intimate that the Law has been taken away or in some way has been altered. One of the best known of these passages is Galatians 3:28:

> *28:* There is neither Jew nor Greek, there is neither slave nor free, there is neither male nor female; for you are all one in Messiah Yeshua.[7]

Similar to this is Colossians 3:9–11:

> *9:* Do not lie to one another, seeing that you have put off the old nature with its practices *10:* and have put on the new nature, which is being renewed in knowledge after the image of its Creator. *11:* Here there cannot be Greek and Jew, circumcised and uncircumcised, barbarian, Scyth'ian, slave, free man, but Messiah is all, and in all.[8]

The distinction between Jew and Gentile is made very clear in the Torah. God chose the people of Israel[9] and separated them from the nations.[10] Yet here in Galatians 3:28 we are told, "There is neither Jew nor Greek . . . ," and in Colossians 3:11, "Here there cannot be Greek and Jew, circumcised and uncircumcised . . ." These two verses are examples of "in Messiah" passages (see chapter 5). A quick review in their respective contexts will clearly show this: Galatians 3:28 proclaims, ". . . for you are all one *in Messiah Yeshua*"; and similarly in Colossians 3:11, ". . . Messiah is all, and in all." They both speak of those who have entered the realm of the new creation. When the new creation has fully come, the Torah will have finished its purpose and will have come to an end. Among those who will equally share in the new creation there indeed will be neither Jew nor Gentile, neither male nor female, neither slave nor free. We have seen, however, that those who are in Messiah have *already* entered the realm of the new creation. Nonetheless, the believer in Yeshua, as we have seen over and over again, is living not only in the realm of the new creation. At the same time he lives in the realm of the

---

7. Gal 3:28 (RSV).
8. Col 3:9–11 (RSV).
9. Exod 19:3–6; Deut 4:34–38.
10. Lev 20:24–26.

new creation, he also lives the realm of the present creation in which these distinctions still exist. Paul would, for instance, never intimate that there is no longer any difference between a man and a woman in the current world that we all know and live in. In the realm of the present creation, then, there is indeed male and female, slave and free, and there is likewise a distinction between Jew and Gentile. Another very significant "in Messiah" passage is found in Ephesians 2:13-16:

> *13:* But now *in Messiah* Yeshua you who once were far off have been brought near in the blood of Messiah. *14:* For he is our peace, who has made us both one, and has broken down the dividing wall of hostility, *15: by abolishing in his flesh the law of commandments* and ordinances, that he might create in himself one new man in place of the two, so making peace, *16:* and might reconcile us both to God in one body through the cross, thereby bringing the hostility to an end.[11]

We have encountered these verses already in chapter 5 as one of the "in Messiah" passages. It is important to remember that although the work of Yeshua's atonement has already been accomplished, the Torah has not expired altogether. We have seen that the atonement of Yeshua is outside of time and effective before and after the day of Yeshua's death. The date that the Law ends is different for each person, according to the day that he accepts Yeshua and enters the new creation.

ALL FOODS CLEAN

In Mark 7:14-23 we read:

> *14:* And he [Yeshua] called the people to him again, and said to them, "Hear me, all of you, and understand: *15:* there is nothing outside a man which by going into him can defile him; but the things which come out of a man are what defile him." *17:* And when he had entered the house, and left the people, his disciples asked him about the parable. *18:* And he said to them, "Then are you also without understanding? Do you not see that whatever goes into a man from outside cannot defile him, *19:* since it enters, not his heart but his stomach, and so passes on?" (Thus he declared all foods clean.) *20:* And he said, "What comes out of a man is what defiles a man. *21:* For from within, out of the heart of man, come evil thoughts, fornication, theft, murder, adultery, *22:* coveting, wickedness, deceit, licentiousness, envy, slander,

11. Eph 2:13-16 (RSV), emphasis added.

pride, foolishness. *23:* All these evil things come from within, and they defile a man."[12]

Some have taken this to mean that Yeshua abrogated the dietary laws of the Torah. It should be recognized from the outset that the topic under discussion in this passage was apparently the pharisaic tradition of washing the hands before eating and not the dietary laws per se. (This is evident from a comparison of this passage with its parallel in Matthew 15:15–20.) Scholars consider the commentary "Thus he declared all foods clean"[13] as a gloss added by a later writer, perhaps a Gentile. If this is so, the writer may have been pressing his cause for the believer's freedom from the Law as a new creature in Messiah. Whether it was written by the author of the book of Mark himself or by a commentator at a much later date, it should be recognized as a commentary on Yeshua's words. Yeshua himself did not state in the passage that he was proclaiming all foods clean. The main point that Yeshua was attempting to get across to his disciples is that the real defilement of a person comes from his sin, which proceeds from within his heart. The commentary about declaring all things clean is a side issue, a concern possibly of a later time and a different culture from that of first-century Judaism. This does not invalidate the comment as a legitimate part of Scripture. It must simply be understood as another example of an "in Messiah" passage. In fact, Yeshua did declare all foods clean for those who put their faith in him and are transformed into a part of the new creation.

PETER'S VISION OF THE SHEET

In Acts 10:9–16 Simon Peter was on the rooftop of Simon the Tanner's house, in the town of Jaffa, praying when he was given a vision.

> *9:* The next day, as they were on their journey and coming near the city, Peter went up on the housetop to pray, about the sixth hour. *10:* And he became hungry and desired something to eat; but while they were preparing it, he fell into a trance *11:* and saw the heaven opened, and something descending, like a great sheet, let down by four corners upon the earth. *12:* In it were all kinds of animals and reptiles and birds of the air. *13:* And there came a voice to him, "Rise, Peter; kill and eat." *14:* But Peter said, "No, Lord; for I have never eaten anything that is common or unclean." *15:* And the voice came to him again a second time,

---

12. Mark 7:14–23 (RSV).
13. Mark 7:19 (RSV).

"What God has cleansed, you must not call common." *16:* This happened three times, and the thing was taken up at once to heaven.[14]

It is argued that God's command "Rise, Peter; kill and eat" unclean animals most clearly demonstrates that the dietary laws of the Torah have been abrogated in the New Testament scriptures. It is important, however, to remember that Peter was seeing a vision that required interpretation. His response was not to jump up and look for a ham sandwich. In fact, Peter was perplexed and did not immediately comprehend the meaning of the vision

> *17:* Now while Peter was inwardly perplexed as to what the vision which he had seen might mean, behold, the men that were sent by Cornelius, having made inquiry for Simon's house, stood before the gate . . .[15]

It was only after the unfolding of the events of Acts 10 that Peter finally grasped the meaning of the vision:

> *28:* and he said to them, "You yourselves know how unlawful it is for a Jew to associate with or to visit any one of another nation; but God has shown me that I should not call any man common or unclean."[16]

The point of the story is that God is calling out a people for himself from among the Gentiles whom he has proclaimed clean by the atonement of Yeshua. This is the meaning of Peter's vision of the sheet, and not that Jews or Jewish believers in Messiah must abandon the dietary laws of the Torah.

LIVING IN THE TWO REALMS

The believer in Yeshua is indeed free from the Law since he has entered the realm of the new creation. However, as we have seen in chapter 5, the believer is paradoxically living in two realms at the same time, the realm of the new creation and the realm of the present creation. Because of this, the Jewish believer is placed in a somewhat unique position. The Torah was given to the nation of Israel as a special covenant. Its ultimate purpose is to lead the Jewish people as a nation to Messiah. Since the Jewish believer in Yeshua has already entered the new creation, he himself is personally totally free from the Law. He is still, however, a member of the Jewish people, that

14. Acts 10:9–16 (RSV).
15. Acts 10:17 (RSV).
16. Acts 10:28 (RSV).

is to say, a part of Israel. As we have seen, Israel is, along with its covenant and constitution the Torah, connected to *the present creation*. The Jewish believer in Yeshua consequently has a duty to observe the Torah, not for his own salvation or righteousness, but with the hope of seeing his people come to Messiah.

The Gentile who comes to belief in Yeshua has no such obligation to the Torah since he does not belong to the Jewish people. He has already fulfilled the demands of the Law by simply believing in Yeshua. The Torah was never given to him as a covenant. Neither he nor his ancestors ever swore to keep it.

LEAST IN THE KINGDOM OF HEAVEN

The Jewish believer, by choosing to surrender some of his freedom in Messiah by keeping the Torah, participates in the effort to lead his people as a nation to Messiah Yeshua. Since a Jewish believer is in no wise less free than his Gentile brother, he can indeed choose and live entirely free from the Torah. In doing so, however, he is shirking the responsibility he has to his people. Yeshua had strong words for those who do this in Matthew 5:19.

> *19:* "Whoever then relaxes one of the least of these commandments and teaches men so, shall be called least in the kingdom of heaven; but he who does them and teaches them shall be called great in the kingdom of heaven."[17]

Yeshua did not say that one who relaxes ones of the least of the commandments of the Torah is out of the kingdom of heaven. The Torah is not the means by which one comes into or, for that matter, stays in the kingdom. It is only by trusting in Messiah and the power of his atonement that one has entrance into and is able to stay in the kingdom. Rather, Yeshua says that he shall be called least in the kingdom. This is evidently because he has set aside God's plan for the redemption of his people, the Jews.

THE GENTILES AND THE TORAH

Yeshua was *not* saying in Matthew 5:19 that *all believers* must keep the commandments of the Law, but rather those to whom it pertains.

---

17. Matt 5:19 (RSV).

> *19:* Now we know that whatever the law says *it speaks to those who are under the law, so that every mouth may be stopped, and the whole world may be held accountable to God.*[18]

The Gentile who has accepted Yeshua and is part of the new creation has no more obligation to the Torah. He has come to faith in Yeshua without the Torah.

ACTS 15

A burning question in the early days of the congregation of believers in Yeshua was whether the Gentiles who accepted Yeshua needed to keep the Torah. Once they had accepted the Jewish Messiah, did it not make sense that they should convert to Judaism and live according to Jewish Law? Those of the circumcision party vehemently insisted that Gentiles who come to faith in Yeshua must be circumcised and keep the Torah. A special meeting was called in Jerusalem by the apostles and elders of the congregation in order to decide this matter. The proceedings of this council meeting are recorded in Acts 15. Peter reported about his encounter with Cornelius, his family, and his friends[19]:

> *9:* and he made no distinction between us and them, but cleansed their hearts by faith. *10:* Now therefore why do you make trial of God by putting a yoke upon the neck of the disciples which neither our fathers nor we have been able to bear? *11:* But we believe that we shall be saved through the grace of the Lord Jesus, just as they will."[20]

Next, they listened to Paul and Barnabas tell about the wonders that God had done through them among the Gentiles. Finally, James, the leader of the Jerusalem congregation, addressed them. He concluded:

> *19:* Therefore my judgment is that we should not trouble those of the Gentiles who turn to God, *20:* but should write to them to abstain from the pollutions of idols and from unchastity and from what is strangled and from blood.[21]

And so they wrote a letter to this effect to the believing Gentiles at Antioch, Syria, and Cilicia:

18. Rom 3:19 (RSV), emphasis added.
19. Acts 10:9–11.
20. Acts 15:9–11 (RSV).
21. Acts 15:19–20 (RSV).

22: Then it seemed good to the apostles and the elders, with the whole church, to choose men from among them and send them to Antioch with Paul and Barnabas. They sent Judas called Barsab'bas, and Silas, leading men among the brethren, *23:* with the following letter: "The brethren, both the apostles and the elders, to the brethren who are of the Gentiles in Antioch and Syria and Cili'cia, greeting. *24:* Since we have heard that some persons from us have troubled you with words, unsettling your minds, although we gave them no instructions, *25:* it has seemed good to us, having come to one accord, to choose men and send them to you with our beloved Barnabas and Paul, *26:* men who have risked their lives for the sake of our Lord Yeshua the Messiah. *27:* We have therefore sent Judas and Silas, who themselves will tell you the same things by word of mouth. *28:* For it has seemed good to the Holy Spirit and to us to lay upon you no greater burden than these necessary things: *29:* that you abstain from what has been sacrificed to idols and from blood and from what is strangled and from unchastity. If you keep yourselves from these, you will do well. Farewell."[22]

THE LAWS OF NOAH

These few demands that were made on the Gentile believers have nothing to do with the Mosaic Law. Rather, they reflect the Laws of Noah (based on Gen 9:1–7), which are seen in Judaism as incumbent upon all men. Even today, Orthodox Judaism prescribes the Laws of Noah as the only requirement for Gentiles. With regard to Jewish believers they gave no new recommendation. In other words, nothing had changed for them; that is to say, they should continue to observe the Law as they had all along.

ACTS 21:19–26

The New Testament scriptures are entirely consistent throughout: while Gentile believers have no need to observe the Torah, Jewish believers are intended to keep it. The clearest illustration of this is found in Acts 21. Paul goes up to Jerusalem in order to be there by Pentecost (the Jewish festival of Shavuot).[23]

---

22. Acts 15:22–29 (RSV).
23. See Acts 20:16; Lev 23:15–21.

19: After greeting them, he related one by one the things that God had done among the Gentiles through his ministry. *20:* And when they heard it, they glorified God. And they said to him, "You see, brother, how many thousands there are among the Jews of those who have believed; they are all zealous for the law, *21:* and they have been told about you that you teach all the Jews who are among the Gentiles to forsake Moses, telling them not to circumcise their children or observe the customs. *22:* What then is to be done? They will certainly hear that you have come. *23:* Do therefore what we tell you. We have four men who are under a vow; *24:* take these men and purify yourself along with them and pay their expenses, so that they may shave their heads. Thus all will know that there is nothing in what they have been told about you *but that you yourself live in observance of the law*. *25:* But as for the Gentiles who have believed, we have sent a letter with our judgment that they should abstain from what has been sacrificed to idols and from blood and from what is strangled and from unchastity." *26:* Then Paul took the men, and the next day he purified himself with them and went into the temple, to give notice when the days of purification would be fulfilled and the offering presented for every one of them.[24]

These preparations were the prescription for the Nazirite vow,[25] which, it should be noted, required bloody Temple sacrifices. This demonstrates that Paul was not keeping merely the "spiritual parts of the Law," but also the "ritual parts" as well (see chapter 9). Here, then, is Paul, the apostle to the Gentiles, the great exponent of the doctrine of grace, the one who wrote to the believers at Corinth, "'. . . eat whatever is set before you'. . ."[26] and "Stand fast therefore in the liberty by which Messiah has made us free . . . ,"[27] making an unequivocal statement that he himself is observant of the Torah. Paul was not merely acquiescing to the demands of James and those believers who were "zealous for the Law." Paul was a man of principle. He would never have compromised on such an important issue. He would not have gone along with this as a show if he himself was not in complete agreement. It is interesting that Paul had earlier, on his own initiative, put himself under a Nazirite vow.[28] This of course does not mean that Paul was always able to eat kosher meals while he was locked away in a Roman prison. Paul not only

24. Acts 21:19–26 (RSV), emphasis added.
25. Num 6:1–21.
26. 1 Cor 10:27.
27. Gal 5:1 (NKJV).
28. Acts 18:18.

kept the commandments of the Law himself, he also admonished all Jewish believers in Yeshua to do likewise.[29]

In short, Jewish believers in Yeshua, though free from the Law, are admonished, like Paul, to faithfully continue keeping the commandments of the Torah, not for their own sake, but in hope of seeing their people as a nation saved.

---

29. 1 Cor 7:17–20; Gal 2:14.

9

Grafted in . . . to What?

GENTILES AND THE TORAH

We have seen that the Torah was given as a covenant by God to the nation of Israel. It was not given to the Gentiles or even to individual Jews. Rather, it was given to all Israel as the example nation. To this day Israel bears the yoke of the Torah on behalf of all mankind. This does not mean that the Gentiles have no relation at all to the Torah. We have seen that through Israel the Torah holds every person in the world accountable to God.

> *19:* Now we know that whatever the law says it speaks to those who are under the law, so that every mouth may be stopped, and the whole world may be held accountable to God.[1]

To be sure, if a Gentile wishes to prove himself righteous before God by his own efforts, then he has no choice but to come to the Torah, since, as we have seen, it alone is God's perfect standard. The very first thing that he must do in order to meet God's standard (of course) is to become Jewish, if he is a man, by means of circumcision. After that he must join Israel and keep the entire Law flawlessly. But as we have also seen,

> *20:* . . . no human being will be justified in his sight by works of the law, since through the law comes knowledge of sin.[2]

---

1. Rom 3:19 (RSV).
2. Rom 3:20 (RSV).

The purpose of the Law is to point out sin, not to make anyone righteous. The fact is that the Gentiles were never asked to keep the commandments of the Law. It is enough that Israel as the example nation took the burden of keeping the Torah for all mankind. A Gentile can learn the lesson from Israel that it is futile to seek salvation by works of the Law. Despite the fact he was never asked to keep the Torah, every Gentile is still nonetheless held accountable to God for his sin. Through reading the Scriptures, he can recognize his sin, skip the step of having to keep the Law, and proceed straight to the gates of salvation. He can avoid experiencing firsthand the painful cycle of striving to obey the commandments, failure, and guilt. He can recognize his sin and go directly to receiving the atonement of Yeshua by faith, completely apart from the Torah. Once he has put his faith in Yeshua, he is absolutely free from the Law. Since he does not belong to the Jewish people, he has no obligation toward them to keep the Law.

We have seen that Yeshua warned that those who break the least commandments of the Torah will be considered least in the kingdom of God.[3] A Gentile believer who is justified by faith in Yeshua is incapable of breaking the Torah's commandments. The Law was never given to him as a covenant, he was never required to keep it. and he has already achieved the Law's aim by his receiving Yeshua's atonement by faith. He is not even able to transgress the Law—that is, with a single exception.

THE ONE EXCEPTION

The only circumstance in which a Gentile believer in Yeshua is able to break the commandments of the Torah is if he comes into contact with the Jewish people or the land of Israel.

A Gentile may be guilty of breaking the commandments of the Torah if he causes someone who is Jewish to break a commandment. There are also specific commandments for Gentiles who live in the land of Israel. The most important of these are the commandments regarding the Sabbath, the Feast of Unleavened Bread (*Hag ha Matzot*), and the Day of Atonement (Yom Kippur).

THE SABBATH

The Gentile who lives in Israel must rest on the Sabbath:

---

3. Matt 5:19; see above chapter 7.

> *8:* "Remember the sabbath day, to keep it holy. *9:* Six days you shall labor, and do all your work; *10:* but the seventh day is a sabbath to the Lord your God; in it you shall not do any work, you, or your son, or your daughter, your manservant, or your maidservant, or your cattle, or *the sojourner who is within your gates; 11:* for in six days the Lord made heaven and earth, the sea, and all that is in them, and rested the seventh day; therefore the Lord blessed the sabbath day and hallowed it."[4]

In addition, fire must not be lit in homes in the land of Israel on the Sabbath.

> *3:* you shall kindle no fire in all your habitations on the sabbath day.[5]

THE FEAST OF UNLEAVENED BREAD (HAG HA MATZOT)

There are also requirements for Gentiles living in the land of Israel during the Feast of Unleavened Bread:

> *17:* And you shall observe the feast of unleavened bread, for on this very day I brought your hosts out of the land of Egypt: therefore you shall observe this day, throughout your generations, as an ordinance for ever. *18:* In the first month, on the fourteenth day of the month at evening, you shall eat unleavened bread, and so until the twenty-first day of the month at evening. *19:* For seven days no leaven shall be found in your houses; for if any one eats what is leavened, that person shall be cut off from the congregation of Israel, *whether he is a sojourner or a native of the land. 20:* You shall eat nothing leavened; in all your dwellings you shall eat unleavened bread."[6]

YOM KIPPUR

Gentiles settled in the land of Israel are also required to observe the Day of Atonement:

---

4. Exod 20:8–11 (RSV), emphasis added.
5. Exod 35:3 (RSV).
6. Exod 12:17–20 (RSV), emphasis added.

> *29:* "And it shall be a statute to you for ever that in the seventh month, on the tenth day of the month, you shall afflict yourselves, and shall do no work, either the native or *the stranger who sojourns among you*; *30:* for on this day shall atonement be made for you, to cleanse you; from all your sins you shall be clean before the Lord. *31:* It is a sabbath of solemn rest to you, and you shall afflict yourselves; it is a statute for ever."[7]

VOMITED OUT BY THE LAND

The land of Israel is God's exclusive possession. It is where he has placed his name and the address on the earth where he has chosen to dwell. He lived among the people of Israel in the portable Tabernacle and moved into the land of Israel with them when they settled there. As we have seen, Israel was shielded from God's wrath against sin by obedience to the Torah and the separations set within the Tabernacle (and later in the Temple) that prevented direct contact with him until the day when the remnant of Israel will be transformed into the new creation (see chapter 6). Even though the Temple is not presently standing and the presence of God does not rest on the Temple Mount in the same way that it did when the Temple stood, the holiness of the place still endures. One day the Temple will be restored and Israel will return to the covenant (see chapter 11). For these reasons, God demanded that those who dwell in the land abstain from immorality and keep the commandments. After listing forbidden sexual practices, God warns the people of Israel,

> *24:* "Do not defile yourselves by any of these things, for by all these the nations I am casting out before you defiled themselves; *25:* and the land became defiled, so that I punished its iniquity, and the land vomited out its inhabitants. *26:* But you shall keep my statutes and my ordinances and do none of these abominations, *either the native or the stranger who sojourns among you 27:* (for all of these abominations the men of the land did, who were before you, so that the land became defiled); *28:* lest the land vomit you out, when you defile it, as it vomited out the nation that was before you."[8]

---

7. Lev 16:29–31 (RSV), emphasis added.
8. Lev 18:24–28 (RSV), emphasis added.

THE LAND, THE COVENANT, AND GOD'S LAW

In his parting speech, Joshua admonished the people of Israel,

> *8:* but cleave to the Lord your God as you have done to this day. *9:* For the Lord has driven out before you great and strong nations; and as for you, no man has been able to withstand you to this day. *10:* One man of you puts to flight a thousand, since it is the Lord your God who fights for you, as he promised you. *11:* Take good heed to yourselves, therefore, to love the Lord your God. *12:* For if you turn back, and join the remnant of these nations left here among you, and make marriages with them, so that you marry their women and they yours, *13:* know assuredly that the Lord your God will not continue to drive out these nations before you; but they shall be a snare and a trap for you, a scourge on your sides, and thorns in your eyes, till you perish from off this good land which the Lord your God has given you.[9]

Israel is God's chosen nation, through whom he is achieving his plan for the salvation of mankind. The land of Israel is God's special possession. He has sovereignly chosen to give it to Israel to carry out his plan of redemption. His people, his plan, and his land are holy and very dear to him. They are inseparably linked to the honor of his name. The prophet wrote, speaking of the nation of Israel,

> *8:* For thus said the Lord of hosts, after his glory sent me to the nations who plundered you, for he who touches you touches the apple of his eye:[10]

Consequently, anyone who comes into contact with the Jewish people or God's plan of redemption for Israel risks becoming guilty of breaking the commandments of the Torah. It is especially important for Gentile believers in Yeshua who come to the land of Israel and wish to stay here to keep the commandments enjoined on the stranger and the sojourner in the land.

CHASTISED BY LIONS!

A fascinating but chilling story is told in 2 Kings 17:24–28. The year 722 BCE is remembered as the year the Assyrians conquered the ten northern tribes of Israel. The Assyrians had a practice intended to inhibit rebellion

---

9. Josh 23:8–13(RSV).
10. Zech 2:8b (RSV).

within their vast empire. They removed entire peoples from their homelands and replaced them with other peoples. They did this also with the tribes of northern Israel. They deported the people of Israel and replaced them with others.

> *24:* And the king of Assyria brought people from Babylon, Cuthah, Avva, Hamath, and Sephar-va'im, and placed them in the cities of Sama'ria instead of the people of Israel; and they took possession of Sama'ria, and dwelt in its cities. *25:* And at the beginning of their dwelling there, they did not fear the Lord; therefore the Lord sent lions among them, which killed some of them. *26:* So the king of Assyria was told, "The nations which you have carried away and placed in the cities of Sama'ria do not know the law of the god of the land; therefore he has sent lions among them, and behold, they are killing them, because they do not know the law of the god of the land." *27:* Then the king of Assyria commanded, "Send there one of the priests whom you carried away thence; and let him go and dwell there, and teach them the law of the god of the land." *28:* So one of the priests whom they had carried away from Sama'ria came and dwelt in Bethel, and taught them how they should fear the Lord[11]

This was the origin of the Samaritans, of whom we read in the New Testament[12] and who played a significant role in the history of Israel after the Jewish people returned from Babylon. God takes his covenant with Israel and their connection with the land very seriously. Therefore it is important that non-Jews who visit the land of Israel do their utmost to observe the commandments pertaining to the sojourner in the land.

GRAFTED IN

In Romans 11 Paul tells his renowned tale of two olive trees, one cultivated and the other wild.

> *17:* But if some of the branches were broken off, and you, a wild olive shoot, were grafted in their place to share the richness of the olive tree, *18:* do not boast over the branches. If you do boast, remember it is not you that support the root, but the root that supports you. *19:* You will say, "Branches were broken off so that I might be grafted in." *20:* That is true. They were broken off because of their unbelief, but you stand fast only through faith.

---

11. 2 Kgs 17:24–28 (RSV).
12. Luke 9:52; 10:33; 17:16; John 4:4–42.

> So do not become proud, but stand in awe. *21:* For if God did not spare the natural branches, neither will he spare you. *22:* Note then the kindness and the severity of God: severity toward those who have fallen, but God's kindness to you, provided you continue in his kindness; otherwise you too will be cut off. *23:* And even the others, if they do not persist in their unbelief, will be grafted in, for God has the power to graft them in again. *24:* For if you have been cut from what is by nature a wild olive tree, and grafted, contrary to nature, into a cultivated olive tree, how much more will these natural branches be grafted back into their own olive tree.[13]

Paul tells the Gentiles who come to faith in Yeshua that they have been grafted in; but into what have they been grafted? This passage is often understood to mean that Gentiles believers are grafted into Israel. I will never forget the enormous gentleman who, with a distinct Texan drawl, informed me, "Ah *luv* the Jewish people 'cuz mah Messiah made *me* a Jew!"

EPHESIANS 2:11-22: THE DIVIDING WALL OF HOSTILITY

In order to better understand what Gentile believers are grafted into, it is helpful to reflect on Ephesians 2:11-22.

> *11:* Therefore remember that at one time you Gentiles in the flesh, called the uncircumcision by what is called the circumcision, which is made in the flesh by hands *12:* remember that you were at that time separated from Messiah, alienated from the commonwealth of Israel, and strangers to the covenants of promise, having no hope and without God in the world. *13:* But now in Messiah Yeshua you who once were far off have been brought near in the blood of Messiah. *14:* For he is our peace, who has made us both one, and has broken down the dividing wall of hostility, *15:* by abolishing in his flesh the law of commandments and ordinances, that he might create in himself one new man in place of the two, so making peace, *16:* and might reconcile us both to God in one body through the cross, thereby bringing the hostility to an end. *17:* And he came and preached peace to you who were far off and peace to those who were near; *18:* for through him we both have access in one Spirit to the Father. *19:* So then you are no longer strangers and sojourners,

---

13. Rom 11:17-24 (RSV).

> but you are fellow citizens with the saints and members of the household of God, 20: built upon the foundation of the apostles and prophets, Messiah Yeshua himself being the cornerstone, 21: in whom the whole structure is joined together and grows into a holy temple in the Lord; 22: in whom you also are built into it for a dwelling place of God in the Spirit.[14]

In our tour of the Temple in chapter 6, we saw that inside the Temple courts there was a wall consisting of a low balustrade separating the inner courts and buildings of the Temple from the Court of the Gentiles. Upon this balustrade, engraved on stone slabs, were inscriptions in both Greek and Latin warning Gentiles not to trespass beyond the wall into the inner temple under pain of death. This was very likely the "dividing wall of hostility" that Paul refers allegorically to here. It was a particularly graphic symbol of the division made by the Torah between Jews and Gentiles.

In Ephesians 2:11–22 Paul does not say that Gentile believers become Jewish. It is rather that *in Messiah* the division between Jew and Gentile is taken away, and the two become one new man. In other words, the Gentile who comes to faith in Messiah does not become a citizen of the nation of Israel but rather a citizen of the new creation, a citizen of God's kingdom.

It is important to remember that the nation of Israel is firmly connected with the celestial and terrestrial powers of this present creation. Its constitution is the Torah, which will pass away with the current heaven and earth. The destiny of Israel, or at least the final redeemed generation of Israel, is to enter the new creation, together with believers in Yeshua from among the nations, throughout the ages. Of the Jewish people Paul wrote:

> 4: They are Israelites, and to them belong the sonship, the glory, the covenants, the giving of the law, the worship, and the promises; 5: to them belong the patriarchs, and of their race, according to the flesh, is the Messiah. God who is over all be blessed for ever. Amen.[15]

The Gentile believer in Yeshua is not grafted into the Israel connected with the present creation, but with what the remnant of Israel shall yet become: fellow inheritors of the kingdom in the new creation. As such, Gentile believers in Yeshua do not have any part in the Israel of the present creation except that they have a shared destination. Neither do Gentile believers have an obligation to Israel's covenant, the Torah. Paul wrote to the Gentile Ephesian believers,

---

14. Eph 2:11–22 (RSV).
15. Rom 9:4–5 (RSV).

12: remember that you were at that time separated from Messiah, alienated from the commonwealth of Israel, and strangers to the covenants of promise, having no hope and without God in the world.[16]

Paul continues by explaining that the Ephesians have been brought near to God, however, Paul did not say that Gentile believers ever became part of the commonwealth of Israel or partakers of Israel's covenants. They have been brought near, not by Israel's covenants, *but rather by the blood* (that is to say the atoning sacrifice) *of Messiah apart from the Torah*. Gentile believers are brought into the family of God, not by becoming part of Israel, but rather by faith in Messiah's sacrifice.

13: But now in Messiah Yeshua you who once were far off *have been brought near in the blood of Messiah*.[17]

Paul goes on to say that they, having been brought into the household of God, together with Jewish believers are being built into a holy temple constructed on the foundation of the prophets and apostles, having the Spirit of God living within.[18] This is the original faith of the fathers as opposed to that of Rabbinic Judaism (see chapter 10). Thus, Gentile believers in Yeshua are not grafted into Israel, but rather into what Israel will eventually become when it is fully redeemed.

ALL ISRAEL IS NOT ISRAEL

In the ninth chapter of his letter to the Romans, Paul wrote about the election of believers in Yeshua and why the Jewish people of his day had not accepted him as a nation:

6: But it is not as though the word of God had failed. For not all who are descended from Israel belong to Israel, *7:* and not all are children of Abraham because they are his descendants; but "Through Isaac shall your descendants be named." *8:* This means that it is not the children of the flesh who are the children of God, but the children of the promise are reckoned as descendants.[19]

---

16. Eph 2:12 (RSV).
17. Eph 2:13 (RSV), emphasis added.
18. Eph 2:20–22.
19. Rom 9:6–8 (RSV).

Some people see this as another proof that God has replaced the Jewish people, the Israel of the flesh, with the true spiritual Israel, the Christian church. However, Derek Prince clarified the true meaning of this passage:

> Paul explains here that to be physically descended from Israel—that is, from Jacob—is not sufficient. To qualify for God's promised blessing, a person must also demonstrate the same faith that characterized Abraham, Isaac, and Jacob; otherwise, he or she is not really entitled to the name *Israel*.
> Let me emphasize once again that Paul is not extending the use of Israel to include all believers, irrespective of national origin. On the contrary, he is restricting its use to include only those descendants of Israel who are in the faith of the Messiah. It is an error to suggest that in this passage Paul uses the word *Israel* to describe all believers.[20]

Paul is not by any means intimating that Gentile believers have become Israel in place of the Jews or that Gentile believers in Yeshua become part of Israel. Those Jews physically descended from Israel who in faith accept Yeshua are true Israel, the "Israel of God."[21] Nevertheless, as we have seen, Gentiles who come to faith in Yeshua will, in the end, share the same destiny as that of Israel. They will enter, along with Jewish believers in Yeshua, as citizens of the kingdom in the new creation.

REMAIN AS YOU ARE CALLED

Accordingly, Paul taught that every man should remain as he was called. While teaching Gentile believers in Yeshua that it was needless for them to observe the Torah, he admonished Jewish believers in Yeshua to continue keeping the Law. Paul, himself being Jewish, was fully observant of the Mosaic Law (Acts 21:17–25). James instructed Paul:

> 24: "take these men and purify yourself along with them and pay their expenses, so that they may shave their heads. Thus all will know that there is nothing in what they have been told about you *but that you yourself live in observance of the law*. 25: But as for the Gentiles who have believed, we have sent a letter with our judgment that they should abstain from what has been

---

20. Prince, *Destiny*, 22.
21. Gal 6:16.

sacrificed to idols and from blood and from what is strangled and from unchastity."²²

Paul was unwaveringly consistent throughout his letters. In 1 Corinthians 7:17-20 he admonished:

> *17:* Only, let every one lead the life which the Lord has assigned to him, and in which God has called him. This is my rule in all the churches [congregations of believers in Yeshua]. *18:* Was any one at the time of his call already circumcised? Let him not seek to remove the marks of circumcision. Was any one at the time of his call uncircumcised? Let him not seek circumcision. *19:* For neither circumcision counts for anything nor uncircumcision, but keeping the commandments of God. *20:* Every one should remain in the state in which he was called.²³

What Paul meant is that if someone is Jewish when he becomes a believer in Yeshua, he should continue to be Jewish, living a Jewish lifestyle according to the commandments of the Torah. If someone is a Gentile at the time he accepts Yeshua, he should not seek to become Jewish through circumcision or keeping the Law.

ALL THINGS TO ALL MEN

Paul was called to be an apostle to the Gentiles, despite the fact that he himself was Jewish.

> *19:* For though I am free from all men, I have made myself a slave to all, that I might win the more. *20:* To the Jews I became as a Jew, in order to win Jews; to those under the law I became as one under the law—though not being myself under the law—that I might win those under the law. *21:* To those outside the law I became as one outside the law—not being without law toward God but under the law of Messiah—that I might win those outside the law. *22:* To the weak I became weak, that I might win the weak. I have become all things to all men, that I might by all means save some. *23:* I do it all for the sake of the gospel, that I may share in its blessings.²⁴

---

22. Acts 21:17-25 (RSV), emphasis added.
23. 1 Cor 7:17-20 (RSV).
24. 1 Cor 9:19-23 (RSV).

Some have taken this to mean that when Paul was among Jews he kept a Jewish lifestyle, but when he was among Gentiles he lived as a Gentile, eating unkosher foods and ignoring the Sabbath and Jewish holidays. As the saying goes, "When in Rome do as the Romans." It is clear, however, that Paul did not act this way. Paul always made known the fact that he was Jewish. He never pretended to be a Gentile. When he was speaking with Jews, he appeared entirely Jewish in his attire, his speech, his dietary habits, and his keeping of the Sabbath and Jewish holidays. When he spoke to Gentiles, he emphasized the freedom that he shared with them as part of the new creation in Messiah. He became all things to all men as a matter of attitude, emphasizing whatever he had in common with whatever people he was dealing with. To Jewish people, Paul could speak as one who knew what it was like to be under the Law; at the same time, he could address Gentiles speaking as one for whom the Law was completely fulfilled, he himself having been set free in Messiah.

Imagine a man whose wife invites him to share a word of encouragement with her ladies group. Desiring to be all things to all men (or in this case to all women), he slips on a dress, dons a long wig, and makes himself up with foundation, mascara, eyeliner, and bright red lipstick. When he speaks to the ladies, he puts on an effeminate manner and speaks to them in a high, falsetto voice. It is doubtful whether the members of the fellowship would feel the least bit encouraged, or that he would ever be invited back. Would not the better way to encourage women to be good wives and mothers be, rather, by being an exemplary husband and father? The point, of course, is that it is not necessary for someone to identify with a group of people whom he is addressing, to renounce all that he is and become in every detail like them. Nevertheless, some people are convinced that this is the manner in which Paul conducted himself: when he was with Jews, he *pretended* to be a Jew; when he was with Gentiles, he *pretended* to be a Gentile. If he had indeed acted in this way, his entire life would have been one of pretense and hypocrisy. This is clearly not the way to be straightforward regarding the truth of the good news of the Messiah.

PETER AT ANTIOCH

It is clear that Paul did not act as a Jew when he was with Jews and act as a Gentile when he was with Gentiles. It was, in fact, for making this very error that Paul reprimanded Peter at Antioch in Galatians 2:11–16:

> *11:* But when Cephas [Peter] came to Antioch I opposed him to his face, because he stood condemned. *12:* For before certain

men came from James, he ate with the Gentiles; but when they came he drew back and separated himself, fearing the circumcision party. *13:* And with him the rest of the Jews acted insincerely, so that even Barnabas was carried away by their insincerity. *14:* But when I saw that they were not straightforward about the truth of the gospel, I said to Cephas before them all, "If you, though a Jew, live like a Gentile and not like a Jew, how can you compel the Gentiles to live like Jews?" *15:* We ourselves, who are Jews by birth and not Gentile sinners, *16:* yet who know that a man is not justified by works of the law but through faith in Yeshua the Messiah, even we have believed in Messiah Yeshua, in order to be justified by faith in Messiah, and not by works of the law, because by works of the law shall no one be justified.[25]

Peter, relying on the liberty that he had in Messiah, was having table fellowship with the Gentile believers at Antioch. This may have even included sharing non-kosher food, however, the Scripture does not make it clear exactly what he was eating. Whatever the case, when a group of Jewish believers came from James, he separated himself from the Gentiles publicly. Paul's accusation was twofold: First, he accused Peter, who was a Jew, for not living as a Jew, in other words, for disregarding the commandments of the Torah (possibly, in this case, the dietary laws). Secondly, he reprimanded Peter for forcing the Gentile believers to live as Jews by separating himself from the Gentile believers. Paul instantly recognized the hypocrisy in this move and called Peter on the carpet. The message Peter gave the Gentile believes was that since they were not Jewish and not keeping the Torah, they were not worthy of his fellowship. They simply were not as good as observant Jewish believers are. The implication was, "If you wish to have fellowship with us begin living a Jewish lifestyle, keep the Torah and we will accept you as being as good as we are." Paul rightfully exposed Peter's hypocrisy and condemned his behavior. This, however, is the logical outcome of the approach of acting as a Jew when in the company of Jews and acting as a Gentile when in the company of Gentiles. One day your Jewish and Gentile friends will inevitably meet and then you must decide on the spot which way you are going to behave, as a Jew or as a Gentile. This is the very predicament in which Peter found himself when the party from James arrived at Antioch. Peter had to decide, and so decide he did. There would have been accusations of hypocrisy and hurt feelings either way he chose. Paul, as the apostle to the Gentiles, understood this dilemma all too well. Paul knew that Gentiles would understand his yielding some of his liberty in Messiah in order to win his Jewish brothers to faith in Yeshua. At the same time, he realized that if he

---

25. Gal 2:11–16 (RSV).

presented himself as a Jew while renouncing the Torah and living a Gentile lifestyle, he would fail to even get his foot in the door with his fellow Jews. It is clear that Paul lived in observance of the Torah all the time, when he was with Jews, with Gentiles, and even alone by himself.

THE CIRCUMCISION OF TIMOTHY

In Acts 16:1–3, we read of how Paul had his fellow disciple Timothy circumcised.

> *1:* And he came also to Derbe and to Lystra. A disciple was there, named Timothy, the son of a Jewish woman who was a believer; but his father was a Greek. *2:* He was well spoken of by the brethren at Lystra and Ico'nium. *3:* Paul wanted Timothy to accompany him; and he took him and circumcised him because of the Jews that were in those places, for they all knew that his father was a Greek.[26]

It may seem somewhat surprising that Paul had Timothy, a believer in Yeshua, circumcised in light of Paul's stern words to the Galatians in 5:2–4:

> *2:* Now I, Paul, say to you that if you receive circumcision, Messiah will be of no advantage to you. *3:* I testify again to every man who receives circumcision that he is bound to keep the whole law. *4:* You are severed from Messiah, you who would be justified by the law; you have fallen away from grace.[27]

There seems to be only one possible explanation why Paul would have circumcised Timothy. He must have considered Timothy already Jewish. As such, Timothy's forefathers, at Mount Sinai, had already committed him to keeping the Torah (Exod 24:3). By circumcising him, Paul was not placing Timothy under the Law because he had, in fact, been born under the Law to begin with. Moreover, under Paul's tutelage, Timothy would have undoubtedly understood with absolute clarity that his righteousness was in Yeshua's atonement and not in obeying the works of the Law.[28] As we have seen with the example of Peter at Antioch, it was imperative that Timothy, especially as a worker in the good news of Messiah, choose correctly, whether he should live a Jewish lifestyle in obedience to the Torah, or rather that of a Gentile entirely free from the Law. It was important that Paul clarify

---

26. Acts 16:1–3 (RSV).
27. Gal 5:2–4 (RSV).
28. Gal 2:16.

Timothy's status when he asked Timothy to join him. Paul was evidently under severe scrutiny by local Jews of the area. Any inconsistency regarding Paul's view on Jewish observance of the Torah might have been construed as hypocrisy, or worse yet, defiance of God's word, as when he visited Jerusalem in Acts 21:19–26 (see above) and was misunderstood to be teaching against the Law of Moses. This would have had the potential danger of damaging Paul's witness and placing an insurmountable stumbling block in the way of his listeners' accepting the good news of Messiah.

WHO IS A JEW?

The case of Timothy's circumcision touches upon the thorny question of who is a Jew according to Scripture. This is important in determining who is held responsible, according to the Scriptures, to observe the Torah. In the ancient patriarchal society, one's father determined whether a person was Jewish. Thus, a number of the patriarchs married foreign wives but their children were still *bnei-Israel* (sons of Israel). Later, Rabbinic Judaism ruled, contrary to the Scriptures, that Jewishness is determined by one's mother.[29] This goes against the teaching of Scripture that declares that one's patronage is determined by one's father. For instance, Israelite patriarchs such as Joseph, Moses, and kings such as David and Solomon married Gentile wives, yet their offspring were still considered Israelites.

THE DAUGHTERS OF ZELOPHEHAD

There is a case that is an interesting exception to this rule recorded in Numbers 27:1–8:

> *1:* Then drew near the daughters of Zeloph'ehad the son of Hepher, son of Gilead, son of Machir, son of Manas'seh, from the families of Manas'seh the son of Joseph. The names of his daughters were: Mahlah, Noah, Hoglah, Milcah, and Tirzah. *2:* And they stood before Moses, and before Elea'zar the priest, and before the leaders and all the congregation, at the door of the tent of meeting, saying, *3:* "Our father died in the wilderness; he was not among the company of those who gathered themselves together against the Lord in the company of Korah, but died for his own sin; and he had no sons. *4:* Why should the name of our father be taken away from his family, because he had no

---

29. Mishnah Kiddushin 3:12.

son? Give to us a possession among our father's brethren." *5:* Moses brought their case before the Lord. *6:* And the Lord said to Moses, *7:* "The daughters of Zeloph'ehad are right; you shall give them possession of an inheritance among their father's brethren and cause the inheritance of their father to pass to them. *8:* And you shall say to the people of Israel, 'If a man dies, and has no son, then you shall cause his inheritance to pass to his daughter.[30]

In other words, the bloodline would be passed down to daughters if no male heir was born. If so, at least in this specific case, membership within Israel might be passed down by the mother.

Was this case of Timothy's mother? Was she born of Jewish parents who had no sons? Scripture does not tell us. Nevertheless, it is clear that Paul must have been convinced that Timothy was indeed Jewish. Evidently his father being Gentile did not change the situation. It is evident, then, that at least in some cases Jewishness may come from one's mother and not only from one's father. In considering who is Jewish under Paul's directive to remain as one is called,[31] this includes a person who has at least one parent who is Jewish, a person who has been brought up Jewish, and a Gentile who has converted to Judaism. Certain factors such as his Jewish identity, his sense of belonging to the Jewish people, and his Jewish education may also figure into the question.

It is important to keep in mind that the reason a Jewish believer should observe the Torah is the hope of seeing those of his nation come to the Messiah. It is not by any means for his own salvation or righteousness. It is not to help him keep his salvation, to make him a better person, or to give him any special status before God or among fellow believers. It is a witness to his people with the ultimate goal of leading them to accept Yeshua as a nation.

JUDAIZING: RETURNING TO THE WEAK AND BEGGARLY ELEMENTS

Within some circles of believers in Yeshua, all Jewish practices and customs are shunned for fear that they might lead some to go "back under the Law." They forbid both Jewish and Gentile believers from participating in anything Jewish, citing passages such as Galatians 4:9–10.

---

30. Num 27:1–8 (RSV); cf. Josh 17:3–6.
31. 1 Cor 7:17–20 (see above).

> 9: But now, after that ye have known God, or rather are known of God, how turn ye again to the weak and beggarly elements, whereunto ye desire again to be in bondage? *10:* Ye observe days, and months, and times, and years.[32]

Some see this as an objection to Jewish believers in Yeshua continuing to keep the commandments of the Torah. They understand that Paul rebuked the Jewish believers who, having been freed from the Law by faith in Yeshua, afterwards returned to keeping the Jewish holidays.

A closer look at this passage, however, shows that Paul was writing to Gentiles rather than to Jewish believers. These were Gentiles who were formerly pagans. In the former worship of their pagan gods, they had observed certain days. These empty practices had brought them no benefit whatsoever, since they had been, in fact, worshiping demons.[33] These deeds did not make them righteous and, needless to say, they most certainly did not point them to Yeshua. These pagans heard the good news about Yeshua and put their faith in him. Afterward, those of the circumcision party convinced them that they must keep the Torah. These exchanged their trust in Yeshua and his atonement for reliance on works of the Law. For this reason Paul equated their keeping of holidays of the Torah with those worthless practices they kept as pagans. This is what Paul meant when he said that they had returned again to "the weak and beggarly elements." Paul, however, encouraged Jewish believers in Yeshua to continue keeping the commandments of the Torah.

THE LAW OF MESSIAH

Few believers realize the extent of the freedom that they have in Messiah. When the question is asked, "Are believers in Yeshua free from the Law?," the response that is often heard is, "Yes, we are free from the Law, but we are not lawless, since we are under the Law of Messiah" (or Law of Christ). Paul mentioned something similar in 1 Corinthians 9:20–21:

> 20: To the Jews I became as a Jew, in order to win Jews; to those under the law I became as one under the law—though not being myself under the law—that I might win those under the law. *21:* To those outside the law I became as one outside the law—not

---

32. Gal 4:9–10 (KJV).
33. 1 Cor 10:20.

being without law toward God but under the Law of Messiah—
that I might win those outside the law.[34]

It is wrongly imagined by some that the keeping the Law of Messiah means observing the "spiritual part" of the Law.

THE SUPPOSED SPIRITUAL AND CARNAL PARTS OF THE LAW

It is widely held by many believers in Yeshua that the Law of Moses can be divided into two parts: the spiritual part of the Law and the carnal part of the Law. The supposed spiritual part of the Law is usually thought to include the Ten Commandments, as well as the commands to love the Lord with all one's heart and to love one's neighbor as one's self[35] and the teachings of the Sermon on the Mount.[36] The carnal or fleshly part of the Law is thought to include the ceremonial Temple sacrifices and rituals (which were merely types and shadows of Messiah) and the "letter of the Law" (see below). It is imagined that the carnal, fleshly part of the Law was in old times what was kept in the flesh, and could not provide salvation. It is supposed that when Yeshua died on the cross he paid for, fulfilled, and did away with the carnal part of the Law. It is furthermore believed that what remains and must be kept by the believer is the spiritual part of the Law. We have seen in chapter 7, however, that the Torah is a single unit, a packaged deal. It is all or nothing. Yeshua said that not an iota would pass from the Law as long as the heaven and earth of this present creation stand.[37] It cannot be separated into spiritual and carnal parts. Moreover, we have seen that Yeshua, by his death and resurrection, fulfilled and paid for the entire Law, not just part of it. After all, which is more important that Yeshua fulfilled by his death and resurrection, the so-called carnal, ceremonial part of the Torah or the supposedly spiritual part of the Law? Does it not make more sense that in order to effect a spiritual change in the hearts of men his sacrifice would deal with the spiritual part of the Law? Yeshua indeed fulfilled both the so-called spiritual and so-called carnal parts of the Law. Nothing whatsoever remains for the believer to keep for his salvation or his continued standing before God. We have seen in chapter 5 how when a person puts his faith in

---

34. I Cor 9:20–21 (RSV).
35. Matt 22:37–39 ; Luke 10:27.
36. Matt 5—7.
37. Matt 5:17–19.

Yeshua's atonement he is transformed and becomes part of the new creation and is set free from all of the Law.

A DEADLY DECEPTION

The notion that a person is initially saved by faith in Yeshua's atonement but his continued standing with God is dependent on observance of some part of the Torah is nothing new. Paul penned his Epistle to the Galatians mainly to counter this false doctrine, which is why it is known as Galatianism:

> *1:* O foolish Galatians! Who has bewitched you, before whose eyes Yeshua Messiah was publicly portrayed as crucified? *2:* Let me ask you only this: Did you receive the Spirit by works of the law, or by hearing with faith? *3:* Are you so foolish? Having begun with the Spirit, are you now ending with the flesh? *4:* Did you experience so many things in vain?—if it really is in vain. *5:* Does he who supplies the Spirit to you and works miracles among you do so by works of the law, or by hearing with faith?[38]

The conviction that the believer must yet keep the spiritual part of the Law is merely a form of Galatianism. The reason that this danger is deadly is that it has the potential to sever one's faith in Messiah's atonement. The Gentile Galatians had been deceived by the circumcision party into believing that they must be circumcised and keep the Torah. The deceived Galatians had begun relying on the works of the Law *instead* of upon Yeshua's atonement for their continued salvation. A person cannot rely on the works of the Torah for his salvation and at the same time trust in the atonement of Messiah. Paul makes this painfully clear:

> *1:* For freedom Messiah has set us free; stand fast therefore, and do not submit again to a yoke of slavery. *2:* Now I, Paul, say to you that if you receive circumcision, Messiah will be of no advantage to you. *3:* I testify again to every man who receives circumcision that he is bound to keep the whole law. *4:* You are severed from Messiah, you who would be justified by the law; you have fallen away from grace. *5:* For through the Spirit, by faith, we wait for the hope of righteousness.[39]

The key here is *reliance* on the Law. Paul himself kept the Law, but he did not rely on it. He relied entirely on the atonement of Yeshua for his salvation and his continued standing before God. He kept the commandments of the Law

---

38. Gal 3:1–5 (RSV).
39. Gal 5:1–5 (RSV).

in the hope of seeing the Jewish people, as a nation, one day accept Yeshua as Messiah. It is likewise imperative that every Jewish believer in Yeshua have it absolutely clear in his mind that the reason he keeps the Torah is not for his own salvation or righteousness, but for the purpose of seeing his people, as a nation, come to Yeshua.

LED BY THE SPIRIT—THE PRINCIPAL OPERATING SYSTEM OF THE BELIEVER

If the believer is not bound by the commandments of the Torah, how is he to live his life in obedience to God's will? John admonishes believers:

> *27*: But as for you, Messiah has poured out his Spirit on you. As long as his Spirit remains in you, you do not need anyone to teach you. For his Spirit teaches you about everything, and what he teaches is true, not false. Obey the Spirit's teaching then, and remain in union with Messiah.[40]

We have seen how the moment a person puts his faith in Yeshua God's Spirit enters his body and bonds with his human spirit, effecting his transformation into a new creature. Jeremiah prophesied of the coming of a new covenant:

> *31:* "Behold, the days are coming, says the Lord, when I will make a new covenant with the house of Israel and the house of Judah, *32:* not like the covenant which I made with their fathers when I took them by the hand to bring them out of the land of Egypt, my covenant which they broke, though I was their husband, says the Lord. *33:* But this is the covenant which I will make with the house of Israel after those days, says the Lord: I will put my law within them, and I will write it upon their hearts; and I will be their God, and they shall be my people. *34:* And no longer shall each man teach his neighbor and each his brother, saying, 'Know the Lord,' for they shall all know me, from the least of them to the greatest, says the Lord; for I will forgive their iniquity, and I will remember their sin no more."[41]

Through the indwelling of his Spirit, God transforms the heart of the believer, impressing on it his Law, so that he delights in his "inner being" to serve him. Led by God's Spirit, he no longer needs the precepts of the Written Torah to restrain or direct him. He also has the correction of fellow

---

40. 1 John 2:27 (Good News Bible).
41. Jer 31:31–34 (RSV).

believers and the Scriptures made alive by the Spirit of God to guide him. It goes without saying that the freedom of the believer is not intended to give him license to sin.

> *1:* What shall we say then? Are we to continue in sin that grace may abound? *2:* By no means! How can we who died to sin still live in it?[42]
>
> *15:* What then? Are we to sin because we are not under law but under grace? By no means! *16:* Do you not know that if you yield yourselves to any one as obedient slaves, you are slaves of the one whom you obey, either of sin, which leads to death, or of obedience, which leads to righteousness?[43]

The believer is set free in order to obey the Lord and serve his fellow believers from his heart.

> *13:* For you were called to freedom, brethren; only do not use your freedom as an opportunity for the flesh, but through love be servants of one another.[44]

WHAT IS THE LAW OF MESSIAH?

The Law of Messiah to which Paul referred in 1 Corinthians 9:20–21 is simply what Yeshua commanded his disciples in John 13:34–35:

> *34:* "A new commandment I give to you, that you love one another; even as I have loved you, that you also love one another. *35:* By this all men will know that you are my disciples, if you have love for one another."[45]

WHAT THE LAW OF MESSIAH IS NOT

The Law of Moses is not a spiritualized reworking of the Law of Moses. Neither is it the supposed spiritual part of the Law. There is no hope for salvation or righteousness through works of the Law, not even the spiritual parts of the Law. These can only come through Yeshua's atonement, to which nothing more can be added. Paul admonished:

42. Rom 6:1–2 (RSV).
43. Rom 6:15–16 (RSV).
44. Gal 5:13 (RSV).
45. John 13:34–35 (RSV).

> *2:* Bear one another's burdens, and so fulfil the law of Messiah.[46]

The Law of Messiah is specifically Yeshua's commandment to "love one another; even as I have loved you," and not the compendium of all the commandments of Yeshua and his apostles.

THE LETTER OF THE LAW

> *4:* And such trust have we through Christ to God-ward *5:* not that we are sufficient of ourselves to think any thing as of ourselves; but our sufficiency is of God; *6:* who also hath made us able ministers of the new testament; not of the letter, but of the spirit: for the letter killeth, but the spirit giveth life.[47]

Those who perceive a division of the Law into spiritual and carnal parts see "the letter" here as meaning a very literal, merciless, eye-for-an-eye, nit-picking, gnat-straining obedience to every jot and tittle of the Law. This they believe is, after all, what Yeshua accused the Pharisees of. They understand "the spirit" here as the spirit of the Law based the higher, universal, spiritual, moral Law embedded in the Law of Moses. In opposition to the letter of the Law, they believe that the spirit of the Law is a more casual, merciful observance of the Law based on what one feels in his heart. This is a terrible misunderstanding of the verse. The letter of the Law is not the literal or the carnal part of the Law, but the *entire Law*, the whole thing. The entire Law, including the Ten Commandments, the Sermon on the Mount, and the commandments to love God and one's neighbor, is a package deal. It has no power whatsoever to give life. In 2 Corinthians 3:7 it is called "the dispensation of death." All it can do is condemn to death and that is in fact its purpose: to convict the world and hold it accountable so that men might seek salvation through Yeshua.

> *19:* Now we know that whatever the law says it speaks to those who are under the law, so that every mouth may be stopped, and the whole world may be held accountable to God.[48]

The "spirit" in 2 Corinthians 3:6 has nothing to do with the "spirit of the Law" or the "spiritual" parts of the Law. Its rather speaks of the Spirit of God, who gives eternal life to the person who puts his faith in Yeshua's atonement and transforms him into a part of the new creation.

---

46. Gal 6:2 (RSV).
47. 2 Cor 3:4–6 (The King James Bible).
48. Rom 3:19–20 (RSV); see also Gal 3:23.

ESTABLISHING THE LAW

In Romans 3:31 Paul asks,

> *31:* Do we then make void the law through faith? Certainly not! On the contrary, we establish the law.[49]

What did Paul mean by this? He was asking if one's relying on faith in Yeshua's atonement instead of relying upon the works of the Law for one's righteousness annuls the Law. The answer is absolutely not! The main purpose of the Torah is to lead people to Messiah. The person who accepts Yeshua has done exactly what the Torah was intended to make him do. At that same moment all his obligations to the Law are met, not through his own righteousness, but through Messiah's. By putting his faith in Yeshua, the believer thus establishes the very purpose for which the Law was created. He moreover demonstrates the genuine value of the Law in its ability to convict men's hearts and turn them to Yeshua, their Savior. Some have taken these words of Paul the wrong way: they understand that when Paul said that through faith we establish the Law, he meant that when a person comes to faith in Yeshua and God's Law is written on his heart he is suddenly enabled by God's Spirit to keep the commandments of the Law. This thinking suggests that before a person comes to Yeshua he is living in the flesh and is thus unable to keep the Law. When, however, he comes to faith in Yeshua and receives the Spirit of God, he is then supernaturally enabled to keep the Law by faith. The end result is once again that he views his salvation as dependent on his keeping some part of the Torah. This is of course not what Paul meant at all. Paul made clear that at the moment when one puts his faith in Yeshua the Law for him personally is fulfilled once and for all.

REPLACEMENT THEOLOGY

There is another danger with seeing the Law divided into a carnal part and a spiritual part that must still be kept by the believer. This thinking logically leads to supersessionism or replacement theology. According to this false doctrine, believers in Yeshua are obeying the spiritual part of the Law and are thus is seen as spiritual Israel, the true inheritor of all the promises of the *Tanakh*. Since the Jewish people rejected Yeshua, God rejected them and the church has now replaced the Jews as God's chosen people. We have seen that Paul wrote the eleventh chapter of the book of Romans mainly in order to refute this error.

---

49. Rom 3:31(NKJV).

> *1:* I ask, then, has God rejected his people? By no means! I myself am an Israelite, a descendant of Abraham, a member of the tribe of Benjamin. *2:* God has not rejected his people whom he foreknew.[50]

In replacement theology the local church building, thought of as the "house of God," replaces the Temple. As we have seen in chapter 6, the Temple was intended to represent, among other things, the body of Messiah, both as Yeshua himself walked upon the earth and his corporate body, the congregation of believers in Yeshua. Notwithstanding, the physical Temple will be rebuilt in the future on Mount Moriah and still has an important role to play, as the centerpiece of the Torah, as the schoolmaster in leading the Jewish people as a nation to Yeshua the Messiah.

In replacement theology, the Saturday Sabbath is thought to have been replaced by Sunday. It seems that the early believers did, in fact, recognize Sunday, the first day of the week upon which Yeshua rose from the dead, as the as "the Lord's Day." a special time for gathering, worship, and prayer. Nevertheless, Sunday, the Lord's Day, was in no way intended to replace the Sabbath as an integral part of the Torah. The Jewish believers of the first centuries continued to observe Saturday as the Sabbath. Later, Sunday became a day of rest in Western countries. This was not initiated by Yeshua's disciples but was originally enacted into Roman law by the emperor, Constantine, in honor of the sun god in 321 CE.[51]

The deception of replacement theology marginalizes the nation of Israel and is a major cause of anti-Semitism. It moreover disrupts God's plan of redemption both for Israel and for the world. The belief that the church has replaced Israel has blinded many Gentile believers in Yeshua from seeing the primary importance of the Jewish people in God's plan. It has kept them from recognizing the tremendous significance of the return of the Jewish people to the land of Israel and its meaning for our times. Consequently, Gentile believers have been apathetic, or even hostile, toward God's chosen people.

To say that the Torah has been replaced by the Law of Messiah misses the mark entirely. It robs the Torah of its power to convict of sin. There is, of course, nothing at all wrong with worshipping in a church building or keeping Sunday as a day of worship, but to say that the church building replaces the Temple and Sunday replaces Saturday as the Sabbath is not in keeping with the teaching of the Scriptures. Removing these two central elements from God's Law disables the Torah from fulfilling its role as a schoolmaster

---

50. Rom 11:1–2a (RSV).
51. *Codex Justinianus*, lib. 3, tit. 12, 3.

to lead Israel as a nation to Yeshua. It might be argued that the Temple not having been standing on Mount Moriah in Jerusalem for nearly two thousand years is proof that God no longer needs or wants a Temple. Not so long ago, a similar argument could have been made that since the nation of Israel has not existed in its own land, God no longer cares about it and it will never return as a nation to its ancient homeland. Just as the promise in the Scriptures that the Jewish people would return to the land[52] has come to pass, God will fulfill his promise that the Temple will once again stand on Mount Moriah.[53] Replacement theology has greatly hindered the good news of Yeshua from reaching the Jewish people over the past two thousand years.

We have seen that the Torah still has an important role as a schoolmaster to lead the Jewish people to Yeshua as Messiah. If Israel is seen as the church and the Torah, the Temple, and the Temple sacrifices are all spiritualized, the Jewish people will never accept Yeshua. If the Jewish people do not recognize Yeshua as the Messiah, he will not return.[54] There will be no resurrection from the dead and the new creation will never happen.

THE ISRAEL OF GOD

In the final chapter of Galatians Paul expands on the grace of God in Messiah:

> *14*: But God forbid that I should boast except in the cross of our Lord Yeshua the Messiah by whom the world has been crucified to me, and I to the world. *15*: For in Messiah Yeshua neither circumcision nor uncircumcision avails anything, but a new creation. *16*: And as many as walk according to this rule, peace and mercy be upon them, and upon the Israel of God.[55]

What Paul intended to say is that in eternity what really counts is that a person accepts Yeshua's atonement and becomes a part of the new creation. By comparison, whether a he is Jewish or Gentile is of little consequence. In the end, at Yeshua's appearance both Jewish and Gentile believers will be transformed and enter together as citizens of the kingdom. Because a believer in Messiah is *already* a part of the new creation, he is able to live according to this reality, now at this present time. It is interesting that Paul spoke of "walking according to this rule." Jewish Law is referred to as *hallachah*,

---

52. Ezek 37; Isa 11:11.
53. Dan 9:27; 2 Thess 2:4; Rev 11:1–2.
54. Acts 3:17; Matt 23:37–39; see above chapter 2.
55. Gal 6:14–16 (NKJV).

"walking." Those who live according Jewish Law walk it out, day by day. Here Paul blessed those who were conducting their daily lives according to the rule of the new creation, that is to say, conducting their daily lives as free from the Law. Then he added "and upon the Israel of God." There has been some dispute about what Paul meant by "the Israel of God." Exactly who is the Israel of God? Is he referring to the Jewish people? Those who hold that Paul rejected the Law and renounced Judaism claim that he could only have been referring to the Christian church. Note, for instance, how Galatians 6:16 reads in the New International Version:

> *16:* Peace and mercy to all who follow this rule, *even* to the Israel of God. (emphasis added)

The small Greek word *kai* is usually translated "and." By rather translating *kai*, in this verse, to read "even," the NIV translators make it sound as though Paul is calling those who live free from the Law "the Israel of God." The NIV translators have undoubtedly engaged here in a bit of unwarranted editorializing, evidently with a theological agenda. It promotes the idea that the Christian church as "spiritual Israel" has replaced "Israel of the flesh." As we have seen, Paul spoke very sternly against replacement theology in chapter 11 of his Letter to the Romans.

Derek Prince, who was educated as a scholar of Greek at Cambridge University, weighed in on the NIV's translation of *kai* in this passage:

> You would have to search the New Testament to find places where that word is legitimately translated "even"— probably fewer than once in five hundred occurrences. Overwhelmingly, *kai* is translated "and."[56]

The "and" here implies a distinction between those who walk by this rule and the Israel of God. You would not, for instance speak of boys *and* boys, but of boys *and* girls. Paul obvious intended by "the Israel of God" to mean others who do *not* conduct their daily lives according to this rule. This "Israel of God," then, is evidently the body of Jewish believers in Yeshua who, in hope of the redemption of Israel and for the sake of their witness to the Jewish people, continue to observe the commandments of the Torah.

If indeed the Torah is intended to serve as a schoolmaster to lead the Jewish people to Yeshua, why has it failed so miserably to do so over the past two thousand years that have elapsed since the first coming of Yeshua? This will be the topic of the next chapters.

---

56. Prince, *Destiny*, 24.

10

What They Came Up with at Yavneh

THE RABBI'S DARING ESCAPE

RABBAN YOHANAN BEN-ZACHAI ASSESSED the dismal situation. The defenders of Jerusalem were starving! It would not be long before the Roman legionaries would pierce the walls of the city and come pouring through the breach, sparing neither man, woman, nor child. He knew that the nation was lost and that the people would be scattered to the four winds.

But the rabbi had a plan. He would exit the dying city in a coffin. Thus he would pass through the Romans, who held a tight clasp on the city, and at the same time outwit the ring of Jewish defenders within the walls, who would have undoubtedly accused him of desertion. The rabbi's disciples bore the casket of their master out through the city gate. But rather than making a break for freedom, the pallbearers, following the instruction of the rabbi, turned and brought the coffin before Vespasian, the general in charge of the Roman army besieging Jerusalem. There before the astonished commander the lid popped off the crate, and up from it rose Rabban Yohanan Ben-Zachai. The rabbi greeted the general with a prophecy that he, Vespasian, would soon rise to be ruler of the entire Roman Empire. Thus finding favor in the eyes of the commander, the rabbi dared to make his request. "Give me Yavneh and its sages," he entreated. Thus the ancient Jewish source *Avoth d' Rabbi Nathan*[1] explained how Rabban Yohanan Ben-Zakai came to head the Yeshiva (academy) at the Roman colony of Yavneh.

1. Schechter, *Abot d' Rabbi Nathan*, version B, ch. 4.5.

In the year 70 CE, on the tenth day of the month of Av, the Temple of Jerusalem, the house of the God of Israel, went up in flames. Along with it went the hopes and aspirations of the Jewish people. The Romans, brutally crushing the revolt against their rule, had set Jerusalem to the torch. Time had stopped for the nation of Israel. It would be led away captive by the edge of the sword and be dispersed to the four corners of the earth. All hope was gone. At Yavneh, on the southern coast of Israel, a tattered remnant of Jewish scholars who had survived the debacle, led by Rabban Yohanan Ben-Zakai, sat down to ponder what they should do next. The town of Yavneh was, at the time, a small colony under Roman autonomy and had remained unaffected by the revolt. Since Rabbi Yohanan had requested a place merely for the study of the Jewish religion, devoid of any apparent political aim, the Romans perceived no danger in permitting the assembly.

The dilemma that Rabbi Yohanan and his disciples faced was no small matter: From the giving of the Torah at Sinai until that day, with the exception of the seventy years of the exile in Babylon, Judaism had been centered about the ancient Tabernacle, followed by the Temple, its service and sacrifices. The religion and indeed the entire way of life of the people of Israel was virtually inseparable from its Temple. So now, with the Temple smoldering in the ashes, the very fabric of the nation was on the verge of disintegration. How could this handful of scholars rescue the chosen people from complete dissolution?

What the scholars at Yavneh came up with was absolutely ingenious: a total remodeling of Judaism so drastic that it was virtually a new religion! It was as if Judaism, like Yohanan Ben-Zakai himself, had risen from the grave. Despite its continuity with age-old tradition, which promoted its general acceptance, in many ways this new Judaism bore little resemblance to its ancient parent faith!

THE THREE TENETS

This new Judaism was based on three tenets: prayer, good works, and giving charity. These replaced atonement through the sacrifices in the Temple.

FROM TEMPLE TO SYNAGOGUE AND HOME

In the absence of the Temple at Jerusalem, the architects of the new Judaism made the synagogue and the individual Jewish home the new main focus of Jewish life. Once again it is important to remember that a synagogue is very different from the ancient Temple. Within the Temple the very presence of God dwelt, at times appearing in the visible form of a cloud. When the Jewish people met at the Temple of Jerusalem, they literally stood in the presence of the Almighty. A synagogue, on the other hand, is merely a place for prayer and study of the Scriptures. Since the worshiper does not come in direct contact with the divine presence, no special ritual purification is required in order to enter the synagogue, as it was in the case of the Temple. Many of the restrictions that existed in the Temple could be dropped.

FROM COHEN TO RABBI

It may seem surprising to some people that rabbis are not found at all in the *Tanakh* (Old Testament). The reason is that they did not exist at the time it was written. Instead we find cohens (priests) and Levites leading and teaching the people of Israel. It was only with the creation of Rabbinic Judaism that the cohen, the priestly leader in the Temple, was replaced by the rabbi, a man learned in oral traditions, as head of the Jewish community. Scripture required that the spiritual leaders of the people, cohens (priests), be only from the priestly families who belonged to the tribe of Levi. Rabbis, however, could be from any tribe of Israel.

THE HISTORY OF RABBINIC JUDAISM

The idea of Judaism practiced without the Temple was not entirely novel. In fact, the Jewish people had once before been forced into making do without the Temple and without Jerusalem. This was the seventy years from 586 to 515 BCE, when the first Temple was destroyed by Nebuchadnezzar and the Jews were deported to Babylon. After seventy years, the Jewish people returned to the land of Israel. The Jewish people rebuilt the Temple at Jerusalem but they never forgot the profound lessons that they had learned during their captivity in Babylon. Their experience of living without the Temple served as a dry run for the two millennia of exile that would follow the Roman destruction.

PHARISEES AND SADDUCEES: WHO HAS THE AUTHORITY?

Toward the end of the Second Temple Period, the Jewish nation was fragmented into many sects and parties. The first-century historian Josephus Flavius named three main sects to which the Jews belonged at this time:

the Sadducees, the Pharisees, and the Essenes.[2] Only the first two concern us here. The Sadducees, or in Hebrew *Tzadukim*, evidently took their name from Zadok, who was the high priest in King David's time.[3] It seems that the party of the Sadducees was comprised of the chief priests and those belonging to the aristocratic class that had grown up around them.[4] The priests had been appointed from the beginning to be the leaders of the people of Israel. As the administrators of the Temple, they clearly held the scriptural mandate to lead and to teach the nation.[5] But in the course of the Second Temple Period the priesthood had undergone drastic and dramatic changes. When the Romans took more direct role in the government of Judea, they exercised more and more control upon the priests and the administration of the Temple. Eventually they demanded the prerogative of appointing and deposing the high priest. This was seen by the people as an abrogation of the scriptural requirements for succession of the high priest and his appointment for life. In their eyes the priesthood became tainted. Furthermore, the priests had become worldly through the influence of Hellenism. Their holding to the letter of the Torah made their interpretation of it rigid and antiquated, incapable of adjustment or adaptation to changing situations within society. As a result this and the superiority of their class and the oppression of the poor, they became detached from the common people and became lax in their responsibilities to teach and lead the nation. They became more and more associated with their Roman sponsors, who were seen as unwelcome conquerors.

Within Israel, from the ranks of every sector of the nation, there arose another sect, that of the Pharisees. Scholars have suggested the name "pharisee" probably came from the Hebrew *parush*, "to divide." The Pharisees, or *Parushim* as they were known in Hebrew, were those who considered themselves as interpreting or "dividing" the Scriptures rightly.[6] A member of the Pharisees did not necessarily have to come from the aristocratic priestly class, as usually did the members of the Sadducees. Rather, the Pharisee could come from any tribe of Israel and from any walk of life. They based their authority on the appointment of elders by Moses from all Israel[7] as well as their abilities as interpreters and teachers of the Scriptures. The Pharisees stepped into the vacuum left by the Sadducees' failure to stay in

2. Josephus, *War* 2:119–166.
3. 2 Sam 20:25; Ezek 48:11–12.
4. Acts 4:1; 5:17.
5. Exod 29:41; Lev 10:11.
6. Cf. 2 Tim 2:15.
7. Exod 18:13–26.

touch with the people. Consequently, the Pharisees became the popular teachers and leaders of the nation, gaining a major role in the great council known as the Sanhedrin, the highest governing body of the day. As a result, the Pharisees gained greater and greater authority in Israel.

THE ORAL LAW

The Pharisees claimed that they were the inheritors of an oral Torah that existed alongside the written Law. This oral Law amplified and elaborated the Written Torah, supposedly explaining the correct manner in which it was to be observed. While the Pharisees claimed that the oral Law was given by God at Sinai and handed down from Moses to Joshua then to the prophets and finally to themselves.[8] In reality, it was for the most part a product of much later times.[9] Most agree that the precepts of the oral Law developed either during or after the first exile to Babylon.[10] Because it was oral and not set down in writing, it retained a good deal of flexibility, which permitted considerable latitude. The oral Law could be adapted to fit the changing social situations and circumstances of the Jewish people. It consequently gave the impression of always staying current.

The oral Law was not written down for many generations. It was intentionally kept oral and was preserved by repetition and memorization. It was the particular possession of the scribes and Pharisees and their pupils, passed down from teacher to disciple. To learn it took much perseverance and determination. It in essence served as secret knowledge for the initiated. In Yeshua's day, everyone was judged according his knowledge of the oral Law, or the lack thereof. Those who had been educated according to pharisaic traditions were called "lettered," while those who had not studied under the tutelage of the scribes and Pharisees were considered uneducated. The Pharisees were amazed that Yeshua had such knowledge despite his not having studied under their teachers.

> *15:* The Jews marveled at it, saying, "How is it that this man has learning, when he has never studied?"[11]

---

8. M. Avot 1:1.
9. Barr and Brosh, *Rabbinic Judaism Debunked*, 21–27.
10. Linfield, "Relation of Jewish to Babylonian Law."
11. John 7:15.

PASSED DOWN BY SUCCESSION

The oral Law was passed down from sage to disciple, and from generation to generation. When a particular passage was quoted, the student was required to recall the source from which the teaching descended. For instance, with regard to the *parochet*, the veil before the holy of holies in the Temple, it was taught:

> R. Shimon b. Gamliel says in the name of R. Shimon the son of the *Segan* (deputy high priest), The curtain was one handbreadth thick, woven on seventy-two strands, and on each strand were twenty-four threads; its length was forty *amot* (cubits) and its width twenty *amot* (cubits), and of eighty-two ten thousands it was made; and they would make two every year, and three hundred *kohanim* (priests) would immerse it.[12]

The way Yeshua taught, however, was quite different. He simply taught them straightforwardly on his own authority:

> 28: And when Yeshua finished these sayings, the crowds were astonished at his teaching, 29: for he taught them as one who had authority, and not as their scribes.[13]

BUILDING FENCES AROUND THE TORAH

In order to prevent the possibility of inadvertently transgressing the Law, the practice of surrounding each commandment with a fence of additional commandments was established. A good example is the commandment not to boil a kid in its mother's milk[14] and the additional fence commandment prohibiting eating milk and meat together. Thus, commandment upon commandment was added, creating an ever greater obligation and burden. Yeshua said of the scribes and Pharisees,

> 4: They bind heavy burdens, hard to bear, and lay them on men's shoulders; but they themselves will not move them with their finger.[15]

---

12. M. Shekalim 8:5 (translated by Levin).
13. Matt 7:28–29 (RSV).
14. Deut 14:21b.
15. Matt 23:4 (RSV).

TAKANOT

At times a specific statute of the Written Torah was deliberately changed out of expediency. The rabbis exalted their authority over the word of God by employing logic and relying on established custom to change a commandment simply because they felt the need to.

PRECEDENCE OF THE ORAL TRADITION OVER THE WRITTEN TORAH

It was inevitable that the oral tradition would eventually take precedence over the Written Torah since it was claimed that it interpreted and explained the Written Torah. Mishnah Sanhedrin 11:3 reads:

> 3. Greater stringency applies to [the observance of] the words of the Scribes than to [the observance] the words of the [written] Law. If a man said, 'There is no obligation to wear phylacteries so that he transgresses the words of the Law, he is not culpable; [but if he said], There should be in them five partitions', so that he adds to the words of the Scribes, he is culpable.[16]

Thus, in Rabbinic Judaism obedience to the tradition of men at times became more important than observance of God's word.

ISAIAH 29:13-14

The roots of Rabbinic Judaism evidently go back to before the destruction of the first Temple. In the book of the pre-exilic prophet Isaiah, God upbraids Israel:

> *13:* And the Lord said: "Because this people draw near with their mouth and honor me with their lips, while their hearts are far from me, and their fear of me is a commandment of men learned by rote; *14:* therefore, behold, I will again do marvelous things with this people, wonderful and marvelous; and the wisdom of their wise men shall perish, and the discernment of their discerning men shall be hid."[17]

Yeshua quoted this verse when speaking with the Pharisees.

---

16. M. Sanhedrin 11:3 (translation by Darbie).
17. Isa 29:13–14 RSV.

6: So, for the sake of your tradition, you have made void the word of God. 7: You hypocrites! Well did Isaiah prophesy of you, when he said: 8: 'This people honors me with their lips, but their heart is far from me; 9: in vain do they worship me, teaching as doctrines the precepts of men.'"[18]

Isaiah 29:13–14 mentions several elements characteristic of Rabbinic Judaism: Prayers are learned according to rote. They are read, today from the *sidur*, the prayer book. In a similar manner, the commandments are a matter of academic instruction, learning and repetition. It is most important in Rabbinic Judaism to obey the letter of the commandment. The intention of the heart is given lesser priority. The emphasis is on speaking the prescribed words and doing the commandment exactly. Rabbinic Judaism also occasionally replaces God's word with human tradition.

THE TRADITION OF THE ELDERS

In Yeshua's day, the oral Law was known as the "Tradition of the Elders" (Matt 15:2). It was from this primitive form of the oral Law from which all rabbinic tradition emanated.

MISHNAH

For the duration of the later Second Temple Period and for over 150 years afterward, the oral Law actually remained oral and loosely organized. With the destruction of the Second Temple and the dispersion of the Jewish people from Jerusalem and the land of Israel, it was feared that the oral traditions might be lost. Therefore, in the year 205 Rabbi Judah ha-Nasi redacted the Mishnah (meaning repetition [teaching]) into six "orders," which were in turn organized into tractates according to subject matter. Eventually the Mishnah was committed to writing, but when this occurred is a matter of debate.

GAMARA: THE TALMUD

After the codification of the Mishnah further explanations and clarification based on reason and tradition were added. This additional material became known as the Gamara (meaning completion) and was produced in

---

18. Matt 15:6–9 (RSV).

two editions, the so-called Jerusalem (or Palestinian) edition and the Babylonian edition. The combination of the Mishnah and Gamara are known as the Talmud, which embodies the earliest layers of the oral Law.

CONTINUATION

Beyond the Gamara, every generation of sages have added their say. Each layer, as it was deposited, became encrusted with the sanctity of tradition.

THE BRANCHES OF MODERN JUDAISM

The three branches or "denominations" of modern Judaism, Orthodox, Reform, and Conservative, may have substantial differences between them but all are expressions of Rabbinic Judaism.

OBEY THE SCRIBES AND PHARISEES

> *1:* Then said Yeshua to the crowds and to his disciples, *2:* "The scribes and the Pharisees sit on Moses' seat; *3:* so practice and observe whatever they tell you, but not what they do; for they preach, but do not practice.[19]

It may be construed from this passage that Yeshua lent his support to the authority of the scribes and Pharisees and their teachings. By implication, this must mean that he also would have given his backing to the authority of rabbis and Rabbinic Judaism that developed out of pharisaic teachings. This, however, does not square with the context of the rest of Matthew 23, in which he upbraids the Pharisees, or with the rest of the New Testament scriptures.

THE SEAT OF MOSES

What exactly is the "seat of Moses" in Matthew 23:2 and what did Yeshua mean when he said the scribes and Pharisees sit on it?

In Exodus 18:13–26, we find a terribly overworked Moses:

> *13:* On the morrow Moses sat to judge the people, and the people stood about Moses from morning till evening. *14:* When

---

19. Matt 23:1–3 (RSV).

Moses' father-in-law saw all that he was doing for the people, he said, "What is this that you are doing for the people? Why do you sit alone, and all the people stand about you from morning till evening?" *15:* And Moses said to his father-in-law, "Because the people come to me to inquire of God; *16:* when they have a dispute, they come to me and I decide between a man and his neighbor, and I make them know the statutes of God and his decisions." *17:* Moses' father-in-law said to him, "What you are doing is not good. *18:* You and the people with you will wear yourselves out, for the thing is too heavy for you; you are not able to perform it alone. *19:* Listen now to my voice; I will give you counsel, and God be with you! You shall represent the people before God, and bring their cases to God; *20:* and you shall teach them the statutes and the decisions, and make them know the way in which they must walk and what they must do. *21:* Moreover choose able men from all the people, such as fear God, men who are trustworthy and who hate a bribe; and place such men over the people as rulers of thousands, of hundreds, of fifties, and of tens. *22:* And let them judge the people at all times; every great matter they shall bring to you, but any small matter they shall decide themselves; so it will be easier for you, and they will bear the burden with you. *23:* If you do this, and God so commands you, then you will be able to endure, and all this people also will go to their place in peace." *24:* So Moses gave heed to the voice of his father-in-law and did all that he had said. *25:* Moses chose able men out of all Israel, and made them heads over the people, rulers of thousands, of hundreds, of fifties, and of tens. *26:* And they judged the people at all times; hard cases they brought to Moses, but any small matter they decided themselves.[20]

We find a similar account in Numbers 11: 16–17

16: And the Lord said to Moses, "Gather for me seventy men of the elders of Israel, whom you know to be the elders of the people and officers over them; and bring them to the tent of meeting, and let them take their stand there with you. *17:* And I will come down and talk with you there; and I will take some of the spirit which is upon you and put it upon them; and they shall bear the burden of the people with you, that you may not bear it yourself alone.[21]

---

20. Exod 18:13–26 (RSV).
21. Num 11:16–17.

From these seventy-plus-one (the one being Moses) developed the Great Sanhedrin of Yeshua's day. This great council, composed of both Sadducees and Pharisees, was the highest Jewish authority in the land. The power of the Pharisees in the council was on the ascent. Note that the seventy elders came from all Israel and not from the priests and Levites only.[22] The Pharisees took their authority and legitimacy of their leadership from these passages. Was Yeshua legitimizing this authority?

Within the ruins of a few ancient synagogues (notably those of Chorazin in the Golan and on the isle of Delos), there were found remains of a stone throne. It may be possible that in other ancient synagogues where they were not discovered such chairs were made of wood or other material that did not withstand the ravages of time. It has been suggested that these chairs represented the *kathedra d'Mosheh*, the seat of Moses in the synagogue. It has furthermore been surmised that the Torah, read on the Sabbath and other days, may have been read by a notable sitting in the chair, possibly a pharisaic scribe acting as the *archos synagogos*, the head of the synagogue. There a number of problems with this scenario. While it is true that the synagogue became the most important institution of Rabbinic Judaism, it is by no means clear that in Yeshua's day the Pharisees had exclusive hegemony in the synagogue.[23] Neither is it clear how the stone chair was used and who if anyone sat in it. L. I. Rahmani has suggested that the Torah scroll itself may have been placed in the chair.[24]

An interesting and important find that sheds some light on Yeshua's directive to obey the Pharisees is the discovery of a Hebrew text of Matthew found within a Jewish polemical treatise by Shem-Tob Ben Isaac Ben Shaprut composed in 1380, and recently published by Dr. George Howard at the University of Georgia.[25] Nehemiah Gordon discovered that in it, Mattew 23:1–3 appears with a slight variation of the Greek-based text:

> Upon the seat of Moses the Pharisees and Sages sit, but now all which *He* will say to you, keep and do, but *their* ordinances and deeds do not do because they say and do not.[26]

It is true according to early sources, particularly Papias, Bishop of Hierapolis in Asia Minor in the middle of the second century, and Iranaeus,

---

22. Exod 18:21; Num 11:16.
23. Levine, *Ancient Synagogue*, 40–41, 466–98.
24. Rahmani, "Stone Synagogue Chairs," 199.
25. Howard, *Hebrew Gospel of Matthew*.
26. Gordon, *Hebrew Yeshua*, 48; Howard, *Hebrew Gospel of Matthew*; Matt 23:1–3 (translated by Shem Tob), emphasis added. The variation pointed out here appears in Shem Tob's Hebrew, but not in Howard's English translation.

Bishop of Lyons, who lived from 120 to 202, that Matthew wrote his gospel in Hebrew[27] and that it was later translated to Greek. It must be kept in mind, however, that Shem-Tob's Matthew is dated to the fourteenth century and is a translation into Hebrew. Consequently, we have no choice other than to rely on the Greek for the original words of Yeshua. Notwithstanding, as Gordon points out, Shem-Tob's Matthew may hint at the original intent of the passage. It says, when he (meaning Moses) speaks (that is to say, when the words of the Written Torah are read to the congregation), his words should be obeyed; however, their (meaning the Pharisees' and sages') ordinances and deeds should not be observed.

In Yeshua's day, the Scriptures were of course not as available as they are today. A community would have been exceptionally fortunate to have a single scroll of the Torah kept in their local synagogue. Although most of the population was evidently literate, they knew the Torah from hearing, rather than reading it themselves.

> *21:* For from early generations Moses has had in every city those who preach him, for he is read every sabbath in the synagogues."[28]

The Pharisees met three times a week, on Tuesday, Thursday, and on the Sabbath, at which times they read from the Torah.

LEAVEN OF THE PHARISEES

In Matthew 16:6–12, Yeshua warns his disciples of the leaven of the Pharisees.

> *6:* Yeshua said to them, "Take heed and beware of the leaven of the Pharisees and Sad'ducees." *7:* And they discussed it among themselves, saying, "We brought no bread." *8:* But Yeshua, aware of this, said, "O men of little faith, why do you discuss among yourselves the fact that you have no bread? *9:* Do you not yet perceive? Do you not remember the five loaves of the five thousand, and how many baskets you gathered? *10:* Or the seven loaves of the four thousand, and how many baskets you gathered? *11:* How is it that you fail to perceive that I did not speak about bread? Beware of the leaven of the Pharisees and Sad'ducees." *12:* Then they understood that he did not tell them

---

27. Bivin and Blizzard, *Difficult Words of Jesus*, 23–24.
28. Acts 15:21 (RSV).

to beware of the leaven of bread, but of the teaching of the Pharisees and Sad'ducees.[29]

In Luke 12:1 Yeshua called the leaven of the Pharisees hypocrisy.

> *1:* In the meantime, when so many thousands of the multitude had gathered together that they trod upon one another, he [Yeshua] began to say to his disciples first, "Beware of the leaven of the Pharisees, which is hypocrisy.[30]

On the one hand, Yeshua calls the leaven of the Pharisees their teaching. On the other, he calls the leaven of the Pharisees hypocrisy. The inevitable conclusion is that Yeshua considered the doctrine of the Pharisees to be hypocrisy. By definition, hypocrisy is preaching to others to do what you yourself do not do. This is precisely what Yeshua accused the Pharisees of in Matthew 23:1–3b: ". . . for they preach, but do not practice." The Pharisees would publicly read the words of Moses but conduct their lives according to their own doctrine. In doing so they behaved in a manner that contradicted Moses' words. In Yeshua's day, their doctrine, which consisted of the "tradition of the elders," was still entirely oral and considered their own special possession. Those who studied under pharisaic scribes were considered "in the know," while the common man was thought to be ignorant and "unlettered." Since the intricacies of the oral Law were not in the public domain, the one sure way that the common could man learn of the etiquette of the Pharisees was by observing how they behaved themselves. It was for this reason that Yeshua warned them:

> *2:* "The scribes and the Pharisees sit on Moses' seat; *3:* so practice and observe whatever they tell you, but not what they do; for they preach, but do not practice.[31]

It is quite obvious from the rest of Yeshua's dealings with the Pharisees that he did not accept the authority of their tradition. For instance, the Pharisees asked Yeshua,

> *2:* "Why do your disciples transgress the tradition of the elders? For they do not wash their hands when they eat." *3:* He answered them, "And why do you transgress the commandment of God for the sake of your tradition?"[32]

---

29. Matt 16:6–12 (RSV).
30. Luke 12:1 (RSV).
31. Matt 23:2–3 (RSV).
32. Matt 15:2–3 (RSV).

It even appears that Yeshua sometimes went out of his way to demonstrate his opposition to their traditions.

> *1:* At that time Yeshua went through the grainfields on the sabbath; his disciples were hungry, and they began to pluck heads of grain and to eat. *2:* But when the Pharisees saw it, they said to him, "Look, your disciples are doing what is not lawful to do on the sabbath." *3:* He said to them, "Have you not read what David did, when he was hungry, and those who were with him: *4:* how he entered the house of God and ate the bread of the Presence, which it was not lawful for him to eat nor for those who were with him, but only for the priests? *5:* Or have you not read in the law how on the sabbath the priests in the temple profane the sabbath, and are guiltless? *6:* I tell you, something greater than the temple is here. *7:* And if you had known what this means, 'I desire mercy, and not sacrifice,' you would not have condemned the guiltless."[33]

In another version of the same story, Luke 6:1 adds the detail that Yeshua's disciples were plucking the heads of grain and rubbing them in their hands. By doing so, according to the oral Law, the disciples were guilty of carrying out two prohibited forms of work on the Sabbath, harvesting and winnowing.[34] There was nothing in the Written Torah that prohibited the disciples from plucking the grain, but only in the tradition of the Pharisees. In fact, whenever Yeshua or his disciples were accused of breaking the Sabbath, it was not according to the Written Torah but only according the teaching of the Pharisees.

> *7:* And the scribes and the Pharisees watched him, to see whether he would heal on the sabbath, so that they might find an accusation against him. *8:* But he knew their thoughts, and he said to the man who had the withered hand, "Come and stand here." And he rose and stood there. *9:* And Jesus said to them, "I ask you, is it lawful on the sabbath to do good or to do harm, to save life or to destroy it?" *10:* And he looked around on them all, and said to him, "Stretch out your hand." And he did so, and his hand was restored. *11:* But they were filled with fury and discussed with one another what they might do to Yeshua.[35]

Scripture makes it very clear that Yeshua never transgressed the Written Torah. He kept all of the Torah, including the commandments regarding the

33. Matt 12:1–7 (RSV).
34. Fruchtenbaum, "Three Sabbath Controversies."
35. Luke 6:7–11 (RSV).

Sabbath. As we have seen in chapter 4, Yeshua submitted completely to the will of his Father, by obeying every word of the Torah, both in letter and in spirit. In doing so, he himself was completely free of sin, and was then able to take upon himself the sins of mankind. Had he abrogated the Law in any single point, he would have disqualified himself from being "the Lamb of God who takes away the sin of the world." Luke describes another incident where Yeshua faced disapproval for his healing on the Sabbath.

> *11:* And there was a woman who had had a spirit of infirmity for eighteen years; she was bent over and could not fully straighten herself. *12:* And when Yeshua saw her, he called her and said to her, "Woman, you are freed from your infirmity." *13:* And he laid his hands upon her, and immediately she was made straight, and she praised God. *14:* But the ruler of the synagogue, indignant because Jesus had healed on the sabbath, said to the people, "There are six days on which work ought to be done; come on those days and be healed, and not on the sabbath day." *15:* Then the Lord answered him, "You hypocrites! Does not each of you on the sabbath untie his ox or his ass from the manger, and lead it away to water it? *16:* And ought not this woman, a daughter of Abraham whom Satan bound for eighteen years, be loosed from this bond on the sabbath day?"[36]

It is interesting that rabbinic law later ruled that it is permitted to break the Sabbath for the sake of *pikuah nefesh*, the saving of a life. This includes healing on the Sabbath.

THE OBJECTIVES OF RABBINIC JUDAISM

With the eventual redemption in view, the architects of Rabbinic Judaism had several objectives in mind: 1) to preserve the Jewish nation and heritage; 2) to keep the Jewish people separate and safe from spiritual influences outside of Rabbinic Judaism, particularly that of Christianity, which was perceived as the primary religious threat; 3) to return the Jewish people to the land of Israel and restore the Temple

No one anticipated that the exile would last two thousand years. In time the practices of Rabbinic Judaism developed their own time-worn sanctity. Over the centuries, it became encrusted in layer upon layer of tradition, each separating it further from its ancient parent, biblical Judaism. In time, it was forgotten that anything else existed. Rabbinic Judaism replaced the Torah, which is God's perfect Law, with traditions of men. Whereas

---

36. Luke 13:11–16 (RSV).

the Torah, God's perfect standard, points out sin, Rabbinic Judaism has no power to do so. Since atonement is not based on the Temple sacrifice, but rather on prayer, good works, and charity, Rabbinic Judaism does not point to Yeshua's sacrifice. Consequently, Rabbinic Judaism is little better than the rest of the religions of mankind, a set of man-made rules kept by the strength of human effort.

What is it that is standing in the way of the Jewish people accepting Yeshua and experiencing redemption today?

Because Yeshua did not give heed to the Pharisee's traditions, they opposed him throughout his ministry, and their opposition was one of the main reasons why he was rejected by the nation. After the remodeling of the Jewish faith at Yavneh, the proponents of Rabbinic Judaism were intolerant of any form of Judaism outside of their own. The Sadducees and the Essenes, finding it difficult to withstand the predominance and opposition of the rabbis, soon dwindled in number and eventually disappeared. Jewish believers in Yeshua faced the same fate. While throughout history there have always been individual Jews who have accepted Yeshua as the Messiah and found salvation through him, as a distinct group, Jewish believers in Yeshua had all but disappeared already by the fourth century.[37]

As the message about Messiah went to the ends of the earth, the number of Gentiles who believed in Yeshua outgrew and overwhelmed those of the Jewish believers. Eventually, Christianity took on more and more Gentile qualities. The Gentile believers flagrantly emphasized their liberty from the Law and soon forgot the Jewish roots of their faith. Moreover, having come out of pagan backgrounds, Gentile believers brought with them many pagan practices and customs into the church.

When the emperor Constantine legalized Christianity and later under Theodosius I it became the official religion of the Roman Empire, the church became largely a political entity, and Christianity finally broke completely free of the moorings to its Hebraic origins. In the end, Constantinian Christianity bore very little resemblance to the faith of the original Jewish believers of the first century. Rabbinic Judaism, ever watchful against foreign influences, perceived Gentilized Christianity, as the major threat against the Jewish community. The rabbis constructed strong barriers to protect Jews from coming into contact with Christianity and accepting Yeshua, whom they had come to see as a pagan god.

Christianity, having shaken free of its Jewish roots, sought a new understanding of the Old Testament scriptures. They produced supersessionism or replacement theology, which made the church the true Israel and

---

37. Bourgel, *Jewish Christians*, 7.

spiritualized the promise, the Law, the Sabbath, and the Temple. The result was an unbridgeable gulf between Judaism and Christianity.

TURNING THE JEWISH PEOPLE AWAY FROM YESHUA

Thus, unlike scriptural Judaism, which points the Jewish people as a nation to Yeshua the Messiah, Rabbinic Judaism, because of its built-in antipathy to Christianity and the good news of Yeshua the Messiah, turns people away from him.

HOLDING THE DOOR OPEN

As we have seen in chapter 2, the rejection of Yeshua by the Jewish people as a nation opened the way for salvation to the rest of the nations of the world.

15: For if their rejection means the reconciliation of the world . . .[38]

Rabbinic Judaism, by promoting the continued rejection of Yeshua, unwittingly serves God's purpose in holding open the door of salvation to the world. As we have seen, this makes it possible at this time for individuals, both Jewish and Gentile, to accept Yeshua and become part of his kingdom.

Thus, Rabbinic Judaism has served two purposes at once: it has kept the door of salvation open for the world and at the same time has protected and preserved the Jewish people as separate and unified until the day when they will be restored to their land and their eyes opened to the identity of Messiah. Having succeeded in accomplishing both these goals, we can clearly see God's hand working behind the scenes in the development of Rabbinic Judaism.

PERPETUATION

While the architects of Rabbinic Judaism intended it to serve until the restoration of the Jewish people to the land of Israel and the rebuilding of the Temple, through centuries of tradition it has become accepted as the normative form of Judaism. Scriptural Judaism, based on God's presence dwelling among his people in the Temple and atonement from sin through the sacrifice, has been all but forgotten.

---

38. Rom 11:15a (RSV).

Originally, Rabbinic Judaism was intended to be only a provisional solution to an immediate problem: the destruction of the Temple and exile of the Jewish people from their land. The people were in no wise released from the strict demands of God's covenant with them. Prayer, charity and righteous works could never replace the need for a sacrifice. The stark reality was that there was no longer any way to perform the demands of the covenant without a Temple and separated from Jerusalem. In this light, the destruction was seen as a particularly harsh punishment by God. Gone, at least for the time, was any hope of a national salvation. The horrors of the Holocaust might be seen as the historical culmination of these disasters. Notwithstanding, it was understood that this situation would not last forever, and that God would eventually have mercy upon his people and restore them to the land. On their return, they would once again rebuild the Temple and begin keeping the covenant once more.

TIME TO PLAY BALL!

The nation of Israel is now being restored to the land; however, the practices of Rabbinic Judaism continue to predominate as the normative form of Judaism. The current situation might be compared to a baseball game that has been temporarily halted because of rain. When the rain begins to fall, the players are called off the field and, in order to appease the potentially restless crowd, the management of the stadium arranges for music to be played. The music, of course, is intended to continue only as long as the rain falls. But let's imagine that the organist seizes this opportunity to show off his talents and gets carried away. The time comes to restart the game, but the music continues and continues. The players are returning to the field, which has sufficiently dried, but no one can hear the umpire's call to "Play ball!" It seems that the organist has forgotten the real purpose for which he has been employed.

11

The Restoration

THE PSALMIST DESCRIBES THE great rejoicing when the Jewish people returned from Babylon in the sixth century BCE:

> A Song of Ascents. *1:* When the Lord restored the fortunes of Zion, we were like those who dream. *2:* Then our mouth was filled with laughter, and our tongue with shouts of joy; then they said among the nations, "The Lord has done great things for them." *3:* The Lord has done great things for us; we are glad. *4:* Restore our fortunes, O Lord, like the watercourses in the Negeb! *5:* May those who sow in tears reap with shouts of joy! *6:* He that goes forth weeping, bearing the seed for sowing, shall come home with shouts of joy, bringing his sheaves with him.[1]

Peter, in Acts 3:21, envisioned a time in the future when there would be a "restoration of all things," preceding Yeshua's return to the earth. One of the main elements indicating the beginning of those times is unquestionably the restoration of the Jewish people to their land. And indeed in our day we are once again witnessing God miraculously returning the Jewish people from all the nations of the world back to their homeland. The Lord is doing great things for them again. He is restoring the fortunes of Zion; the restoration has begun!

In the eleventh chapter of the book of Revelation we encounter two individuals who will play an important role in this promised "restoration of all things."

---

1. Ps 126:1–6 (RSV).

> *3:* And I will grant my two witnesses power to prophesy for one thousand two hundred and sixty days, clothed in sackcloth." *4:* These are the two olive trees and the two lampstands which stand before the Lord of the earth. *5:* And if any one would harm them, fire pours out from their mouth and consumes their foes; if any one would harm them, thus he is doomed to be killed. *6:* They have power to shut the sky, that no rain may fall during the days of their prophesying, and they have power over the waters to turn them into blood, and to smite the earth with every plague, as often as they desire.[2]

By means of clues that hark back to passages in the *Tanakh* (the Old Testament), the scripture gives us vital information about the identity of these two individuals and tells us details of the extraordinary task that they will be sent to accomplish.

THE IDENTITY OF THE TWO WITNESSES

We are told of the two witnesses that "if any one would harm them, fire pours out from their mouth and consumes their foes." This recalls how Elijah dealt with the envoys of King Ahab in 2 Kings 1:9–12:

> *9:* Then the king sent to him a captain of fifty men with his fifty. He went up to Eli'jah, who was sitting on the top of a hill, and said to him, "O man of God, the king says, 'Come down.'" *10:* But Eli'jah answered the captain of fifty, "If I am a man of God, let fire come down from heaven and consume you and your fifty." Then fire came down from heaven, and consumed him and his fifty. *11:* Again the king sent to him another captain of fifty men with his fifty. And he went up and said to him, "O man of God, this is the king's order, 'Come down quickly!'" *12:* But Eli'jah answered them, "If I am a man of God, let fire come down from heaven and consume you and your fifty." Then the fire of God came down from heaven and consumed him and his fifty.[3]

We are informed in the sixth verse of Revelation 11 that the two witnesses "have power to shut the sky, that no rain may fall during the days of their prophesying." Again, this reminds us of Elijah's words to Ahab in 1 Kings 17:1

---

2. Rev 11:3–6 (RSV).
3. 2 Kgs 1:9–12 (RSV).

> *1:* Now Eli'jah the Tishbite, of Tishbe in Gilead, said to Ahab, "As the Lord the God of Israel lives, before whom I stand, there shall be neither dew nor rain these years, except by my word."[4]

The duration of this drought was three and a half years.[5] This is also how long "the days of their[the witnesses'] prophesying" will last.[6]

Revelation 11:6 continues, ". . . and they have power over the waters to turn them into blood, and to smite the earth with every plague, as often as they desire." This of course brings to mind how Moses was commanded in Exodus 7 to smite the waters of the Nile with his staff and turn them into blood.

> *20:* Moses and Aaron did as the Lord commanded; in the sight of Pharaoh and in the sight of his servants, he lifted up the rod and struck the water that was in the Nile, and all the water that was in the Nile turned to blood. *21:* And the fish in the Nile died; and the Nile became foul, so that the Egyptians could not drink water from the Nile; and there was blood throughout all the land of Egypt.[7]

Moreover, Moses was instrumental in bringing plagues upon Egypt. Jewish tradition counts ten plagues with which God, working with Moses, struck the Egyptians.

Moses and Elijah are often closely associated in Scripture. For instance, both men appear with Yeshua in the transfiguration.

> *28:* Now about eight days after these sayings he [Yeshua] took with him Peter and John and James, and went up on the mountain to pray. *29:* And as he was praying, the appearance of his countenance was altered, and his raiment became dazzling white. *30:* And behold, two men talked with him, Moses and Eli'jah, *31:* who appeared in glory and spoke of his departure, which he was to accomplish at Jerusalem.

In 1 Kings 19, when Elijah flees Jezebel, the place that he runs to is Mount Horeb, another name for Mount Sinai, the very place where Moses had received the Torah from God.

> *13:* And when Eli'jah heard it, he wrapped his face in his mantle and went out and stood at the entrance of the cave. And behold,

---

4. 1 Kgs 17:1 (RVS).
5. Jas 5:17.
6. Rev 11:3.
7. Exod 7:20–21 (RSV).

there came a voice to him, and said, "What are you doing here, Eli'jah?" *14:* He said, "I have been very jealous for the Lord, the God of hosts; for the people of Israel have forsaken thy covenant, thrown down thy altars, and slain thy prophets with the sword; and I, even I only, am left; and they seek my life, to take it away."[8]

THE PROMISE OF ELIJAH TO COME

Once again, Moses and Elijah are mentioned together in Malachi 4:4-6.

> *4:* "Remember the law of my servant Moses, the statutes and ordinances that I commanded him at Horeb for all Israel. *5:* "Behold, I will send you Eli'jah the prophet before the great and terrible day of the Lord comes. *6:* And he will turn the hearts of fathers to their children and the hearts of children to their fathers, lest I come and smite the land with a curse."[9]

THE ROLE OF MOSES

Moses is, of course, the one who delivered the Torah to the people of Israel at Mount Sinai. As such, he is ever associated with God's Law, its precepts and statutes.

THE ROLE OF ELIJAH

Elijah is the quintessential prophet of the Scriptures. The historic Elijah had a long, illustrious career. However, he is best remembered for his contention with the prophets of Ba'al (1 Kgs 18:20-40). Who can forget Elijah's challenge to Israel:

> *21:* And Eli'jah came near to all the people, and said, "How long will you go limping with two different opinions? If the Lord is God, follow him; but if Ba'al, then follow him." And the people did not answer him a word.[10]

---

8. 1 Kgs 19:13-14 (RSV).
9. Mal 4:4-6 (RSV).
10. 1 Kgs 18:21 (RSV).

Empowered by God's Spirit, Elijah performed a mighty miracle before the eyes of the nation.

> *36:* And at the time of the offering of the oblation, Eli'jah the prophet came near and said, "O Lord, God of Abraham, Isaac, and Israel, let it be known this day that thou art God in Israel, and that I am thy servant, and that I have done all these things at thy word. *37:* Answer me, O Lord, answer me, that this people may know that thou, O Lord, art God, and that thou hast turned their hearts back." *38:* Then the fire of the Lord fell, and consumed the burnt offering, and the wood, and the stones, and the dust, and licked up the water that was in the trench. *39:* And when all the people saw it, they fell on their faces; and they said, "The Lord, he is God; the Lord, he is God."[11]

Thus Elijah succeeded in single-handedly turning Israel back to God. In the end, Elijah did not die, but was taken directly up alive into heaven. It is promised that Elijah will be sent again before the day of the Lord in order to turn the hearts of the people back once more, lest, finding an unrepentant people, God smite the land with a curse.

Yeshua's disciples understood that Elijah was expected to precede the coming of the Messiah. When they saw Yeshua transfigured, they recognized that he was indeed the promised Messiah.

> *10:* And the disciples asked him, saying, Why then say the scribes that Elias [Elijah] must first come? *11:* And Yeshua answered and said unto them, Elias truly shall first come, and restore all things, *12:* But I say unto you, That Elias is come already, and they knew him not, but have done unto him whatsoever they listed. Likewise shall the Son of man suffer of them. *13:* Then the disciples understood that he spake unto them of John the Baptist.[12]

ELIJAH AND JOHN THE BAPTIST

John the Baptist came from a family of cohens (priests). The angel Gabriel appeared to John's father, Zechariah, as he served in the Temple.

> *13:* But the angel said to him, "Do not be afraid, Zechari'ah, for your prayer is heard, and your wife Elizabeth will bear you a

---

11. 1 Kings 18:36–39 (RSV).
12. Matt 17:10–13 (KJV).

> son, and you shall call his name John. *14:* And you will have joy and gladness, and many will rejoice at his birth; *15:* for he will be great before the Lord, and he shall drink no wine nor strong drink, and he will be filled with the Holy Spirit, even from his mother's womb. *16: And he will turn many of the sons of Israel to the Lord their God, 17: and he will go before him in the spirit and power of Eli'jah,* to turn the hearts of the fathers to the children, and the disobedient to the wisdom of the just, to make ready for the Lord a people prepared."[13]

John, then, was to be the forerunner of the Messiah, to prepare a people before him. He was not Elijah himself, but would come in the spirit and power of Elijah. True to the angel's word, John appeared in the desert calling the nation of Israel to repentance. It is interesting how John answered the entourage from Jerusalem that was sent to interrogate him.

> *19:* And this is the testimony of John, when the Jews sent priests and Levites from Jerusalem to ask him, "Who are you?" *20:* He confessed, he did not deny, but confessed, "I am not the Messiah." *21:* And they asked him, "What then? Are you Elijah?" He said, "I am not." "Are you the prophet?" And he answered, "No."[14]

If John came in the spirit and power of Elijah, and Yeshua had intimated that he was Elijah, then why did John himself answer that he was not Elijah?

THE DESTRUCTION OF THE YEAR 70

The backdrop of John's preaching, and that of Yeshua's as well, was the impending destruction of the Temple and Jerusalem.

> *7:* But when he [John the Baptist] saw many of the Pharisees and Sad'ducees coming for baptism, he said to them, "You brood of vipers! Who warned you to flee from *the wrath to come*? *8:* Bear fruit that befits repentance, *9:* and do not presume to say to yourselves, 'We have Abraham as our father'; for I tell you, God is able from these stones to raise up children to Abraham. *10: Even now the axe is laid to the root of the trees; every tree therefore that does not bear good fruit is cut down and thrown into the fire. 11:* "I baptize you with water for repentance, but he who is coming after me is mightier than I, whose sandals I am not worthy to

---

13. Luke 1:13–17 (RSV), emphasis added.
14. John 1:19–23.

carry; he will baptize you with the Holy Spirit and with fire. *12: His winnowing fork is in his hand, and he will clear his threshing floor and gather his wheat into the granary, but the chaff he will burn with unquenchable fire.*"[15]

The imagery of God's threshing floor being cleared is especially to the point. The Temple had been built upon the threshing floor of Ornan the Jebusite[16] (see chapter 6). In a manner to similar John the Baptist, Yeshua prophesied the coming destruction:

> *37:* "O Jerusalem, Jerusalem, killing the prophets and stoning those who are sent to you! How often would I have gathered your children together as a hen gathers her brood under her wings, and you would not! *38:* Behold, your house [the Temple] is forsaken and desolate. *39:* For I tell you, you will not see me again, until you say, 'Blessed is he who comes in the name of the Lord.'"[17]

Again Yeshua warned of the destruction of the Temple:

> *1:* Yeshua left the temple and was going away, when his disciples came to point out to him the buildings of the temple. *2:* But he answered them, "You see all these, do you not? Truly, I say to you, there will not be left here one stone upon another, that will not be thrown down."[18]

It seems that by the end of the Second Temple Period the social and political situation of the nation of Israel had deteriorated to a point similar to that when the First Temple was destroyed by the Babylonians. It was inevitable that the Jewish people would clash with the Romans, the Temple and Jerusalem would be destroyed, and the nation would be led away captive. The one chance of their escaping the destruction was to welcome Yeshua as Messiah. Had they done so, he evidently would have restored the kingdom at that time to Israel and brought in everlasting peace.

> *41:* And when he[Yeshua] drew near and saw the city he wept over it, *42:* saying, "Would that even today you knew the things that make for peace! But now they are hid from your eyes. *43:* For the days shall come upon you, when your enemies will cast up a bank about you and surround you, and hem you in on

---

15. Matt 3:7–12 (RSV), emphasis added.
16. 1 Chr 21:18–22:1.
17. Matt 23:37–39 (RSV).
18. Matt 24:1–2 (RSV).

every side, *44:* and dash you to the ground, you and your children within you, and they will not leave one stone upon another in you; because you did not know the time of your visitation."[19]

Yeshua called the people of his day an evil generation[20] and warned of the wrath that would come upon it.[21] The nation was given the grace of about forty years (a biblical generation), from Yeshua's death resurrection and ascension, to accept him. At the end of that time, in the year 70, the destruction came upon the nation. John the Baptist had been sent before Yeshua to prepare them. However, since the nation did not heed John's message, when Yeshua appeared, they failed to recognize him as the Messiah and rejected him. Therefore, there was no escape for them. God had warned,

> *5:* "Behold, I will send you Eli'jah the prophet before the great and terrible day of the Lord comes. *6:* And he will turn the hearts of fathers to their children and the hearts of children to their fathers, lest I come and smite the land with a curse."[22]

Nevertheless, God had sent John in the spirit and power of Elijah, and since his message was rejected God had indeed struck the land and the nation with a curse, a desolation that would last for nearly two thousand years. Yeshua warned,

> *20:* "But when you see Jerusalem surrounded by armies, then know that its desolation has come near. *21:* Then let those who are in Judea flee to the mountains, and let those who are inside the city depart, and let not those who are out in the country enter it; *22:* for these are days of vengeance, to fulfil all that is written. *23:* Alas for those who are with child and for those who give suck in those days! For great distress shall be upon the earth [land] and wrath upon this people; *24:* they will fall by the edge of the sword, and be led captive among all nations; and Jerusalem will be trodden down by the Gentiles, until the times of the Gentiles are fulfilled.[23]

John failed (though by no fault of his own) in his role as Elijah to turn the nation back to God in preparation for the coming of Messiah. Despite this, a large number of the sons of Israel did accept John's message, even as the

---

19. Luke 19:41–44 (RSV).
20. Luke 11:29–30.
21. Matt 23:34–36; Luke 11:49–51.
22. Mal 4:5–6 (RSV).
23. Luke 21:20–24 (RSV).

angel had promised.[24] Those who heard John's message and accepted Yeshua not only received atonement though Yeshua's sacrifice; they would also have undoubtedly heeded Yeshua's warning and escaped being caught in Jerusalem when it was destroyed. Therefore, Yeshua, speaking to the people of John the Baptist, said,

> *13:* For all the prophets and the law prophesied until John; *14:* and *if you are willing to accept it*, he is Eli'jah who is to come. *15:* He who has ears to hear, let him hear.[25]

Notice that Yeshua did not say here that John was without qualification Elijah, but rather that he is Elijah to come *"if you are willing to accept it."* Had the nation listened to John and repented in preparation for Yeshua's coming, John would have indeed been Elijah to his generation. He was indeed Elijah to those individuals who heard his message and in turn accepted Yeshua. However, since John's message was not received by the nation, Yeshua was rejected and taken up into heaven. Peter, speaking at the Temple, addressing the people of his day, admonished them,

> 19 "Repent, then, and turn to God, so that your sins may be wiped out, that times of refreshing may come from the Lord, 20 and that he may send the Messiah, who has been appointed for you — even Yeshua. 21 He must remain in heaven *until the time comes for God to restore everything, as he promised long ago through his holy prophets.*"[26]

Peter spoke of the time "for God to restore everything" preceding Yeshua's return. It sounds amazingly similar to Yeshua's own words in Matthew 17:11, "Elijah truly shall first come, and restore all things . . ." Thus, the promise that Elijah is to be sent before the coming of Messiah was not entirely fulfilled by John. It is yet for the future. The Elijah yet to come will succeed, whereas John failed, to turn the Jewish people back to God in preparation for Yeshua's return. This is the very role that the two witnesses will play.

By studying John the Baptist in the role of Elijah, we can learn a great deal about the two witnesses and their future activities. The description of the witnesses suggests that they are not actually the historical characters of Moses and Elijah who lived in time past, but, as in the case of John the Baptist, they will come in the "spirit and power" of Moses and Elijah. John's message was, "Repent, for the kingdom of heaven is at hand."[27] The witnesses

24. Luke 1:6.
25. Matt 11:13–15 (RSV), emphasis added.
26. Acts 3:19–21 (NIV), emphasis added.
27. Matt 3:2 (RSV).

will undoubtedly also preach repentance. The repentance that they will call for will involve the turning of the hearts of the people back to God, but it will also require specific actions, namely, a return to the keeping of the commands of the Written Torah. This is why the witnesses are described in terms of both Elijah *and* Moses. In fact, whenever God calls the Jewish people to return to him in repentance, they are expected to return to the terms of his covenant with them, that is to say, the keeping of the Torah. Repentance in the Jewish mindset is always a return to the commandments of the Law.

There are two more very significant clues that hark back to the *Tanakh* that indicate the nature of the task that the witnesses will be sent to accomplish.

MEASURING THE TEMPLE: SHOWING THE HOUSE TO THE HOUSE.

Chapter 11 of Revelation, which tells about the witnesses, begins with the measuring of the Temple.

> *1:* Then I was given a measuring rod like a staff, and I was told: "Rise and measure the temple of God and the altar and those who worship there, *2:* but do not measure the court outside the temple; leave that out, for it is given over to the nations, and they will trample over the holy city for forty-two months."[28]

This measuring of the Temple recalls the measuring of the Temple in Ezekiel 40–43 (cf. Zech 2). Here the prophet Ezekiel looks on as an angel with a measuring reed proceeds to tell the height and breadth of each of the components of the sacred house. The purpose of this exercise is explained in Ezekiel 43:10–11.

> *10:* "And you, son of man, describe to the house of Israel the temple and its appearance and plan, that they may be ashamed of their iniquities. *11:* And if they are ashamed of all that they have done, portray the temple, its arrangement, its exits and its entrances, and its whole form; and make known to them all its ordinances and all its laws; and write it down in their sight, so that they may observe and perform all its laws and all its ordinances."[29]

---

28. Rev 11:1–2 (RSV).
29. Ezek 43:10–11 (RSV).

When these words were penned by Ezekiel the prophet, Israel was still in Babylon following the destruction of the first Temple by the Babylonians in the year 586 BCE. At that time, the Temple lay in ruins. As the appointed end of that diaspora approached, and the time when the Jewish people would return to the land of Israel drew near,[30] Ezekiel was given his vision of the Temple in order to restore the people of Israel *as a nation* to the true worship of the God of Israel. God tells the prophet that if Israel is ready to repent from their sins and turn to God, then he should show them the details of the Temple's structures in order that they might rebuild it and keep its ordinances.

THE TWO LAMPSTANDS

The second clue to the identity and task of the two witnesses is found in Revelation 11:4. Here the angel speaking of the two witnesses says of them,

> *4:* These are the two olive trees and the two lampstands which stand before the Lord of the earth.[31]

These words recall the vision of Zechariah 4:1–14.

> *1:* And the angel who talked with me came again, and waked me, like a man that is wakened out of his sleep. *2:* And he said to me, "What do you see?" I said, "I see, and behold, a lampstand all of gold, with a bowl on the top of it, and seven lamps on it, with seven lips on each of the lamps which are on the top of it. *3:* And there are two olive trees by it, one on the right of the bowl and the other on its left." *4:* And I said to the angel who talked with me, "What are these, my lord?" Then the angel who talked with me answered me, "Do you not know what these are?" I said, "No, my lord."[32]
> *11:* Then I said to him, "What are these two olive trees on the right and the left of the lampstand?" *12:* And a second time I said to him, "What are these two branches of the olive trees, which are beside the two golden pipes from which the oil is poured out?" *13:* He said to me, "Do you not know what these are?" I said, "No, my lord." *14:* Then he said, "These are the two anointed who stand by the Lord of the whole earth."[33]

---

30. Jer 25:11–12; 29:10; Dan 9:2.
31. Rev 11:4 (RSV).
32. Zech 4:1–5 (RSV).
33. Zech 4:11–14 (RSV).

This rather peculiar vision was given to the prophet Zechariah concerning two notable leaders of the period of the return of the Jewish people to Jerusalem after the first destruction of the Temple and the Babylonian captivity, Zerubbabel ben Shealtiel, governor of Judah, and Yeshua ben Jehoz'adak, the high priest. The details of the golden lampstand in the vision are clearly similar to those of the menorah, the lampstand that stood in the holy place of the Temple, before the *parochet*, the veil separating the holy place from the holy of holies. The illumination of the menorah's seven lamps made visible the way into the holy of holies, the dwelling place of God in the Temple. The two olive trees on either side of the lampstand facilitated the lampstand's light by giving their oil. Zerubbabel and Yeshua the high priest are remembered in Scripture mainly as the builders of the Second Temple.[34] The Temple that stood in Yeshua's day is often called the Temple of Herod the Great, but Herod did not build the Second Temple; he only enlarged and refurbished it. Likewise, the Maccabees did not rebuild the Temple; they only rededicated it after the Greek Syrians defiled it. (This rededication is commemorated by the holiday Chanukah.) The Temple that the Maccabees rededicated and Herod later refurbished was the very same one originally built by Zerubbabel and Yeshua the high priest. They were the builders of the last Temple, which stood in Jerusalem until the year 70 CE.

The measuring of the Temple (recalling Ezek 40–43) and the two witnesses as "the two olive trees and the two lampstands which stand before the Lord of the earth" (recalling Zech 4:14) are fairly unmistakable clues that the two witnesses will be two prominent Jewish leaders, the primary agents in rebuilding the future Third Temple at Jerusalem. The rebuilding of the Temple on Mount Moriah will be far more than the construction of a building. It will require revolutionary changes throughout Israeli society.

RESURRECTION!

Revelation 11 continues:

> *7:* And when they [the two witnesses] have finished their testimony, the beast that ascends from the bottomless pit will make war upon them and conquer them and kill them, *8:* and their dead bodies will lie in the street of the great city which is allegorically called Sodom and Egypt, where their Lord was crucified. *9:* For three days and a half men from the peoples and tribes and tongues and nations gaze at their dead bodies and refuse to let them be placed in a tomb, *10:* and those who dwell on

---

34. Hag 1:14.

the earth will rejoice over them and make merry and exchange presents, because these two prophets had been a torment to those who dwell on the earth. *11:* But after the three and a half days a breath of life from God entered them, and they stood up on their feet, and great fear fell on those who saw them. *12:* Then they heard a loud voice from heaven saying to them, "Come up hither!" And in the sight of their foes they went up to heaven in a cloud. *13:* And at that hour there was a great earthquake, and a tenth of the city fell; seven thousand people were killed in the earthquake, and the rest were terrified and gave glory to the God of heaven.[35]

This beast that ascends from the bottomless pit is evidently the wicked adversary called "the man of sin" in 2 Thessalonians 2:8 (and popularly known as the antichrist). He is described in terms of Antiochus IV Epiphanes, the king of the south, in Daniel 11:5–45, and allegorically as the "little horn" of Daniel 7: 8–11, 23–26. At the end of the testimony of these two agents, this enemy will publicly execute them and their bodies will lie in Jerusalem, but after three and a half days they will be resurrected and ascend bodily into heaven before the eyes of their foes.

"THEIR LORD"

In verse 8 the witnesses are executed in the city (Jerusalem) "where their Lord was crucified." Some ancient Greek manuscripts read *"their* Lord," while others read *"our* Lord." If *"their* Lord" (as the RSV, NIV, Jerusalem Bible and others prefer) is correct, then this confirms that the two witnesses are Jewish believers in Yeshua. Anyhow, whether it is "their Lord" or "our Lord" is really of little consequence, since the context of the chapter indicates that they are quite assuredly Jewish believers in Yeshua.

THE MESSAGE OF THE WITNESSES: PUTTING IT ALL TOGETHER

The two witnesses described in terms of Moses and Elijah are evidently the personification of the Law and the Prophets, which, as we have seen over and over, are intended to lead the Jewish people to Yeshua the Messiah. They will call the nation of Israel to repentance by returning it to the Law of Moses.

35. Rev 11:7–13 (RSV).

Scripture says that Elijah will "restore all things," but what exactly is it that Elijah is expected to restore? We saw, in the last chapter, how Rabbinic Judaism came to replace scriptural Judaism; how the synagogue took the place of the Temple; and how prayer, good works, and charity became the means of atonement instead of the Temple sacrifice. We saw how Rabbinic Judaism turns Jewish people away from Yeshua rather than toward him. In order to point the Jewish people as a nation to Yeshua Messiah, the two witnesses will restore scriptural Judaism in order to show the Jewish people the true meaning of the Law.

BRINGING ISRAEL BACK TO GOD

Just as Moses delivered the Law to Israel, they will teach the Jewish people the true meaning of the Law in its role as a schoolmaster to lead them to Messiah. Just as Elijah turned Israel back from idolatry to worship of the true God, these two individuals will turn Israel back to God by turning them from Rabbinic Judaism and restoring scriptural Judaism. Thus they will turn the hearts of the fathers (the patriarchs of old) to the hearts of the children (the Israel of today). They will restore obedience and worship of God to the Jewish people, even as it was commanded of Moses.

AN ANCIENT TEXT ABOUT ELIJAH'S COMING

The great theologian Augustine (354–430), philosopher and bishop of Hippo, on the North African coast, and a contemporary of Jerome, wrote *The City of God*, which became one of the most influential works of the Middle Ages. In it he speaks of Elijah who is to come:

> That this great and mighty prophet Elijah shall convert the Jews unto Christ before the judgement, by expounding them the law is most commonly believed and taught by us Christians, and is held as a point of infallible truth. For we may well hope for the coming of him before the judgment of Christ, whom we do truly believe to live in the body at this present hours (sic) without having tasted of death. He was taken up by a fiery chariot, body and soul from this mortal world, as the scriptures plainly avouch. Therefore when he comes to give the law a spiritual exposition, which the Jews do now understand wholly in a carnal sense "Then shall he turn the hearts of the fathers unto the children" (or, "the heart of the father unto the child: for the Seventy [The

writers of the Septuagint[36]] do often use the singular number for the plural); that is, the Jews shall then understand the law as their holy forefathers had done before them, Moses, the prophets and the rest. For the understanding of the fathers being brought to the understanding of the children, is the turning of the fathers' hearts unto the children; and the children's consent unto the understanding of the fathers, is the turning of their hearts unto the fathers. And whereas the Seventy say: "And the heart of a man unto his kinsman"; fathers and children being the nearest of kindred are consequently meant in this place. There may be a farther and more choice interpretation of this place, namely, that Elijah should turn the heart of the Father unto the Child; not by making the Father to love the Child, but by teaching that the Father loves Him, that the Jews who hated Him before, may henceforth love Him also.[37]

Despite the distinct antipathy toward the Jews and the brooding specter of replacement theology present in this text, it preserves an ancient tradition held by the early believers in Yeshua, still extant in the fourth century. Elijah would appear before the return of Yeshua to teach the true meaning of the Torah to the Jewish people and so turn their hearts to faith in Yeshua. Augustine emphatically affirmed that this was commonly believed *by all* Christians of his day and held to be an infallible truth.

Joel A. Weaver has compiled a number of similar ancient Christian texts, the earliest dating to the first half of the second century, that speak of this Elijah who is to come and his future mission.[38] These writings surely originated in the teachings of Yeshua and his disciples and were held to by the entire early Christian community.

THE BUILDING OF THE THIRD TEMPLE

The main instrument witnesses will use to restore scriptural Judaism will undoubtedly be the rebuilding of the Temple, which they will use in a bold and clear manner to demonstrate to the nation of Israel that Yeshua is indeed the Messiah. They will use the Temple sacrifices to show the meaning of the great sacrifice that Yeshua accomplished for their atonement. They

---

36. The Septuagint is the Greek translation of the Tanakh (the Old Testament). Traditionally, the first five books of the Torah were believed to have been composed by seventy elders in the third century BCE. Mulder, *Mikra*, 81.

37. Augustine, *City of God* 20:29.

38. Weaver, *Theodoret of Cyprus*, 119–41.

will explain with great skill how each minute detail of the Temple points to Messiah and his atonement.

PREVIOUS ATTEMPTS TO REBUILD THE TEMPLE

During the course of the two-thousand-year diaspora, several attempts were made to reestablish the Temple. There was what the Jewish people understood to be a promise by the emperor Hadrian to rebuild the Temple in the early second century CE. The emperor's reneging on his promise to do so was one of the reasons cited for the Second Revolt of the Jews against the Romans,[39] the so-called Bar Kochba Revolt. Then there was another attempt in the fourth century by the emperor Julian (nicknamed the Apostate), who believed that he could prove Christianity to be false by rebuilding the Temple. There were reportedly signs of divine disfavor with Julian's scheme, including a terrible earthquake that devastated the entire land of Israel in the year 363 and the appearance of a mysterious fireball from heaven. This effort was ended when Julian was killed before he could carry out his plan.[40]

In 1967, when in the Six-Day War the Old City of Jerusalem and the Temple Mount were finally captured by Israeli forces, there was renewed hope that the Temple might be rebuilt. Those hopes were dashed when Defense Minister Moshe Dayan immediately returned the Mount to autonomous Muslim control.[41] More recently, in 1998, there was a failed attempt to symbolically carry on to the Temple Mount what the Temple Mount Faithful organization proclaimed to be the foundation stone of the Third Temple. This resulted in the Arabs rioting and many deaths. Israel was widely condemned for the incident.[42]

SEEING IS BELIEVING

It is not enough that the witnesses explain the Law and the Temple to the Jewish people. They must show them. The Sidur, the daily Jewish prayer book, contains prayers imploring God to reestablish the Temple "speedily in our day."[43] By succeeding to build the Temple on Mount Moriah, some-

---

39. Wright, "After the Star," 9.
40. Simmons, "Emperor Julian's Order."
41. Dunetz, "Moshe Dayan."
42. Inbari, *Jewish Fundamentalism*, 79.
43. The *Amida* (*Eighteen Benedictions*).

thing that no one else over the past two thousand years has been able to accomplish, they will demonstrate undeniably God's support and approval. By rebuilding the Temple they will be able to show that Yeshua is the fulfillment of all the aspirations of the Jewish people, the culmination of their history. Revelation 11:10 informs us that these two men will be prophets. Equipped with a direct line of communication with God, they will be able to sort out the myriad of knotty details and difficulties associated with the reconstruction of the Temple and the vast social, religious, and political changes in Israeli society that will necessarily go along with it. Moreover, it is clear that their message will be accompanied by powerful miracles that will be witnessed by the entire people. As we have seen in chapter 7, the Torah has not passed away or in the slightest detail changed. There is no reason to doubt that if the conditions are met the cloud of God's presence[44] will once again come to rest upon the rebuilt Temple. With this divine endorsement, these two witnesses will be able to effectively open the eyes of the nation of Israel, proving to them through the Law and the Prophets that Yeshua is indeed their long-waited Messiah.

THE ISRAEL OF GOD

These two messengers will be the leaders of a large community "who keep the commandments of God and bear testimony to Yeshua."[45] They will be key figures of a movement that will sweep through Israel. While many will accept their message, others will reserve judgement. As we have seen, in the end their adversary, the one called the "man of sin" (popularly known as the antichrist) will publicly execute them and place their dead bodies on display for all the world to see.

THE HATRED AGAINST THE WITNESSES

Although the witnesses' message is primarily to Israel, their deaths will bring much rejoicing to the world. Revelation 11:10 informs us that the dwellers of the earth will rejoice, make merry, and even exchange presents among themselves. The reason we are told that the world rejoices is "because these two prophets had been a torment to those who dwell on the earth." We have seen that the purpose of the Law of Moses is to point out sin. By boldly preaching the Torah, and by their unwavering moral stance,

---

44. Exod 40:35; 2 Chr 5:13–14; Isa 6:4; Ezek 10:3–4.
45. Rev 12:17.

these two messengers will convict the world of its sin, very much as Yeshua himself did in the days when he was upon earth.

THE DECISIVE MOMENT

Suddenly, after three and a half days, the two witnesses will stand upon their feet, and before the astonished nation they will ascend into a cloud, even as Yeshua himself did.[46] Their ascension will be accompanied by a powerful earthquake that will cause much death and destruction. It will confirm once and for all the divine authority behind the witnesses' message. This will be the decisive moment for Israel. The Jewish people will at last be convinced that Yeshua is indeed the Messiah.

---

46. Acts 1:9.

12

The Master Plan Revealed

THE KINGDOM IS AT HAND

THE KINGDOM IS COMING! It is a world-wide kingdom of peace in which there will be perfect righteousness. It will be ruled by God's Messiah, Yeshua, from his throne on Mount Zion (Mount Moriah). The kingdom belongs to the remnant of the nation of Israel and those of the nations who have put their trust in Messiah. They will inherit the kingdom and those who are his at Yeshua's coming. Notwithstanding, the kingdoms of this world, under Satan's hand, will not easily yield their power to Yeshua. Even now, the influential people of this present age resist him and the hatred of the nations is turned against Israel.

> 1: Why do the heathen rage and the people imagine a vain thing? 2: The kings of the earth set themselves and the rulers take counsel together, against the Lord, and against his anointed [Hebrew: His Messiah], saying 3: Let us break their bands asunder and cast away their cords from us. 4: He that sitteth in the heavens shall laugh: the Lord shall have them in derision. 5: Then shall he speak unto them in his wrath, and vex them in his sore displeasure. 6: Yet have I set my King upon my holy hill of Zion. 7: I will declare the decree: the Lord hath said unto me, Thou art my Son; this day have I begotten thee. 8: Ask of me, and I shall give thee the heathen for thine inheritance, and the uttermost parts of the earth for thy possession. 9: Thou shalt break them

with a rod of iron; thou shalt dash them in pieces like a potter's vessel. *10*: Be wise now therefore, O ye kings: be instructed, ye judges of the earth. *11: Serve the Lord with fear and rejoice with trembling. 12*: Kiss the Son, lest he be angry, and ye perish from the way when his wrath is kindled but a little. Blessed are all they that put their trust in him.[1]

SATAN KNOWS THAT HIS TIME IS SHORT

From the time that Satan beguiled man in the garden he has ruled over the nations of the world with an iron fist. He inspired the many forms of human religion so that in serving the "gods" of this world the entire earth has unwittingly worshiped him. He has held mankind captive in untold strife, sickness, and death. But the day is coming when his rule will end. Satan knows that the day for his judgment is nearing. He understands that he cannot by any means stop the decree. It is inevitable. All he can hope to do is to delay it. This has been his tactic: to put the brakes on and obstruct and delay God's plan at every opportunity. In chapter 12 of Revelation the curtain rises on the drama of the final stage of Israel's redemption, the transfer of the dominion of this world by Satan to the glorious rule of Israel's Messiah. This drama opens with a vision of a heavenly battle:

> *7:* Now war arose in heaven, Michael and his angels fighting against the dragon; and the dragon and his angels fought, *8:* but they were defeated and there was no longer any place for them in heaven. *9:* And the great dragon was thrown down, that ancient serpent, who is called the Devil and Satan, the deceiver of the whole world—he was thrown down to the earth, and his angels were thrown down with him. *10:* And I heard a loud voice in heaven, saying, "Now the salvation and the power and the kingdom of our God and the authority of his Messiah have come, for the accuser of our brethren has been thrown down, who accuses them day and night before our God. *11:* And they have conquered him by the blood of the Lamb and by the word of their testimony, for they loved not their lives even unto death. *12:* Rejoice then, O heaven and you that dwell therein! But woe to you, O earth and sea, for the devil has come down to you in great wrath, because he knows that his time is short!"[2]

---

1. Ps 2 (KJV).
2. Rev 12:7–12 (RSV).

The instrument that Satan uses to prolong his rule over the world is a mysterious individual described allegorically in the book of Revelation as "the beast." The writer of the book of Revelation evidently borrows this sobriquet from Daniel 7:11. Moreover, Daniel, speaking of this same individual, describes him in terms of Antiochus IV Epiphanes (Dan 11:30–45), the villain of the Chanukah story, Israel's quintessential enemy, in the same way we might speak of "another Hitler." The "beast" stands at the head of the government of a global empire. Paul calls him "that man of sin"[3] in the King James Version, or in the Revised Standard Version "the man of lawlessness."

DANIEL'S "SEVENTY WEEKS"

Daniel, living among the captives in Babylon, was studying the words of Jeremiah[4] when he realized that the seventy years of the captivity for the people of Israel was drawing to an end and it was time for them to return to their land. He diligently began to pray. He repented on behalf of his people and pleaded for their redemption (Dan 9:3–19). In answer to his prayer, the angel Gabriel was sent to him to reveal to him the future of his nation, the master plan for the redemption of Israel (Dan 9:24–27). In this prophetic vision, Israel's future is laid out, spanning over seventy weeks of years, *shevuim* in Hebrew, in total 490 years.

> *24:* "Seventy weeks are determined
> For your people and for your holy city,
> To finish the transgression,
> To make an end of sins,
> To make reconciliation for iniquity,
> To bring in everlasting righteousness,
> To seal up vision and prophecy,
> And to anoint the Most Holy.
> *25:* "Know therefore and understand,
> That from the going forth of the command
> To restore and build Jerusalem
> Until Messiah the Prince,
> There shall be seven weeks and sixty-two weeks:
> The street shall be built again, and the wall.
> Even in troublesome times.
> *26:* And after the sixty-two weeks
> Messiah shall be cut off, But not for Himself;

---

3. 2 Thess 2:3.
4. Jer 25:11–12; 29:10.

And the people of the prince who is to come
Shall destroy the city and the sanctuary:
The end of it shall be with a flood,
And till the end of the war desolations are determined.
27: Then he shall confirm a covenant with many for one week;
But in the middle of the week
He shall bring an end to sacrifice and offering.
And on the wing of abominations shall be one who makes desolate.
Even until the consummation, which is determined,
Is poured out on the desolate."[5]

THE REDEMPTION

The redemption of Israel is described in verse 24: "To finish the transgression, To make an end of sins, To make reconciliation for iniquity, To bring in everlasting righteousness, To seal up vision and prophecy, And to anoint the Most Holy." Transgression is the breaking of the Law (see chapter 3). Paul proclaimed, ". . . where there is no law there is no transgression."[6] When the Law has at last finished its purpose the world will be transformed in the new creation. Sin will be removed entirely. It was Yeshua who made reconciliation for iniquity by his sacrifice.[7] Everlasting righteousness will be ushered in with the return of Yeshua and the coming of his kingdom. Vision and prophecy in Scripture point to Yeshua. With his return to earth the prophecies will be fulfilled. The anointing of the Most Holy[8] may refer to the anointing of Messiah and the beginning of his earthly reign. A king begins his reign with an anointing. This is likely another way of saying the inauguration of the king. In short, what this means is the fulfillment of Gods promise to Abraham: the redemption of Israel and through it the redemption of the world.

The grouping of years into sevens may have to do with the sabbatical year that occurred every seven years.[9] Among the sins for which Israel was sent into the first exile was its failure to allow the land of Israel to rest on the sabbatical year. The denominator of seventy may have to do with the seventy

---

5. Dan 9:24–27 (NKJV).
6. Rom 4:15 (RSV).
7. Isa 53:6,12.
8. In Hebrew literally "Holy of Holies," considered by some commentators to refer rather to the Holy of Holies in the Temple.
9. Lev 25:1–6, 8.

years of the first exile,[10] which is the focus of Daniel's prayer in 9:24–27. The use of the Hebrew term *Shevuim* (translated as "weeks") may also recall the countdown for the Feast of Weeks (Shavuot) in which seven weeks (forty-nine days) were counted to Pentecost[11] (see chapter 15).

The most sensible starting point for the counting of the seventy weeks of years is the date of the commission obtained by Nehemiah in the first month (Nissan) of the year 445 BCE, specifically permitting him to rebuild the walls of Jerusalem. The reasoning for this date is discussed in detail by Sir Robert Anderson.[12]

MESSIAH ARRIVES ON THE SCENE

According to the prophecy, in the sixty-ninth "week" the Messiah is revealed and "cut off" (sacrificed). Sir Robert Anderson, fixing the first day of the first month (Nissan) 445 as the starting point and reckoning a 360-day Jewish year, calculated the day of Messiah's appearance to be the tenth day of the first month (Nissan), April 6 of the year 32 CE.[13] This he determined was the very day of Yeshua's triumphal entry into Jerusalem, just five days before his crucifixion. If this calculation is indeed correct, it demonstrates the amazing accuracy of scriptural prophecy by foretelling the very day on which this event would occur hundreds of years before it would happen. After the sixty-ninth "week," Jerusalem and the Temple were destroyed. "The people of the prince who is to come" (Dan 9:26) evidently refers to the Romans who destroyed the Temple in 70 CE.

THE MYSTERIOUS SEVENTIETH WEEK

> 27: Then he shall confirm a covenant with many for one week;
> But in the middle of the week He shall bring an end to sacrifice and offering.[14]

The final, seventieth week forms the basis of the chronology for Jewish eschatology. In the book of Daniel, these seven last years of the prophecy lead up to the final redemption of Israel. The eschatology of Jewish literature of

---

10. Jer 25:12.
11. Lev 23..
12. Anderson, *Coming Prince*, 37–39.
13. Anderson, *Coming Prince*, 51.
14. Dan 9:27a (NKJV).

the intertestamental period is also arranged according to the last "week" of Daniel. For instance, in the apocryphal books of Enoch[15] the last seven years of final events lead up to the end of days. The structure of the book of Revelation is built on Daniel's seventieth week.

THE GAP

The counting of the seventy weeks of years for Israel came to a temporary halt. The final, seventieth week is postponed until a date still in the future when the counting will be resumed. How do we explain the delay of the completion of these last seven years? Why is it that they did not immediately follow the appearance and crucifixion of Messiah?

THE MYSTERY OF GOD

We have seen that the rejection of Messiah by the Jewish people opened the door of salvation for all individuals, both Jewish and Gentile, to accept Yeshua, to be spiritually transformed as part of the new creation, and to enter into the kingdom of God. This was God's plan right from the beginning. Through the Jewish people, as the example nation, he made salvation available for all mankind. It was in fact it for this very reason that he created and chose the Jewish people; not for their own salvation only, but as a means by which he might redeem people chosen from every nation. We have also seen that when the full number of Gentiles have come in God will open the eyes of the Jewish people, who will accept Yeshua and welcome him. At his return, Yeshua will resurrect those have trusted in him and will physically transform those of Israel along with those from among the Gentiles who have believed in him throughout the ages. They will reign together with him as coinheritors of the kingdom of God. That God would choose a people for himself from among the Gentiles and afterwards restore the kingdom to Israel is called in Scripture "the Mystery of God" or "the Mystery of Messiah." In Ephesians 3:1–12 Paul wrote:

> *1:* For this reason I, Paul, a prisoner for Messiah Yeshua on behalf of you Gentiles—*2:* assuming that you have heard of the stewardship of God's grace that was given to me for you, *3:* how the mystery was made known to me by revelation, as I have written briefly. *4:* When you read this you can perceive my insight into the mystery of Messiah, *5:* which was not made

---

15. Price, "Daniel's Prophecy."

known to the sons of men in other generations as it has now been revealed to his holy apostles and prophets by the Spirit; *6:* that is, how the Gentiles are fellow heirs, members of the same body, and partakers of the promise in Messiah Yeshua through the gospel. *7:* Of this gospel I was made a minister according to the gift of God's grace which was given me by the working of his power. *8:* To me, though I am the very least of all the saints [believers in Yeshua], this grace was given, to preach to the Gentiles the unsearchable riches of Messiah, *9:* and to make all men see what is the plan of the mystery hidden for ages in God who created all things; *10:* that through the church [body of believers in Yeshua] the manifold wisdom of God might now be made known to the principalities and powers in the heavenly places. *11:* This was according to the eternal purpose which he has realized in Messiah Yeshua our Lord, *12:* in whom we have boldness and confidence of access through our faith in him.[16]

Moreover, as we have already seen in a passage that has become very familiar, Romans 11:25–27, he wrote:

> *25:* Lest you be wise in your own conceits, I want you to understand this mystery, brethren: a hardening has come upon part of Israel, until the full number of the Gentiles come in, *26:* and so all Israel will be saved; as it is written,
> "The Deliverer will come from Zion, he will banish ungodliness from Jacob";
> *27:* "and this will be my covenant with them when I take away their sins."[17]

REBUILDING OF THE TABERNACLE OF DAVID

Speaking of this same matter, Yaakov (James), the brother of Yeshua, addresses the council of the leaders of the early Jewish believers in Yeshua in Acts 15:13–18.

> *13:* And after they had become silent, James answered, saying , "Men and brethren, listen to me: *14:* "Simon has declared how God at the first visited the Gentiles to take out of them a people for His name. *15:* And with this the words of the prophets agree, just as it is written: *16:* 'After this I will return And will rebuild the tabernacle of David which has fallen down: I will rebuild its

---

16. Eph 3:1–12 (RSV).
17. Rom 11:26–27 (RSV).

ruins, And I will set it up; *17:* So that the rest of mankind may seek the Lord. Even all the Gentiles who are called by My name, Says the Lord who does all these things." *18:* "Known to God from eternity are all His works"[18]

James was quoting Amos 9:11–12. At the time in which Amos wrote, the First Temple was yet standing. Amos 9:1 envisions the coming destruction of the first Temple, representing the first destruction and dispersion of the Jewish people by Assyria and Babylon.

> *1:* I Saw the Lord standing by the alter and He said:
> "Strike the doorposts, that the thresholds may shake
> And break them on the heads of them all.
> I will slay the last of them with the sword.
> He who flees from them shall not go away,
> And he who escapes from them shall not be delivered.[19]

In the context of Amos 9:11, the rebuilding of the tabernacle of David sounds very much like promise of the restoration of the Temple at Jerusalem.

> *11:* On that day I will raise up
> The tabernacle of David which has fallen down,
> And repair its damages;
> I will raise up its ruins,
> And rebuild it as in the days of old . . .[20]

The curious term that Amos and James after him uses for this structure, the "tabernacle of David," needs explanation. David did indeed build a tabernacle upon Mount Moriah, where he housed the ark of the covenant, the predecessor of the Temple built by his son, Solomon. Just as the destruction of the Temple in Amos 9:1 represents the destruction of the nation, the rebuilding of the Tabernacle of David in Amos 9:11 is evidently used to represent the reparation of the nation of Israel. Most commentators conclude that the "tabernacle of David" here in fact refers to the restoration of the dynasty of David. God had promised David through the prophet Nathan,

> *16:* "And your house and your kingdom shall be made sure for ever before me; your throne shall be established for ever."[21]

---

18. Acts 15:13–18 (NKJV).
19. Amos 9:1 (NKJV).
20. Amos 9:11 (NKJV).
21. 2 Sam 7:16 (RSV).

The eternal establishment of David's throne will be fulfilled by the everlasting reign of Messiah. The prophet Isaiah, in that famous passage about David's descendant the Messiah, prophesied,

> 6: For to us a child is born, to us a son is given; and the government will be upon his shoulder, and his name will be called "Wonderful Counselor, Mighty God, Everlasting Father, Prince of Peace." 7: Of the increase of his government and of peace there will be no end, upon the throne of David, and over his kingdom, to establish it, and to uphold it with justice and with righteousness from this time forth and for evermore. The zeal of the Lord of hosts will do this.[22]

Likewise, Ezekiel prophesied,

> 24: "My servant David shall be king over them; and they shall all have one shepherd. They shall follow my ordinances and be careful to observe my statutes. 25: They shall dwell in the land where your fathers dwelt that I gave to my servant Jacob; they and their children and their children's children shall dwell there for ever; and David my servant shall be their prince for ever.[23]

AFTER WHAT?

What does James intend in Acts 5:16 when he says, quoting Amos 9:11–12, "*After this* I will return and will rebuild the tabernacle of David which has fallen down . . ."? After *what* does he mean? James is clearly saying that it is after God has visited the Gentiles to take out of them a people for his name that he will return and reestablish David's throne. In other words, God will at that time restore the kingdom to Israel. This restoration includes the rebuilding of the Temple, allegorically envisioned as the "tabernacle of David." This was undoubtedly what the disciples had in mind when they asked Yeshua after his resurrection if he would at that time restore the kingdom to Israel.[24] What they wanted to know was if Yeshua, as David's descendant, would restore the Davidic kingdom, that is, the "tabernacle of David." Yeshua tells his disciples that they must first bring the good news to all the world. Thus, in both Acts 1 and Acts 15 the pattern is the same: God first (as a result of Israel's rejection) calls out a people for himself from

---

22. Isa 9:6–7 (RSV).
23. Ezek 37:24–25 (RSV).
24. Acts 1:6.

among the Gentiles. Only afterward, God regathers Israel from the exile. Yeshua returns (as a result of Israel's acceptance) and restores the Davidic kingdom (the Tabernacle of David) to Israel.

NO MORE DELAY!

John, in chapter 10 of Revelation, just preceding the measuring of the Temple and the testimony of the two witnesses in chapter 11, writes,

> *5:* And the angel whom I saw standing on sea and land lifted up his right hand to heaven *6:* and swore by him who lives for ever and ever, who created heaven and what is in it, the earth and what is in it, and the sea and what is in it, that there should be no more delay, *7:* but that in the days of the trumpet call to be sounded by the seventh angel, the mystery of God, as he announced to his servants the prophets, should be fulfilled.[25]

The delay of which the angel speaks here is, of course, the delay of the seventieth week and the redemption of Israel. The seventieth week was delayed so that the mystery of God might be carried out. When the full number of Gentiles has come in, the counting of the seventy weeks will resume.

THE RESTORATION

The events of the last seven years of Daniel's prophecy are the final stage leading to the complete redemption of Israel. A comparison of Daniel 9:27 with Matthew 24, Revelation 11, and 2 Thessalonians 2:2–8 brings into focus the chronology of these events yet to come. The counting of the final week of seven years resumes with the Torah covenant between God and Israel being "confirmed."

IS THE COVENANT MADE, CONFIRMED, OR STRENGTHENED?

Daniel 9:27 describes this crucial seventieth week. In the Revised Standard Version this verse begins: "And he shall make a strong covenant with many for one week . . ." The King James Version reads somewhat differently: "And he shall confirm the covenant with many for one week . . ." However, the Hebrew word *ve-higbir*, translated as "and he shall make" in the RSV and as "he

---

25. Rev 10:5–7 (RSV).

shall confirm" in the KJV, is better translated as "he shall amplify." Indeed, Young's Literal Translation reads, "And he hath strengthened a covenant with many–one week . . ." So, what is the difference if the word is translated as "make," "confirm," "amplify," or "strengthen"? The word "make" implies that the covenant is something new, that it is being enacted for the first time. "Confirm," "amplify," and "strengthen" all imply that the covenant is already in existence. You cannot strengthen something unless it is already there.

THE IDENTITY OF THE COVENANT

Can we determine exactly what this covenant is? Some claim that it is nothing more than an agreement or treaty.[26] However, notice that verse 27 continues, ". . . and in the midst of the week he shall cause the sacrifice and the oblation to cease . . ." What covenant involves sacrifice and oblation? This matter becomes more clear in the light of Daniel 12:11:

> *11:* And from the time that the continual burnt offering is taken away, and the abomination that makes desolate is set up, there shall be a thousand two hundred and ninety days.[27]

1290 days add up to three and a half years, exactly half of seven years. In other words, the continual sacrifice is among those sacrifices that will cease in the middle of the week. What covenant involves the continual sacrifice? It is none other than the Mosaic covenant! As it is commanded in Exodus 29:38–42:

> *38:* "Now this is what you shall offer upon the altar: two lambs a year old day by day continually. *39:* One lamb you shall offer in the morning, and the other lamb you shall offer in the evening; *40:* and with the first lamb a tenth measure of fine flour mingled with a fourth of a hin of beaten oil, and a fourth of a hin of wine for a libation. *41:* And the other lamb you shall offer in the evening, and shall offer with it a cereal offering and its libation, as in the morning, for a pleasing odor, an offering by fire to the Lord. *42:* It shall be a continual burnt offering throughout your generations at the door of the tent of meeting before the Lord, where I will meet with you, to speak there to you."[28]

---

26. Swanson, "Earth's Final Hours," 29.
27. Dan 12:11 (RSV).
28. Exod 29:38–42 (RSV).

Daniel 9:27 says that the covenant will be strengthened. As we have seen, the Mosaic covenant, the Torah, has not been taken away or changed in any detail since it was given by God at Mount Sinai. So why then would the Mosaic covenant need to be strengthened? The reason is that the Mosaic covenant has been made weak because it cannot possibly be put into practice without the existence of the Temple. In order for the covenant to be strengthened, the Temple must be reestablished.

This is the reason why the eleventh chapter of Revelation, which tells about the two witnesses, begins with the measuring of the Temple. It is indicating that at that time the Temple will be rebuilt. Finally, the true purpose of the Torah as a schoolmaster to lead the Jewish nation to Yeshua their Messiah will be realized. This is precisely what is meant by Daniel 9:27, "And he shall confirm [strengthen] the covenant with many for one week . . ." At the culmination of the restoration movement, the two witnesses will effectively use the elements of the Temple to open the eyes of Israel and demonstrate to them that faith in Yeshua is the true purpose of the Law and the Prophets. The testimony of the two witnesses and their activity will continue for three and a half years,[29] that is, the first half of the final seven years. At the midpoint of the seven years, the one who is called the "lawless one" or "man of sin" (and popularly called the antichrist) will attempt to crush the restoration movement. This one whom Scripture portrays as Israel's supreme enemy is the instrument of Satan himself. He will kill the two leaders:

> 7: And when they have finished their testimony, the beast that ascends from the bottomless pit will make war upon them and conquer them and kill them . . .[30]

He will end the Temple sacrifice:

> 27: . . . and in the midst of the week, he shall cause the sacrifice and the oblation to cease . . .[31]
> 11: And from the time that the continual burnt offering is taken away, and the abomination that makes desolate is set up, there shall be a thousand two hundred and ninety days.[32]

This continual sacrifice was the permanent sign of the operation of the covenant was offered twice daily, morning and evening.[33] He will attempt to

29. Rev 11:3.
30. Rev 11:7 (RSV).
31. Dan 9:27b (KJV).
32. Dan 12:11 (RSV); cf. Dan 11:31.
33. Exod 29:38–42; see above chapter 6.

change times and the Law. This is evidently the reason he is known as "the man of lawlessness."

> *25:* He shall speak words against the Most High, and shall wear out the saints of the Most High, and shall think to change the times and the law; and they shall be given into his hand for a time, two times, and half a time.[34]

The "times" that he will attempt to change are the appointed feasts[35] of the Torah, the appointed times that keep the Torah on schedule. For this reason it is extremely important that these feasts be kept precisely in the time appointed by God: "These are the appointed feasts of the Lord, the holy convocations, which you shall proclaim at the time appointed for them."[36]

By changing the Torah and the timing of the Torah, the Man of Lawlessness will attempt to disrupt God's covenant with the Jewish people and so put an end to the restoration. He defiles and occupies the Temple, proclaiming himself to be God:

> *3:* Let no one deceive you in any way; for that day will not come, unless the rebellion comes first, and the man of lawlessness is revealed, the son of perdition, *4:* who opposes and exalts himself against every so-called god or object of worship, so that he takes his seat in the temple of God, proclaiming himself to be God.[37]

The word for "Temple" here in the Greek, *naos*, makes it clear that it is the inner building of the Temple that the man of sin will occupy. His defilement of the Temple is known as "the abomination of desolation." This likely includes setting up a statue, possibly of himself.[38]

> *11:* And from the time that the continual burnt offering is taken away, and the abomination that makes desolate is set up, there shall be a thousand two hundred and ninety days.[39]

Yeshua, speaking of this time, warned:

> *15:* "So when you see the desolating sacrilege spoken of by the prophet Daniel, standing in the holy place (let the reader understand), *16:* then let those who are in Judea flee to the mountains;

---

34. Dan 7:25 (RSV).
35. Lev 23.
36. Lev 23:4 RSV.
37. 2 Thess 2:3–4 (RSV).
38. Rev 13:14.
39. Dan 12:11 (RSV); cf. Dan 11:31.

> *17:* let him who is on the housetop not go down to take what is in his house; *18:* and let him who is in the field not turn back to take his mantle.[40]

At the same time, the man of sin initiates a worldwide holocaust against the followers of Yeshua, and particularly against believing Israel, the Jews who have embraced Yeshua as Messiah.

> *17:* Then the dragon [an allegorical personification of Satan] was angry with the woman, and went off to make war on the rest of her offspring, on those who keep the commandments of God and bear testimony to Yeshua. And he stood on the sand of the sea.[41]

Yeshua also described this time of persecution in Matthew 24: 21–22.

> *21:* For then there will be great tribulation, such as has not been from the beginning of the world until now, no, and never will be. *22:* And if those days had not been shortened, no human being would be saved; but for the sake of the elect those days will be shortened.[42]

All these actions have a single aim: Satan will use the man of sin to put an end to the restoration that he knows will inevitably lead to Yeshua's return and the dissolution of Satan's rule. However, the plans of Satan will completely boomerang. His killing of the two witnesses will result in their resurrection and ascension, and the recognition of the Jewish people that Yeshua is indeed the Messiah.

THE CRUSHING OF THE HOLY PEOPLE

In the crucible of persecution by the man of sin, Israel will cry out even as they did under the abuse of Pharaoh in Egypt.[43] They will cry out for Messiah Yeshua, who in reply will descend bodily to destroy the "lawless one" and end the holocaust.

> *8:* Then will the lawless one be revealed, whom the Lord Yeshua will remove with the breath of His mouth, and bring to an end by the visible manifestation of His coming.[44]

---

40. Matt 24:15–18 (RSV); see also Rev 13:14–15.
41. Rev 12:17 (RSV).
42. Matt 24:21–22 (RSV); cf. Dan 12:1.
43. Exod 2:23.
44. 2 Thess 2:8 (Revised Berkeley Version).

The persecution of the man of sin is referred to in the book of Daniel as "shattering of the power of the holy people." It evidently forces the Jewish people to give up any self-reliance and to place their trust entirely in the power of God to save them.

> 6: And I said to the man [angel] clothed in linen, who was above the waters of the stream, "How long shall it be till the end of these wonders?" 7: The man clothed in linen, who was above the waters of the stream, raised his right hand and his left hand toward heaven; and I heard him swear by him who lives for ever that it would be for a time, two times, and half a time; and that when the shattering of the power of the holy people comes to an end all these things would be accomplished.[45]

As we saw in chapter 7, this phrase "all these things would be accomplished," *cal tichlena eleh* in Hebrew, refers to the completion of all the events leading up to the coming of Yeshua. This phrase may be compared with "to seal up vision and prophecy" in Daniel 9:24 and to "so all Israel will be saved" in Romans 11:26. The "time, two times, and half a time" equal the two and a half years, the second half of the seventieth week.

THE SEVENTH TRUMPET SOUNDS

We have seen in the book of Revelation that

> 7: . . . in the days of the trumpet call to be sounded by the seventh angel, the mystery of God, as he announced to his servants the prophets, should be fulfilled.[46]

That is to say, God, having finished his program to choose from among the nations a people for himself, will then restore the kingdom to Israel. Immediately following the resurrection of the two witnesses and the earthquake that convince Israel that Yeshua is the Messiah, the seventh angel blows his trumpet:

> 15: Then the seventh angel blew his trumpet, and there were loud voices in heaven, saying, "The kingdom of the world has become the kingdom of our Lord and of his Messiah, and he shall reign for ever and ever." 16: And the twenty-four elders who sit on their thrones before God fell on their faces and worshiped God, 17: saying, "We give thanks to thee, Lord God

---

45. Dan 12:6–7 (RSV).
46. Rev 10:7 (RSV).

> Almighty, who art and who wast, that thou hast taken thy great power and begun to reign. *18:* The nations raged, but thy wrath came, and the time for the dead to be judged, for rewarding thy servants, the prophets and saints, and those who fear thy name, both small and great, and for destroying the destroyers of the earth." *19:* Then God's temple in heaven was opened, and the ark of his covenant was seen within his temple; and there were flashes of lightning, voices, peals of thunder, an earthquake, and heavy hail.[47]

The Temple of God in heaven is that after which the earthly Tabernacle, and later the Temple in Jerusalem, were patterned. When the ark of the covenant is seen in the heavenly Temple, it indicates that the covenant between God and Israel has been fulfilled. The Torah has fulfilled its role as a schoolmaster, having led Israel as a nation to accept of Yeshua.

The seventh trumpet is the final trumpet of the book of Revelation. It is undoubtedly the last trumpet of 1 Corinthians 15:52 and of 1 Thessalonians 4:16.

> *51:* Lo! I tell you a mystery. We shall not all sleep, but we shall all be changed, *52:* in a moment, in the twinkling of an eye, at the last trumpet. For the trumpet will sound, and the dead will be raised imperishable, and we shall be changed. *53:* For this perishable nature must put on the imperishable, and this mortal nature must put on immortality. *54:* When the perishable puts on the imperishable, and the mortal puts on immortality, then shall come to pass the saying that is written: "Death is swallowed up in victory." *55:* "O death, where is thy victory? O death, where is thy sting?" *56:* The sting of death is sin, and the power of sin is the law. But thanks be to God, who gives us the victory through our Lord Yeshua the Messiah[48]
>
> *16:* For the Lord himself will descend from heaven with a cry of command, with the archangel's call, and with the sound of the trumpet of God. And the dead in Messiah will rise first; *17:* then we who are alive, who are left, shall be caught up together with them in the clouds to meet the Lord in the air; and so we shall always be with the Lord.[49]

Daniel described the very same occurrence:

---

47. Rev 11:15–19 (RSV).
48. 1 Cor 15:51–56 (RSV).
49. 1 Thess 4:16 (RSV).

1: ". . . And there shall be a time of trouble, such as never has been since there was a nation till that time; but at that time your people shall be delivered, every one whose name shall be found written in the book. *2:* And many of those who sleep in the dust of the earth shall awake, some to everlasting life, and some to shame and everlasting contempt. *3:* And those who are wise shall shine like the brightness of the firmament; and those who turn many to righteousness, like the stars for ever and ever."[50]

The book mentioned here is, of course, the Lamb's "Book of Life,"[51] in which are written the names of those who trusted in Yeshua and received his atonement. At the sounding of this final trumpet, Yeshua will return and raise to life those who have been faithful to him throughout the ages and restore David's Tabernacle, that is, his kingdom on the earth. At last he will bring Israel's long-awaited redemption.

---

50. Dan 12:1b–3 (RSV).
51. Rev 3:5; 13:8; 20:12, 15; 21:27.

13

Recognizing Our Times

THE JEWISH LEADERS OF Yeshua's day failed to recognize the day of their visitation.[1] They did not read the signs that God had given them in the writings of the prophets to understand clearly that they were living in the time of Messiah's coming. As a result of their failure to recognize Yeshua as the Messiah, they missed out on their single opportunity to escape the destruction of Jerusalem and the Temple and the dispersion of their nation.

> *1:* And the Pharisees and Sad'ducees came, and to test him [Yeshua] they asked him to show them a sign from heaven. *2:* He answered them, "When it is evening, you say, 'It will be fair weather; for the sky is red.' *3:* And in the morning, 'It will be stormy today, for the sky is red and threatening.' You know how to interpret the appearance of the sky, but you cannot interpret the signs of the times."[2]

Yeshua chided the Jewish leaders of his day for failing to recognize the signs of their times. Will we be able to recognize the signs of our own times?

After taking a look at an overview of God's plan for the redemption of Israel and glimpsing into future events, it is important that we ask ourselves, "Where do we currently stand on this timetable?" Our present location is clear if we recognize a number of landmarks in light of the Scriptures.

---

1. Luke 19:44 (RSV).
2. Matt 16:1–3 (RSV).

LANDMARK 1: THE RETURN OF THE JEWISH PEOPLE TO THE LAND OF ISRAEL

When the Jewish people as a nation failed to recognize Yeshua as the Messiah, the restoration of the kingdom to Israel was postponed. Time stopped for Israel and the nation stood on the brink of the two-thousand-year exile.

> *20:* "But when you see Jerusalem surrounded by armies, then know that its desolation has come near. *21:* Then let those who are in Judea flee to the mountains, and let those who are inside the city depart, and let not those who are out in the country enter it; *22:* for these are days of vengeance, to fulfil all that is written. *23:* Alas for those who are with child and for those who give suck in those days! For great distress shall be upon the earth [land] and wrath upon this people; *24:* they will fall by the edge of the sword, and be led captive among all nations . . ."[3]

In our own day this exile is drawing to an end. As it was prophesied long ago, God is restoring, once again, his people to their land.

> *21:* then say to them, Thus says the Lord GOD: Behold, I will take the people of Israel from the nations among which they have gone, and will gather them from all sides, and bring them to their own land . . .[4]

This is the first stage of restoration, indicating that the redemption has indeed already begun.

LANDMARK 2: RESTORATION OF JEWISH SOVEREIGNTY OVER JERUSALEM: THE SET TIME

After Yeshua's resurrection, his disciples approached him and dared to ask the most crucial question about the time in which they were living:

> *6:* So when they met together, they asked him, "Lord are you *at this time* going to restore the kingdom to Israel?" *7:* He said to them: "It is not for you to know *the times or dates the Father has set by his own authority.* 8: But you will receive power when the Holy Spirit comes on you; and you will be my witnesses in Jerusalem, and in all Judea and Samaria, and to the ends of the earth."[5]

---

3. Luke 21:20–24a (RSV).
4. Ezek 37:21 (RSV).
5. Acts 1:6–7 (NIV), emphasis added.

Yeshua informed them that they were not to know this time when the kingdom would be restored to Israel. It was very distant for them. The next important event in God's program was the coming of the Holy Spirit to empower Yeshua's disciples to bring the good news of Messiah to the ends of the earth. As for Israel, the nation was to be dispersed and Jerusalem laid waste.

The time set by the Father for the restoration of the kingdom to Israel could only come when the Jewish people regained sovereignty over Jerusalem. Yeshua promised that this would happen only when the age of the Gentiles was completely over.

> *24:* "... and Jerusalem will be trodden down by the Gentiles, *until* the times of the Gentiles are fulfilled."[6]

The time set by the Father for the restoration of the kingdom to Israel would come only when the Jewish people returned to the land and Zion and Jerusalem were restored to them.

> *13:* Thou shalt arise, and have mercy upon Zion: for the time to favor her, *yea, the set time, is come. 14:* For thy servants take pleasure in her stones, and favor the dust thereof. *15:* So the heathen shall fear the name of the Lord, and all the kings of the earth thy glory. *16:* When the Lord shall build up Zion, he shall appear in his glory.[7]

The Lord's appearing in his glory is surely Yeshua's physical appearance and return to the earth to restore the kingdom to Israel.[8]

A MIRROR OF FIRST-CENTURY JERUSALEM

Jerusalem today is in a sense a mirror reflection of what it was in the first century, with everything appearing as it was in reverse. It is as though we are peeking through the other side of the looking glass. In the first century, the Messiah, Yeshua, was crucified, died, rose, and ascended into heaven. Forty years later the Temple was destroyed, and Jerusalem was lost. Jewish society was dissolved and finally the people of Israel were forced to leave the land. Today we are watching everything happening in reverse: The people of Israel have returned to the land and established the Jewish state. With much work they have built a prosperous, vibrant modern society. About twenty years after the establishment of the state, the Old City of Jerusalem was recaptured

---

6. Luke 21:24 (RSV), emphasis added.
7. Ps 102:13–16 (KJV), emphasis added.
8. Matt 24:27, 30; 2 Thess 2:1–8.

by Israel. If this trend continues, we should expect to eventually see the restoration of the Temple and the return of Yeshua himself. It is interesting in this regard to recall the words of the two angels that attended as Yeshua's disciples watched him ascend into the sky above the Mount of Olives.

> *10:* And while they were gazing into heaven as he went, behold, two men stood by them in white robes, *11:* and said, "Men of Galilee, why do you stand looking into heaven? This Yeshua, who was taken up from you into heaven, will come in the same way as you saw him go into heaven."[9]

LANDMARK 3: THE GOOD NEWS OF MESSIAH HAS GONE TO THE ENDS OF THE EARTH

At the time Yeshua left this earth, the good news of the Messiah was known to only a handful of Jewish disciples. Those who were meeting after Yeshua's ascension numbered about 120 persons.[10] Yeshua commanded them to, starting at Jerusalem, be his witnesses to the ends of the earth.[11] The idea that many of the Gentile world would believe in Yeshua and receive the atonement of the Messiah must have been a nearly impossible concept for those early disciples to have grasped. This, as we have seen, the mystery of Messiah is the first half of the story. The second half is that, after choosing out a people for himself from among the Gentiles, God would return and restore the kingdom to Israel. Likewise, Paul informed us that that the partial hardening of the Jewish people would last only until the full number of Gentiles has come in and then all Israel would be saved.[12] Yeshua himself said,

> *14:* And this gospel of the kingdom will be preached throughout the whole world, as a testimony to all nations; and then the end will come.[13]

In our day, the message of Yeshua the Messiah has indeed gone throughout the earth, to an extent that the early believers would surely have found difficult to comprehend. While it may not yet have reached every single nook and cranny of the world, in essence, Yeshua's words have already been

---

9. Acts 1:10–11.
10. Acts 1:5.
11. Acts 1:8.
12. Rom 11:25.
13. Matt 24:14 (RSV).

fulfilled. Even now, vast efforts are being made to bring the good news to the unreached peoples of the earth.

LANDMARK 4: THE REBIRTH OF MESSIANIC JUDAISM

Messianic Judaism is a movement of Jewish people who accept Yeshua as the Messiah while remaining fully Jewish and holding to Jewish practice. Many individual Jewish people have believed in Yeshua throughout the ages, however, as a large distinct group, Jewish believers in Yeshua ceased to exist sometime around the fourth century. For the first time since then, Messianic Jews have reappeared. It is generally accepted that Messianic Judaism was reborn in 1967, the same year as the reunification of Jerusalem. More than forty years (a biblical generation) have passed since then and Messianic Judaism is now coming of age (see below, chapter 14).

LANDMARK 5: A GROWING INTEREST IN THE REBUILDING OF THE TEMPLE

In the year 70 CE, the Temple went up in flames. For hundreds of years the restoration of the Temple has been merely an abstract concept, far from reality. It was and still is believed by some ultra-orthodox Jews that the Temple already fully constructed will descend out of heaven. Despite this, in recent years there have been practical steps taken toward the rebuilding of the Temple. There are growing movements sponsored by organizations whose purpose is to reestablish the Temple. These include the groups like the Temple Mount Faithful,[14] whose aim is to lay the foundation stone of the Third Temple. Yeshivat Ataret ha Cohenim[15] is an institution that is instructing young men of Cohen (priestly) families in the way of sacrifice and other Temple practices. The Temple Institute[16] is preparing vessels of the Third Temple and the garments to be worn by the high priest and the other priests pre-70 according to the Scriptures and other ancient texts. The excavations outside the Western and Southern Walls of the Temple Mount, first by Benjamin Mazar and Meir ben Dov[17] and later by Ronnie Reich

---

14. Inbari, *Jewish Fundamentalism and the Temple Mount*, 79–96.
15. Inbari, *Jewish Fundamentalism and the Temple Mount*, 123.
16. Inbari, *Jewish Fundamentalism and the Temple Mount*, 31–51.
17. Ben Dov, *In the Shadow of the Temple*.

RECOGNIZING OUR TIMES   203

and Yakov Billig,[18] have drawn much attention to the history of the Temple structures and have sparked new interest in all aspects of the Temple.

THE TEMPLE MOUNT OCCUPIED

That the Temple area is dominated by the Dome of the Rock and the Al-Aqsa Mosque under Islamic authority is also an important sign in determining where we stand on the timetable of God's program for the redemption of Israel. The final seventh week begins with the amplification of the covenant. This may be triggered by the return of Jewish sovereignty over the Temple Mount, which will permit rebuilding of the Temple. Evidently, though, at least part of the Temple area will remain occupied even at the climax of the restoration. In Revelation 11, the same chapter that tells about the two leaders of the restoration, the prophet is commanded to measure the Temple. With regard to the outer court he is told,

> 2: but do not measure the court outside the temple; leave that out, for it is given over to the nations [the Gentiles], and they will trample over the holy city for forty-two months.[19]

THE SINGLE BLUE THREAD

There is also a growing interest in restoring the practices that have disappeared since the destruction of the Second Temple. One example is the restoration of the one blue thread in the tassels worn by Jewish men on the corners of their garments.

In Leviticus 15:37–39 God commands the people of Israel to put *tzitzit* (tassels) on the corners of their clothing.

> 37: The Lord said to Moses, 38: "Speak to the people of Israel, and bid them to make tassels on the corners of their garments throughout their generations..."[20]

He furthermore required them to put upon each tassel a single thread of *techelet* (sky blue color).

> 38: ... and to put upon the tassel of each corner a cord of blue;
> 39: and it shall be to you a tassel to look upon and remember all

---

18. Reich and Billig, *Robinson's Arch Area*.
19. Rev 11:2 (RSV).
20. Num15:37–38 (RSV).

> the commandments of the Lord, to do them, not to follow after your own heart and your own eyes, which you are inclined to go after wantonly.[21]

Because the method of obtaining the blue color of this thread was lost, the practice of including the thread in the tassel was abandoned and observant Jews wore only white tassels without the blue thread for many years. Tradition has it that it was imperative that the color be obtained from a type of sea worm.[22] In recent years scientists have succeeded in producing a dye from the murex shellfish that can be manipulated to appear in various hues of red, purple, and blue.[23] In ancient times, murex dye was, because of its extreme costliness, reserved for royalty. Thus we find in Yeshua's story of the rich man and Lazarus in Luke 16:19–31:

> *19:* "There was a rich man, who was clothed in purple and fine linen and who feasted sumptuously every day. *20:* And at his gate lay a poor man named Laz'arus, full of sores . . ."[24]

Likewise, when the soldiers at Yeshua's trial mocked his kingship, they dressed him in a purple robe.

> *2:* And the soldiers plaited a crown of thorns, and put it on his head, and arrayed him in a purple robe; *3:* they came up to him, saying, "Hail, King of the Jews!" and struck him with their hands.[25]

The blue in this single thread evidently symbolizes heaven. As such, it is a reminder that the nation of Israel is the special possession on God himself and alludes to the royal, heavenly citizenship of the remnant of Israel in the kingdom of God. As a result of the rediscovery of the technology of producing *techelet* dye from the murex shellfish, some observant Jews have begun to tie the blue thread into their tassels. The return to observing this commandment has become seen a means of bringing the redemption in some small measure. Certain *Haredim* (ultra-Orthodox Jews), however, tenaciously refuse to include the blue thread in their tassels.

---

21. Num 15:38–39 (RSV).
22. Garr, *Hem of His Garment*, 49–56.
23. Borschel, "Ancient Cloth."
24. Luke 16:19–20 (RSV).
25. John 19:2–3 (RSV).

LANDMARK 6: A RECENT ATTEMPT TO REESTABLISH THE SANHEDRIN

The ancient council of Jewish elders, the Sanhedrin, disappeared in roughly the year 425 CE. During the Second Temple Period, the Sanhedrin constituted the highest legal authority in the land. An ancient prophecy foretold that the Sanhedrin would one day be restored in the city of Tiberias on the southern shore of the Sea of Galilee.[26] On October 14, 2004 a group notable rabbis met in Tiberias with the aim convening the council for the first time in over 1,600 years. It is hoped that this assembly of seventy-plus-one will develop into the modern counterpart of the Sanhedrin of ancient days. This is significant because so many biblical practices have been put off as long as the Sanhedrin is not sitting in Jerusalem. These practices include adhering to the biblical calendar (see below, chapter 15) and the right of the nation to enact capital punishment. One of the first orders of business being discussed by the new "Sanhedrin" is the rebuilding of the Temple.[27]

This is at a time when so much of Israeli society and institutions are rapidly being restored. Everything is being prepared. It will be for the leaders of the restoration movement to complete the job.

LANDMARK 7: RELIGIOUS ZIONISTS

A sector of Israeli society is daily living in the hope of bringing the redemption to the Jewish people. These are the Religious Zionists. They are easily recognized. Guided by their deep, energetic faith, they give their lives to settling the land. They often live in settlements under very difficult and dangerous circumstances, making great sacrifices because they believe that rebuilding Israel sanctifies God's name. For all this they have earned the scorn of the world and the secular Israeli press, who demonize them as religious extremists.

The roots of Religious Zionism reach back to the pragmatic political movement Mizrahi, which was established in 1902 by R. Yitzak Ya'kcov Reines of Kerolin, Belorussia (White Russia).[28] Reine's revolutionary school taught traditional religion together with secular subjects. He encouraged his students to go settle the land of Israel, combining religious studies with physical labor. Reines himself was one of the first rabbis to join the Zionist

---

26. Gilor, "Sanhedrin Reestablished?"
27. Ice, "Is It Time for the Temple?"
28. Weiss, *Rabbi Isaac Jacob Reines*.

movement. It was R. Abraham Yitzak Kook,[29] the first Chief Rabbi of Israel, born in Latvia in 1865, who really transformed the Religious Zionist movement. In contrast to Reines, Kook envisioned the state as "the foundation of God's throne in the world," the beginning of the redemption of the Jewish people, imbued with messianic significance. After his death in 1935, R. Kook's s,on, R. Zvi Yehudah Kook,[30] inherited the spiritual and political mantle of Religious Zionism. Zvi Yehuda's main contribution was the establishment of the *Gush Emunim* (Block of the Faithful) movement, whose objective was to settle the lands captured in the Six-Day War of 1967, the West Bank and the Gaza Strip. The so-called West Bank of the Jordan, biblical Judea, and Samaria constitute the heartland of ancient Israel. The Gaza Strip, a stretch of land on the southern coast of the Mediterranean Sea, was for the most part a sandy desert wasteland when Israel captured it in the Six-Day War. Religious Zionist settlers, creating a "miracle in the desert," within three decades turned it into a paradise producing terrific quantities of fruits and vegetables both for Israel and for export to other lands. Sadly, this ended when the Israeli government chose to unilaterally disengage from Gaza in 2005. Through settling the land, those of the *Gush Emunim* movement sought to hasten the redemption of Israel.

Some Religious Zionists have begun to waken to the common interests that they share with evangelical Christians and Christians Zionists and have expressed a willingness to work with them. This has come through much patience and persistence of organizations such as the International Christian Embassy,[31] Christian Friends of Israel,[32] and Christians United for Israel,[33] which have over many years demonstrated unwavering support for Israel and the Jewish people. At long last, their perseverance is bearing fruit. This rapprochement between believing Christians and religious Jews over the issue of the land of Israel is a unique phenomenon in the past two thousand years of Jewish-Christian relations. Jewish Religious Zionists share amazingly similar political and spiritual values and viewpoints with Messianic Jews, especially with regard to Israel and the redemption. While Religious Zionists have no qualms about non-Jews accepting Yeshua, they have the built-in resistance to the message of Messiah that most Rabbinic Jews share. They consequently look with much disdain upon Jews believing in Yeshua. The cooperation between Jewish Religious Zionists and Christian

---

29. Student, *Religious Zionism Debate*, 28.
30. Student, *Religious Zionism Debate*, 28.
31. Knarud, "Bringing God's Chosen People Home," 23–34.
32. Knarud, "Bringing God's Chosen People Home," 28.
33. Christians United for Israel homepage, https://cufi.org/.

Zionists may one day help to bridge the differences between Jewish Religious Zionists and Messianic Jews.

LANDMARK: 8: THE RISE OF A NEW FORM OF ANTI-SEMITISM

A new anti-Semitism is on the rise, primarily in Europe, disguised as anti-Israel political sentiment. It is also taking hold worldwide, and is expressed, for example, in the multitude of United Nations resolutions against Israel. It has become politically correct to bash Israel. It is claimed that this animosity is aimed against Israel and its policies and not against Jewish people per se. In some ways this is a reflection of the culture war that is sweeping the West that includes growing amorality and increasing enmity against the scriptural world view. Behind the new anti-Semitism it is possible to see that we are moving toward the time of redemption. As we draw closer to the time of the redemption, the new Anti-Semitism and hatred of Israel can be expected to increase. Satan knows that the day for his judgment is nearing (see above, chapter 12). He also knows that the Jewish people have an important role in bringing the downfall of his kingdom. He understands that he cannot by any means stop the decree. It is inevitable. All he can hope to do is to delay it. This is his tactic: to put the brakes on. Eventually, when the two leaders of the restoration appear, the full force of this anti-Jewish hatred will be aimed at them.

THE BOOK OF DANIEL UNSEALED

When the Daniel wrote his book, he was commanded to seal it up.

> *4:* "But you, Daniel, shut up the words, and seal the book until the time of the end . . ."[34]

Some of the visions and their meanings were at times even puzzling to the prophet himself.

> *8:* Although I heard, I did not understand. Then I said, "My lord, what shall be the end of these things? *9:* And he said, "Go your way, Daniel, for the words are closed up and sealed till the time of the end. *10:* "Many shall be purified, made white, and refined,

---

34. Dan 12:4 (NKJV).

but the wicked shall do wickedly; and none of the wicked shall understand, but the wise shall understand."[35]

The time of the end speaks of the consummation when Yeshua will return and there will be the resurrection of the dead in Messiah; then the end will come.[36] The fact that it is now possible to comprehend the prophetic events of the book of Daniel reasonably well, within their proper context, indicates that we are now living close to that time of the end to which this passage refers.

CONCLUSIONS

When we view these landmarks together, the general picture is that we are standing on the threshold of the moment spoken of in Scripture as "the time of the restoration of all things," which will culminate in the return of Yeshua to earth. This last chapter leading to the redemption of Israel will only be brought to completion by the activity of the two leaders of the restoration movement. It promises to be the most difficult and yet exciting epoch in the history of mankind. Even now we should expect to see the beginnings of the restoration movement and be prepared to take an active role in it.

---

35. Dan 12:8–10 (KJV).
36. Matt 24:29–35.

14

Israel Coming Alive!

THE PROPHET EZEKIEL, IN his famous vision of the dry bones, describes the restoration of the nation of Israel in its land:

> *1:* The hand of the Lord was upon me, and he brought me out by the Spirit of the Lord, and set me down in the midst of the valley; it was full of bones. *2:* And he led me round among them; and behold, there were very many upon the valley; and lo, they were very dry. *3:* And he said to me, "Son of man, can these bones live?" And I answered, "O Lord GOD, thou knowest." *4:* Again he said to me, "Prophesy to these bones, and say to them, O dry bones, hear the word of the Lord. *5:* Thus says the Lord GOD to these bones: Behold, I will cause breath to enter you, and you shall live. *6:* And I will lay sinews upon you, and will cause flesh to come upon you, and cover you with skin, and put breath in you, and you shall live; and you shall know that I am the Lord." *7:* So I prophesied as I was commanded; and as I prophesied, there was a noise, and behold, a rattling; and the bones came together, bone to its bone. *8:* And as I looked, there were sinews on them, and flesh had come upon them, and skin had covered them; but there was no breath in them. *9:* Then he said to me, "Prophesy to the breath, prophesy, son of man, and say to the breath, Thus says the Lord GOD: Come from the four winds, O breath, and breathe upon these slain, that they may live." *10:* So I prophesied as he commanded me, and the breath came into them, and they lived, and stood upon their feet, an exceedingly great host. *11:* Then he said to me, "Son of man, these bones are the whole house of Israel. Behold, they say, 'Our

bones are dried up, and our hope is lost; we are clean cut off. *12:* Therefore prophesy, and say to them, Thus says the Lord GOD: Behold, I will open your graves, and raise you from your graves, O my people; and I will bring you home into the land of Israel. *13:* And you shall know that I am the Lord, when I open your graves, and raise you from your graves, O my people. *14:* And I will put my Spirit within you, and you shall live, and I will place you in your own land; then you shall know that I, the Lord, have spoken, and I have done it, says the Lord.[1]"

SOMETHING MUCH GREATER

After years of war, terrorism, and economic constraints, many Israelis are disillusioned. Zionism, which was primarily intended to bring the Jewish people back to the land of Israel, has more or less fulfilled its purpose and holds little inspiration for Israelis today. Consequently, Israelis speak disparagingly of our living in the era of post-Zionism. Most are secular, being discontent with established Judaism. There is an unspoken feeling among Israelis that in returning to the land they had expected to be a part of something greater, even miraculous, that never fully materialized. For this reason Israelis have sought meaning through many different avenues. They attempted and failed to create through the kibbutz movement a socialist utopia. They have tried to find deeper significance in the settlement of the land itself. They have delved into Jewish mysticism and reached out to Eastern religions. Some have sought meaning and fulfillment in the peace process, believing that it would bring security and a better life. But the peace process has brought nothing but agony. With its collapse, many Israelis who had hoped in it have fallen into deep despair. None of these things have brought the spiritual fulfillment which they desperately seek.

Alarmingly, the new generation in Israel has, following the young people of the West, turned to materialism and escape through alcohol and drugs. True hope for the nation, however, promises to come from an unexpected quarter.

THE BIRTH OF MESSIANIC JUDAISM

In 1967, the same year that Jerusalem was liberated and united, the Messianic Jewish movement was born. Throughout the two-thousand-year

---

1. Ezek 37:1–14 (RSV).

diaspora, there have always been Jews who believed in Yeshua as the Messiah. The significant difference is that Messianic Jews identify themselves as Jews who have come to faith in Yeshua and yet remain entirely Jewish.

We have seen how the rejection by the Jewish people of Yeshua flung open the door of salvation to the rest of the world, and how by sheer numbers non-Jews who came to faith in Yeshua quickly overwhelmed those of the Jewish believers. A number of historical events came together to further this process, including the destruction of the Temple and the fall of Jerusalem, the reforms of Yavneh, and within the church the development of replacement theology, resulting in an unbridgeable chasm between Rabbinic Judaism and Constantinian Christianity. These circumstances, on the one hand, assured that the Jewish people as a nation would continue to reject the Messiah until the appointed time, holding open the door of salvation for the world, while, on the other hand, they preserved the Jewish people as a separate, more or less unified nation until the time for the restoration. Jews who came to faith in Yeshua had little other choice than to join the Christian church and assimilate. They were made to renounce any and all Jewish practices and thoroughly repudiate Judaism in all its forms.[2] Christians, for their part, could not possibly comprehend the unique role that the Jewish people have yet to play in the redemption of mankind. Moreover, Christians could not understand why Jews so vehemently resist the Gospel despite the fact that it is clearly spelled out in Scripture. This situation was not to change until the late nineteenth century.

A BRIEF HISTORY OF MESSIANIC JUDAISM

In surveying the history of Messianic Judaism, we must recognize two major stages in its development: firstly, that of Hebrew Christianity (Hebrew Christians are believers in Yeshua who identify themselves as Christians of Jewish descent), and secondly, that Messianic Judaism itself. Both of these developments are intimately intertwined with the restoration of the nation of Israel and the return the Jewish people to their land.

HEBREW CHRISTIANITY

In his book *Messianic Judaism: Its History, Theology, and Polity*, David Rausch commented, "The beginning of the nineteenth century was the beginning of

---

2. "Constantinian Creed," 105.

a renaissance for the 'Hebrew' Christian."[3] Rausch documented the remarkable confluence of world events that contributed to this restoration. Among them, he cited the French Revolution, which was directly responsible for the revival of interest in biblical prophecy; the French National Assembly "Declaration of the Rights of Man and of the Citizen," which led to the granting of legal emancipation to the Jew; and the birth of the American Christian Fundamentalist movement with its premillennial view of the future. Also, the nineteenth century saw the first great waves of *aliya* (immigration to the land of Israel), as large numbers of Jews began making their way back to their homeland.

Another factor in the rise of Hebrew Christianity was in connection with the worldwide Second Great Awakening and the church's subsequent missionary zeal to "win the world" to Jesus Christ and "remake" society.[4] Through the activities of exceptional personalities such as Joseph Samuel Frey, "the father of Jewish Missions,"[5] born in 1771 of a German Jewish family and with a thorough traditional training in Jewish practice, a number of missionary societies were birthed. These included *Benei Avraham* and the London Jew's Society in England, as well as the Society for Meliorating the Condition of the Jews in the United States. These organizations held regular meetings for worship and fellowship with the aim of encouraging Jewish converts to Christianity and assisting them with their needs and struggles. Hebrew Christian fellowships and societies began organizing alliances on both sides of the Atlantic. In London in 1866 the Hebrew Christian Alliance was formed with the objective of providing regular fellowship between "Christian Israelites," uniting with and caring for their brethren, and studying the Scriptures regarding Israel and Israel's king.[6] While members of the Alliance often belonged to various churches, they considered it important at the same time to have fellowship with other Hebrew Christians.

In 1903 the "First Hebrew Christian Conference in the United States" met at Mountain Lake Park, Maryland, under the chairmanship of A. R. Kuldell, the pastor of St. Paul's Evangelical Lutheran Church in Allegheny, Pennsylvania. The purpose of the conference was to organize a Hebrew Christian Alliance of America.[7]

American Fundamentalists perceived the growing return of Jewish people to the land of Israel as fulfillment of prophecy and supported the

---

3. Rausch, *Messianic Judaism*, 21.
4. Rausch, *Messianic Judaism*, 21–22.
5. Rausch, *Messianic Judaism*, 22–24.
6. Rausch, *Messianic Judaism*, 26.
7. Rausch, *Messianic Judaism*, 29.

Jewish people's inherent right to the land of Israel. As such they were pro-Zionist. In turn, Hebrew Christians were drawn to the early Fundamentalist movement and became very involved in it[8]

The birth of Hebrew Christianity corresponded with the rebirth of Jewish nationalism and was a natural consequence of it. This renaissance of Jewish nationalism culminated in the establishment of the state of Israel in 1948. Jewish believers in Yeshua began to take pride and interest in their national identity as a heritage to be proud of and embrace. Moreover, with the regathering of the Jewish people into the land of Israel, both Jewish and non-Jewish believers in Yeshua perceived God's hand in the fulfillment of prophecy and recognized that the time of Israel's redemption was drawing near.

MESSIANIC JUDAISM

It was a pivotal year in prophetic history. Three monumental events occurred in 1967. The first was the reunification of Jerusalem and its restoration as the capital of the nation of Israel. The second event was the beginning of a worldwide outpouring of God's Spirit, manifested in the Jesus Movement and the Charismatic renewal within denominational churches. The third event was the awakening of Messianic Judaism. Without a doubt, these three events were linked and interrelated. It is clear that Messianic Jewish concepts were already being discussed and debated long before 1967 and that the term "Messianic Judaism" itself was coined at a much earlier date.[9] It was, however, the other two events occurring in 1967, the restoration of Jerusalem and the outpouring of God's Spirit manifested in the Jesus Movement, that were largely responsible for Messianic Judaism suddenly being propelled into a dynamic, rapidly growing movement.

THE JESUS MOVEMENT

The young people affected by the Jesus Movement fueled Messianic Judaism. Manny Brotman, who had recently graduated from the Jewish Studies program at Moody Bible Institute in Chicago, was instrumental in forming a "Young Hebrew Christian branch" of the Hebrew Christian Alliance of America.[10] Joe and Debbie Finkelstein, from Philadelphia, both believers

---

8. Rausch, *Messianic Judaism*, 30.
9. Rausch, *Messianic Judaism*, 33.
10. Rausch, *Messianic Judaism*, 72.

in Yeshua and married in a Conservative Jewish wedding, created in their home a refuge for those involved in the Jesus Movement in the latter 1960s, many of whom were Jewish.[11] Their home became known as "Fink's Zoo." Martin Chernoff, a Hebrew Christian in Cincinnati, had been active in Jewish evangelism for thirty years. His nominally Christian sons, David and Joel, along with a number of their friends, "turned on" to Jesus at a prayer meeting in Martin Chernoff's home. Joel believes that the Six-Day War and the "movement of the Spirit of God during the Jesus people generation" was largely responsible for their group of young people moving out of "nominal" Christian roles and becoming "on fire for God."[12] The Chernoffs began a local congregation called Beth Messiah.

At a momentous Alliance conference in Detroit 1971, Martin Chernoff brought a considerable number of young people and Joe Finkelstein also showed up with twenty-five hippie young people. Largely as a result of this conference the Alliance changed to more of a youthful orientation.[13]

SIX-DAY WAR

The Six-Day War in 1967 was a principal catalyst for the Messianic Jewish movement. In much the same way as the regathering of the Jewish people and the founding of the state of Israel had been pivotal for the formation of Hebrew Christianity, the restoration of the Old City of Jerusalem to Israel was seen as evidence of God's faithfulness toward his chosen people.[14] Moreover, this was viewed as the most significant fulfillment of prophecy leading to the return of Yeshua.

Yeshua, speaking to his disciples, foretold the coming destruction by the Romans:

> 22: "for these are days of vengeance, to fulfill all that is written. 23: Alas for those who are with child and for those who give suck in those days! For great distress shall be upon the earth [land] and wrath upon this people; 24: they will fall by the edge of the sword, and be led captive among all nations; and Jerusalem will be trodden down by the Gentiles, *until the times of the Gentiles are fulfilled.*"[15]

---

11. Rausch, *Messianic Judaism*, 72.
12. Rausch, *Messianic Judaism*, 73.
13. Rausch, *Messianic Judaism*, 74.
14. Rausch, *Messianic Judaism*, 73.
15. Luke 21:22–24 (RSV), emphasis added.

As we have seen, "the times of the Gentiles" refers to the period in which the Gentiles ruled over Jerusalem (see chapter 2). Suddenly, after two thousand years, the Old City of Jerusalem was in the hands of the Jewish people. The euphoria of capturing the Jewish capital, combined with the realization that the ancient prophecy had been fulfilled, infused Hebrew Christianity with new life. Suddenly there was a much greater desire among Jewish believers to be a part of the Jewish people and to express their Jewishness. That God had kept his promise to restore Jerusalem to the Jewish people gave added assurance that he would also keep his promise to send Yeshua their Messiah and that he would return to Jerusalem and the Jewish people.

Another factor in the development of Messianic Judaism was the popular concept of the indigenous church in missions.[16] Rather than missionaries imposing their own culture on a church, they were encouraged to preserve the local culture of its congregants and appoint leaders from the local community. With these views in mind, it became accepted that those working in Jewish evangelism should preserve Jewish tradition and include as much Jewish practice as possible in Messianic Jewish services.

CHANGE OF NAME, CHANGE IN CONCEPT

The Chernoff group in Cincinnati found that the term "Hebrew Christian" was awkward. They began to describe themselves rather as Jews who believe in Messiah Jesus.[17] They pioneered messianic music, launching the avidly popular group Lamb.[18] When Manny Brotman changed his base of operations from Chicago to Florida, he also changed its name from Shalom International to The Messianic Jewish Movement International.[19]

At the 1973 conference of the Hebrew Christian Alliance of America in Dunedin, Florida, a motion was brought to the floor to change its name to the Messianic Jewish Alliance.[20] This proposal was met with such resistance that it threatened to split the Alliance asunder. However, policies were rapidly changing within the Alliance. The concept of Messianic Judaism represented an evolution in the thought processes and religious philosophical outlook toward a more fervent expression of Jewish identity.[21]

---

16. Rausch, *Messianic Judaism*, 79.
17. Rausch, *Messianic Judaism*, 74.
18. Rausch, *Messianic Judaism*, 75.
19. Rausch, *Messianic Judaism*, 75.
20. Rausch, *Messianic Judaism*, 76.
21. Rausch, *Messianic Judaism*, 77.

Only two years later, at the 1975 conference at Messiah College in Grantham, Pennsylvania, the number of Messianic Jews had grown, outnumbering the Hebrew Christians at the conference. This time, the name change to the Messianic Jewish Alliance of America went into effect without any problems.[22] Moreover, the name of the quarterly publication of the Alliance was also changed to *The American Messianic Jewish Quarterly*.

At the Alliance conferences in 1979 and 1980, nearly a thousand participants showed up. As Rausch put it, "the New guard had arrived."[23]

THE DIFFERENCE BETWEEN HEBREW CHRISTIANITY AND MESSIANIC JUDAISM

David Stern, in his seminal work, *Messianic Jewish Manifesto*, noted that the difference between Hebrew Christianity and Messianic Judaism was one of emphasis.

> *Hebrew Christianity*. An older term, dating from the nineteenth century—today it sounds a bit quaint to call a Jew a "Hebrew." Nevertheless, the term is important, since it is used by Jews believing in Yeshua who wish to stress the priority of their Christianity over their Jewishness . . . The terms "Hebrew Christian" and "Messianic Jew" (in the narrower sense) describe different streams or ways of being a Jewish believer in Yeshua.[24]

In the term "Hebrew Christian," the emphasis is on the noun, *Christian*, and the adjective, *Hebrew*, describes the sort of Christian one is. In the term "Messianic Jew," the emphasis is on the noun, *Jew*, and the adjective, *Messianic*, describes what sort of Jew one is. Hebrew Christians see themselves as being those of Hebrew birth who have converted to Christianity. Messianic Jews do not perceive themselves as having left Judaism at all. They rather see themselves as Jews who have discovered and embraced Yeshua, the Jewish Messiah. As such they continue to be a part of the Jewish people. This is highly significant since Messianic Jews consequently represent a portion of the Jewish people that have accepted Yeshua and have experienced the spiritual transformation (see chapter 7). Furthermore, as Jewish believers who remain a part of the Jewish people, they are highly effective in introducing other Jews to Yeshua as Messiah.

---

22. Rausch, *Messianic Judaism*, 76.
23. Rausch, *Messianic Judaism*, 77.
24. Stern, *Messianic Jewish Manifesto*, 28.

ISRAEL COMES ALIVE!

In Ezekiel's vision of the dry bones (Ezekiel 37), the prophet is commanded to prophecy to bones, representing "the whole house of Israel," spread out over a valley. When he speaks to the bones they come together and flesh comes upon them. He is told that God will in this way gather the Jewish people together and place them back in their own land. However, the bones, when they have joined together and are covered with flesh and skin, have no breath in them. They are dead bodies! Then the prophet is told to speak to the breath to come from the four winds, and breathe upon these dead bodies. As a result, the Spirit of God comes into them and the bodies come to life. Their coming to life may be compared with Paul's proclamation that the day is coming when "all Israel shall be saved." This, of course, will happen when the Jewish people as a nation accept Yeshua as Messiah.

Today, the Jewish people, like the dry bones, have indeed been gathered together from all over the world back into the land of Israel. However, like the dead bodies in the vision, they are spiritually lifeless. They are waiting for the Spirit of God to enter them. And yet, despite this, Israel is not entirely without spiritual life.

THE BREATH FROM THE FOUR WINDS

The four winds of Ezekiel 37:9–10 are the four winds of heaven[25] which move upon peoples from the four corners of the earth,[26] that is to say, from all over the world. The use of the "wind" here is a play on words. In Hebrew, the word *ruah* may be translated as "wind" or "spirit." At first it might seem that the breath from four winds from the four corners of the earth might appear to be a second allegory for the regathering of Jewish people from all over the world back to the land of Israel. Nonetheless, when we take a closer look we see that the breath coming from the four winds is actually a part of the same allegory as the joining of the dry bones. The breath coming from the four winds must then represent an event subsequent to the bones coming together.

Christians who foresaw the restoration of Israel expected that the Jewish people as a nation would accept Yeshua *before* being gathered back into the land. When they studied the Scriptures, including Ezekiel's vision of the dry bones, however, they realized that, according to prophecy, it was only

---

25. Cf. Dan 7:2.
26. Isa 11:12; cf. Matt 24:31.

after the people had returned to the land and they were settled in it that they would come to faith in Yeshua as a nation.²⁷

Today, we find ourselves between these two stages. The dry bones have indeed come together. The Jewish people have returned to the land and have created the state of Israel. They are waiting for the breath to enter into them, that is to say, spiritual life. Despite its important role in preserving the Jewish people, Rabbinic Judaism cannot offer them the kind of spiritual life spoken of in Ezekiel 37:10, 14. Neither can Kabala (Jewish mysticism) or the Eastern religions that many Israelis have delved into give them this life. Furthermore, most Israelis are secular, having found no use for any religion. Although the bones have come together and there is flesh and skin upon them, they need that breath within them to be complete. They appear spiritually lifeless, waiting for the Spirit of God to enter them. This, however, is not an entirely accurate picture.

To illustrate my point, let me tell you an interesting true story: Mel Tari, writing about the Indonesian revival of the late 1960s and 70s in which many amazing miracles took place, related an incident that occurred when he was invited to a funeral.²⁸ When Mel arrived, the man had already been dead for two days and in the Indonesian heat, without the benefit of embalming fluid, the body had already started to reek. Mel and his team had agreed to come to give a word of comfort to the grieving family. To his surprise, God spoke to a member of Mel's team and told him to sing hymns and that the man would be raised back to life. Mel and his group gathered around the body and obediently began to sing a song. The corpse remained as lifeless as ever. Still convinced that God had spoken, they decided to sing a second hymn. Still nothing happened. Not giving up, they sang more songs. When they finished the fifth song still nothing happened. But on the sixth hymn they became frightened when the toes of the man began to wiggle. As they continued to sing the dead man woke up, and began speaking with those around him. Mel relates what the man said to them:

> "I want to tell you something. First, life never ends when you die. I've been dead for two days, and I've experienced it." The second thing he said was "Hell and heaven are real. I have experienced it. The third thing I want to tell you is you don't find Jesus in this life, you will never go to heaven You will be condemned to hell for sure."²⁹

---

27. Knarud, "Bringing God's Chosen People Home," 12.
28. Tari, *Like a Mighty Wind*, 76–78.
29 Tari, *Like a Mighty Wind*, 78.

It is true that Israel is for the most part spiritually lifeless, but not altogether. Messianic Jews represent a part of the Jewish people that have already received God's Spirit. We have seen how when an individual puts his faith in Yeshua a transformation takes place. God's Spirit enters the individual and bonds with his human spirit, causing him to become a new creation. Thus, Messianic Jews represent a portion of the Jewish people who have put their faith in Yeshua and have *already* been filled with God's Spirit. The key is that, unlike Hebrew Christians, who perceive themselves as having converted to Christianity, Messianic Jews see themselves as continuing to be Jewish and a vital part of the Jewish people. Thus, while Israel today appears to be spiritually dead, Jewish individuals are in fact being filled with God's Spirit one by one as they put their faith in Yeshua. Thus Israel is slowly coming alive before our very eyes. The toes have already begun to wiggle!

This process, however, is happening very slowly and only a small part of Israel has until now actually become messianic. What is needed to change this situation is the Torah being presented rightly as a schoolmaster to lead the nation to Messiah. We have seen that the Jewish people as a nation will in the future accept Yeshua as a result of the restoration movement headed by the two leaders who come in the power of Moses and Elijah. They will preach repentance and a return to the Law of Moses, demonstrating with power how it points to Yeshua.

THE NEW ISRAEL

It is unlikely, however, that these two leaders will suddenly drop out of the sky. Rather, they shall appear from within a community that holds the same teachings and values that they do. Scripture envisions such a Jewish community, in the end times, of those "who keep the commandments of God and bear testimony to Yeshua."[30] This group will form the kernel of the Israel that will eventually accept Yeshua and will act as the catalyst to cause all Israel to be saved! In fact, a nascent form of this community already exists. It is the worldwide body of Messianic Jews.

FOR SUCH A TIME AS THIS

The problem is that Messianic Jews are presently in a rather confused state. Until now, they have failed to realize their place and purpose in history.

---

30. Rev 12:17.

When Mordechai urged queenly Ester to take action on behalf of the Jewish people, he admonished her by saying,

> *14:* For if you keep silence at such a time as this, relief and deliverance will rise for the Jews from another quarter, but you and your father's house will perish. And who knows whether you have not come to the kingdom for such a time as this?[31]

Like queenly Ester, Messianic Jews do not understand that they have been called into existence and placed where they are by God in order to fulfill a historic and courageous role. To answer this challenge, they need the insight to recognize the times in which they live, and so take action. Too many have bought the lie that the Law has passed away and no longer has any authority. They need to learn the skill of using the Torah and the Prophets as a schoolmaster to open the eyes of the Jewish people to Yeshua. Teaching through words, however, will not be enough. Messianic Jews, by actually living scriptural Torah, must demonstrate God's covenant with the Jewish people.

THE IDENTITY OF THE BREATH FROM THE FOUR WINDS

We have seen how, in Ezekiel's vision of the dry bones, that after the bones have come together and flesh has come upon them, they are still lifeless. Only after the prophet speaks to the breath emanating from the four winds (evidently representing the most distant parts of the earth) and commands them to "blow on these slain" does the Spirit of God fill them, causing them to live. The question is, why does the Spirit of God come from the four corners of the earth rather than from heaven? The answer, it seems, is that God's Spirit indeed *already* came from heaven at the time when the disciples of Yeshua were gathered together on the day of Shavuot (Pentecost).

> *1:* When the day of Pentecost had come, they were all together in one place. *2:* And suddenly a sound came *from heaven* like the rush of a mighty wind, and it filled all the house where they were sitting.[32]

Yeshua told his disciples:

---

31. Esth 4:14 (RSV).
32. Acts 2:1–2 (RSV), emphasis added.

> *8:* "But you shall receive power when the Holy Spirit has come upon you; and you shall be my witnesses in Jerusalem and in all Judea and Sama'ria and *to the end of the earth.*"[33]

The disciples obeyed Yeshua, going to the ends of the earth, taking with them the good news of the Messiah in their mouths and God's Spirit within their bodies. When Ezekiel prophesied to the dry bones to come together, in actuality, he was speaking not to bones, but to the Jewish people. It may be that when he calls the breath from the four winds he is also addressing people. We read that Yeshua after his resurrection met with his disciples and breathed on them in order that they might receive God's Spirit.

> *21:* Yeshua said to them again, "Peace be with you. As the Father has sent me, even so I send you." *22:* And when he had said this, *he breathed on them, and said to them, "Receive the Holy Spirit."*[34]

This was a symbolic act of transferring the Spirit that was within him to his disciples. He did not only breathe on them. Of course, along with this symbolic act Yeshua enabled them to receive the Holy Spirit by means of his death and resurrection. Moreover, he gave his disciples *the knowledge* that they needed to appropriate his atonement and receive God's Spirit.

Might not the breath coming from the four winds represent Yeshua's disciples? After receiving God's Spirit, they brought him with them to the ends of the earth. That being so, when Ezekiel calls to the breath from the four winds, he may actually be calling to those who have Yeshua living inside them by his Spirit to return from the ends of the earth, back to the land of Israel, back to Jerusalem. He is calling them to breath upon the Jewish people even as Yeshua himself breathed upon his disciples. He is calling these to bring with them the knowledge that the Jewish people need to recognize Yeshua as Messiah and receive his atonement. And so will they receive God's Spirit. He is calling his present-day followers to open of the minds of the Jewish people, even as Yeshua himself opened the minds of his own Jewish disciples by means of the Torah and the Prophets. Yeshua gave his followers a directive to take the good news of his kingdom to all lands. Now with the dry bones having been gathered together in the land of Israel, God's Spirit is seeking those both Jewish and Gentile believers, his voice is calling throughout the earth,

---

33. Acts 1:8 (RSV), emphasis added.
34. John 20:21–22 (RSV), emphasis added.

> *9:* "... Thus says the Lord GOD: Come from the four winds, O breath, and breathe upon these slain, that they may live."[35]

Together, Messianic Jews and Christian Zionists can fulfill this vision by testifying of Yeshua and teaching the Torah as a schoolmaster and so bring the *Ruach ha Kodesh* (Holy Spirit) from the four corners of the earth back to Jerusalem, to spiritually enliven regathered Israel!

---

35. Ezek 37:9b (RSV).

15

Messianic Judaism Comes of Age

JOEL CHERNOFF REMINISCES ABOUT the heady days shortly after the Six-Day War when Messianic Judaism as a movement suddenly burst forth.

> As a young college age man in the early 1970s, I recall the sudden emergence and great enthusiasm for all things Jewish that accompanied the new Messianic Jewish revival. This phenomena (sic) was not just resident in me but in all of the youth and many of the adult members of our young Messianic congregation. Not only did God set us on fire spiritually but he also stirred up a tremendous love of all things Jewish. At that time most of us sported long hair, mustaches and beards, which was not only the "look" of the day but also reflected a time when new and free ideas were being explored.
>
> We took great pleasure in wearing our *kippot, tallitot,* and ten-pound Stars of David at our services. We were militantly pro-Israel and Zionist. This was only natural given the fact that we were "on fire" for the God of Israel and saw the restoration of physical Israel as the completion of prophecies that were to be fulfilled right before Messiah returns. Any newly discovered Jewish expression was embraced and explored.[1]

---

1. Chernoff, "Messianic Jewish Revival and Liturgy," 11–12.

A TWOFOLD VISION

The messianic vision was twofold: (1) to proclaim the messiahship of Yeshua within its biblical Jewish context, and (2) to restore an authentic messianic Jewish lifestyle and worship expression for those who had come to believe that Yeshua is the Messiah. This vision was expressed in (1) the normalization of the concept of Jews for Jesus; that a Jewish believer in Yeshua retains his Jewishness and remains a member of the Jewish people; and (2) the formation of Messianic synagogues and congregations.

THEOLOGY LAGGED BEHIND

Developing from the great outpouring of God's Spirit and the excitement surrounding the restoration of Jerusalem to the Jewish people, Messianic Judaism was an overwhelming spiritual and emotional experience. Unfortunately, sound theology lagged woefully behind. The young Jews who came to faith in Yeshua at that time acted on intuition, knowing that what was happening was in one way or another connected with Judaism. As Chernoff noted, they became excited about all things Jewish. What they knew as essentially Jewish was the Synagogue, so they created Messianic synagogues that honored Yeshua. They knew Jewish leaders were rabbis, so they aspired to become Messianic rabbis who taught Yeshua's message. Within the Synagogue, the *Siddur* is read, so they modified the words of the *Siddur* so that it honored Yeshua.

THE DEVELOPMENT OF MESSIANIC JEWISH THEOLOGY

Eventually, Messianic Jewish theology and literature began to develop, and over the years there have been a number of significant advances in these fields. A survey of the works of three outstanding Messianic Jewish theologians serves to demonstrate the wide range of theological views held within Messianic Judaism. Two pivotal questions in particular will be addressed in each case: 1) the purpose of Messianic Judaism; 2) the view of Torah and Jewish practice.

ARNOLD FRUCTENBAUM

Arnold Fructenbaum has long been hailed as a shining star of Messianic Jewish scholarship. Fructenbaum's *Israelology: The Missing Link in Systematic Theology*[2] is an expanded version of his doctoral dissertation for New York University. His objective in writing it was to provide a complete Israeology: to identify and systematize the doctrine of Israel in covenant theology and in dispensational theology. Fruchtenbaum examined the doctrine of Israel in covenant theology according to its three facets, premillennial, postmillennial and amillennial, mainly as a foil against which to rationalize his own dispensationalist position.

Fruchtenbaum holds that the Mosaic Law was disannulled and made inoperative as a result of Yeshua's death and resurrection. This is a distinctly Hebrew Christian belief as opposed to the Messianic Jewish view, which holds that the Law, according to Yeshua's word in Matthew 5:17-19, is still operative, having a continued role and purpose. The reason Fruchtenbaum suggested for the keeping Jewish practices is appreciation of the beauty of Jewish culture and tradition and the enrichment that they bring.[3] The chief contribution of Frucchtenbaum's book is that it presents for the first time a systematic theology of Hebrew Christianity.

DAVID H. STERN

David H. Stern is an accomplished professor at UCLA. His writings, which include *Jewish New Testament*[4] and *Complete Jewish Study Bible*,[5] have made an enormous contribution to Messianic Judaism. In *Messianic Jewish Manifesto*,[6] later revised as *Messianic Judaism: A Modern Movement With an Ancient Past*,[7] Stern laid out his views on Messianic Judaism. The crux of Stern's book is that Messianic Jews are part of both the Jewish people and the church. As such, they are in a unique position to bring reconciliation between the two. Stern's view of Jewish Law with regard to Messianic Jews is rather complex. In its fullest form, it includes not only the written law found in the Scriptures but also the entire compendium of rabbinical law from the Talmud to the legal rulings of our day. He claimed that the Law has not

2. Fructenbaum, *Israelology*.
3. Fruchtenbaum, *Israelogy*,.
4. Stern, *Jewish New Testament*.
5. Stern, *Complete Jewish Study Bible*.
6. Stern, *Messianic Jewish Manifesto*.
7. Stern, *Messianic Judaism*.

passed away, but that the Torah is in fact an integral part of the Gospel, the observance of which is of benefit for both Jewish and Gentile believers in Yeshua. Keeping the Torah is not prerequisite for salvation. In his view, Messianic Jews are free to keep or not keep Jewish Law as a matter of personal conscience. He defines Jews who convert to Christianity and reject Jewish practice as "Jews who are saved and are free to choose to express their faith in a non-Jewish context."

Manifesto envisions the destiny of Messianic Judaism as healing the historic split between the church and the Jewish people.

DANIEL JUSTER

Daniel Juster, a pastor and a messianic rabbi, has been a major figure in Messianic Judaism since 1972. He was the senior pastor of Beth Messiah Congregation and has founded many other messianic congregations as well. He is a prolific writer, having authored or coauthored at least twelve books. In 1986, Juster published *Jewish Roots: A Foundation of Biblical Theology for Messianic Judaism*,[8] in which he presented his basic views regarding Messianic Judaism.

According to Juster, Messianic Judaism ". . . is a movement among Jewish and non-Jewish followers of Jesus of Nazareth who believe that it is proper and desirable for Jewish followers of Jesus to recognize and identify with their Jewishness."[9] He presents Messianic Judaism in the historical and theological context of its being the logical continuation of Old Testament Israel's role as a witness to God's truth and faithfulness. Somewhat like Stern, Juster believes that the messianic congregation ". . . can be a living bridge of understanding between the Church and the Synagogue."[10]

Juster sees the Mosaic covenant, the Torah, as just and holy. It did not pass away at Yeshua's death and resurrection. However, on the other side of the cross, the Law and the purpose of the Law have been to some extent modified. According to Juster, "the Torah as a covenant is no longer in full effect and God has sovereignly removed the possibility of following it as a covenant by allowing the Temple to be destroyed."[11] However, when we come to faith in Yeshua, the Law of God (which Juster understands to be none other than the Mosaic Law[12]) is written, by the Holy Spirit, on our

8. Juster, *Jewish Roots*.
9. Juster, *Jewish Roots*, vii.
10. Juster, *Jewish Roots*, 165.
11. Juster, *Jewish Roots*, 121.
12. Juster, *Jewish Roots*, 166.

hearts.[13] "Hence, the Spirit enables us to fulfill the Law."[14] "The Law will now be kept [by the believer] progressively in Spirit and truth in response to God's mercy and grace."[15] By "progressively," what Juster means is that the believer will daily grow to obey the commandments of the Torah more faithfully as he matures spiritually.[16] The believer no longer feels condemnation when, in his faltering attempts, he fails to keep the Law perfectly, since he is now under grace. "We may still fall, but we now have the power to obey. From our position in Yeshua, we can grow to progressive obedience in love."[17]

Regarding Jewish practice, the Messianic Jew, in Juster's view, should seek to observe not merely the letter of the commandment, but strive to keep "the spirit of the Law." For him, the spirit of the Law is not always literal but may be symbolic and subject to interpretation. For instance, Juster states,

> The Spirit of the Law allows freedom in the usage of these memory practices [*tzitzit* (Deuteronomy 2:12), *tefillin* (Deuteronomy 6:8), and *mezuzot* (Deuteronomy 6:9),] and emphasizes the memory purpose of the command. Perhaps a modern rendition would be to write the Sh'ma [Deuteronomy 6:4–9] on our dashboards so as to remember it while driving to work, or to place it on other visible spots (e.g. the bathroom mirror while shaving).[18]

TWO MAIN TRENDS OF MESSIANIC JEWISH THEOLOGY

These three examples give us an idea of the current state of Messianic Jewish theology. Jewish believers in Yeshua have generally gone down one of two paths: The first proclaims that the Torah has been entirely nullified and rendered inoperative by the death and resurrection of Yeshua. Jewish believers who hold this doctrine feel that they have no obligation to the Law but are free in the Lord to pick and choose to observe whatever Jewish practices will bring them greater cultural and spiritual enrichment. The second is that the

---

13. Jer 31:33; Ezek 36:26.
14. Juster, *Jewish Roots*, 167.
15. Juster, *Jewish Roots*, 94.
16. Juster, *Jewish Roots*, 94, 167.
17. Juster, *Jewish Roots*, 167.
18. Juster, *Jewish Roots*, 215.

Torah has not passed away but that Jewish believers in Yeshua are empowered by the Holy Spirit to keep all or part of the Law.

Let's look more closely at the difficulties with both of these approaches.

THE TORAH NULLIFIED

The teaching that the Torah has been entirely nullified and rendered inoperative by the death and resurrection of Yeshua is held by many believers in Yeshua, both Jewish and non-Jewish. This doctrine stands in clear contradiction to the teaching of Yeshua in Matthew 5:17–19 that he had not come to destroy the Law but that it would continue without the slightest change and in full force as long as heaven and earth remained (see chapter 7). Moreover, if God has nullified the Law, then not only is his covenant with Israel ended, but he has also abdicated his own right to judge. The sinner is completely free to do as he pleases, and God is obliged to permit him entrance into his kingdom, no questions asked. Neither does the sinner have any need whatsoever of Yeshua or his sacrifice (see chapters 3 and 8).

As we have seen, the Law was not changed one iota by Yeshua's death and resurrection. Rather, it is the believer who is changed when he puts his faith in Yeshua's atonement. At that moment he becomes part of the new creation and he himself is completely free from the Law. The Law, however, still has an important role to play as a schoolmaster to lead the Jewish people as a nation to Yeshua the Messiah. Consequently, Paul advocated for Jewish believers to live a fully Jewish lifestyle, keeping the commandments and remaining a part of the Jewish people.

DOES THE HOLY SPIRIT EMPOWER US TO KEEP THE LAW AFTER WE COME TO FAITH?

The teaching that a Jew who comes to faith in Yeshua is obliged to keep some or all of the Law, albeit in the strength of the Holy Spirit, is beset with difficulties. It is a version of the belief that we are saved by faith but kept by works, and that something more than the completed work of Yeshua's death and resurrection is required to bring about our sanctification.

When Paul asserted, "Do we then make void the law through faith? Certainly not! On the contrary, we establish the law" (Rom 3:31 NKJV), Paul was not saying that we establish the Law by keeping its commandments in faith by the power of the Holy Spirit. Rather, what he meant is that the whole aim of the Law is to bring us to faith in Messiah.[19] The moment an individual puts his faith and trust in Yeshua, he becomes a new creation and immediately, just like that, he has completed everything that the Law was trying to get him to do. In accepting Yeshua he has shown that the Law's judgment of him as a sinner is just. Moreover, by doing so, he demonstrates the true value of the Law and God's wisdom in giving it as a schoolmaster to lead us to Messiah. Therefore, by simply receiving Yeshua the believer's faith establishes the Law. This does not mean that after coming to faith he is obliged to go back and keep the commandments of the Torah "in the Spirit." For him personally, the Law is finished, having achieved its aim.[20] In Messiah, the believer has died and risen and is a new creation. Having already died, the Law has no more demands on him. Neither has it any more jurisdiction over him.[21]

Scripture teaches that the moment someone comes to faith in Yeshua and receives the Holy Spirit he is totally free from the Law. The fact is that the believer is no more capable of keeping the Mosaic Law after coming to faith than he was before coming to faith. This is true for the Jew as well as the non-Jew. The question is, why then should a Jewish believer keep the commandments of the Law? Why did Paul admonish Jewish believers in Yeshua to live a Jewish lifestyle and why did Paul himself obediently observe the commandments of the Torah? The answer is that a Jewish believer does not need to keep it for his own sake. Personally, he is free, but he is at the same time also part of the Jewish people (chapter 9). He himself has come to faith in Messiah, but his nation has not yet believed. A Messianic Jew keeps the commandments of the Torah in hope of seeing all Israel saved. Scriptural Torah will yet be God's primary tool to lead the Jewish people as a nation to Yeshua (see chapter 3).

Messianic Judaism may indeed one day heal the separation between the church and the Synagogue. Nevertheless, the real purpose of Messianic Judaism should not be so much that of healing the rift between Jews and Christians as bringing them resurrection from the dead, both spiritually and physically, by turning the Jewish people as a nation to Yeshua their Messiah!

> *15:* For if their rejection means the reconciliation of the world, what will their acceptance mean but life [resurrection] from the dead?[22]

---

19. Rom 10:4; see above chapter 9.
20. Rom 10:4.
21. Col 3:3; see above chapter 5.
22. Rom 11:15 (RSV).

MIMICKING RABBINIC JUDAISM

Jewish believers have fallen into the mistake of seeing Messianic Judaism as the poor stepchild of Rabbinic Judaism. They view Messianic Judaism as the fourth branch of Judaism, along with Orthodox, Conservative, and Reform Judaism. They gather into Messianic synagogues to read the *Sidur* and they call their leaders "Messianic rabbis." While these practices are meant to connect Jewish believers in Yeshua to their tradition, the truth is that by imitating Rabbinic Judaism, Messianic Jews set themselves at cross purposes with their own intentions to share the good news of the Messiah with their fellow Jews. Rabbinic Judaism will never lead Israel as a nation to Messiah. It cannot. This is because one of the primary aims of Rabbinic Judaism is to turn them away from Yeshua (see chapter 10).

WHICH PRACTICES?

Messianic Jews see themselves as Jews who have accepted the Jewish Messiah. Therefore, Jewish practice plays an important part in their lives. The question is, what Jewish practices should they keep? Should Messianic Jews keep time-honored traditions of men or should they rather observe the Torah commandments given to them by God, which in their keeping have the power to turn the Jewish people as a nation to a knowledge of Messiah?

Messianic Jews must wake up to the realization that they need not play second fiddle to Rabbinic Jews. As they begin to use the scriptural Torah as a schoolmaster to direct the nation to Messiah, they will be returning to the ancient, original faith of the fathers, becoming the true Israel that will finally experience the fullness of the redemption.

It might be argued that is important for Messianic Jews to follow rabbinical tradition in order to express their unity and solidarity with the rest of the Jewish people. There may have been some truth to this back in the infancy of the Messianic Jewish movement. Today, however, as Messianic Judaism comes of age, it is high time for it to break free from the apron strings tying it to Rabbinic Judaism in order to fulfill the historic role to which it is called. The task set before Messianic Jews is to peel away the obstructions of Rabbinic Judaism to reveal the true scriptural Torah, which as a schoolmaster has the power to lead the Jewish people as a nation to Messiah. Most importantly, this must include, in its proper time, the rebuilding of the Temple on its ancient site at Mount Moriah.

16

Revealing Joseph to the Sons of Israel

THE SAGA OF THE patriarch Joseph is one of the most intriguing and beloved stories in the *Tanakh*. It spans ten long chapters of the book of Genesis: chapters 37 and 39 through 47.

Joseph, the second youngest of the twelve sons of Jacob (also known as Israel), was the darling of his father, who gave him his celebrated "coat of many colors." Joseph had prophetic dreams of how he would save his family and be preeminent over them. When he shared these dreams with his older brothers, they despised him out of jealousy. So jealous were they that they abducted him and sold him to traveling Ishmaelites. The Scriptures chronicle Joseph's trials and woes and he how he overcame them through his faithfulness to his God: how, by his favor with God, he rose from the depths of prison to the highest position in Egypt, second only to Pharaoh himself. When a famine devastated Egypt and the Levant, Joseph, by his God-given prophetic abilities and wisdom, brought relief to nations and saved a great many lives. Hearing that there was grain in Egypt, Jacob also sent his sons down to buy there, and so they stood before Joseph, their exalted brother, howbeit they did not recognize him.

The tale of Joseph has long been acknowledged as a prophetic picture of the Messiah. Many parallels, some down to very minute and intricate details, link it with the story of Yeshua, for instance, the focus on Joseph's cup[1] and Yeshua's cup of the new covenant shared at the Last Supper[2] with his disciples

---

1. Gen 44.
2. Luke 22:20.

as well as the cup in the garden.³ Then there is the "coat of many colors,"⁴ stripped from Joseph when he was thrown into the pit, and the seamless coat stripped from Yeshua by the Romans⁵ when they hung him upon the cross. These hints all assure us of the connection between the two stories. The great point of similarity, however, is the irony that Yeshua, like Joseph, the great savior of the world, was the brother of the sons of Israel but incredibly they did not know him. Joseph's appearance to his brothers was that of a foreigner, an Egyptian ruler. When Joseph suddenly revealed himself to the sons of Israel and they realized who he was, they were filled with dread and remorse, however, Joseph comforted his brothers. He told them,

> 20: "But as for you, you meant evil against me; but God meant it for good, in order to bring it about as it is today, to save many people alive."⁶

Likewise, Yeshua, by whom multitudes of people have found salvation, and who is destined to rule and reign over the world from Mount Zion in Jerusalem, is ironically unrecognized by his own brothers, the sons of Israel. The problem is largely that his appearance has become so gentilized that it is difficult for them to realize that he is indeed the very Messiah of Israel, the one for whom they have hoped and pined.

JOSEPH DOWN IN EGYPT

As the message about Yeshua went to the ends of the earth, the number of Gentiles who believed grew and rather quickly overwhelmed that of believing Jews. Consequently, Christianity took on more and more Gentile characteristics, resulting in Christians forgetting and abandoning their Jewish roots entirely. Gentile believers naturally emphasized their liberty from the Law. Moreover, since many of the early Gentile believers in Yeshua came out of pagan backgrounds, many pagan practices and customs crept into the church. After the sweeping changes brought about by Constantine in the fourth century, the Christian church bore little resemblance to the original body of Jewish believers in Yeshua of the first century. Moreover, the Gentile Christian fathers did their utmost to consciously distance the church from any similarity to Judaism.⁷

3. Luke 22:42.
4. Gen 37:3, 31–33.
5. John 19:23–24.
6. Gen 50:20 (NKJV).
7. "Constantinian Creed," 105.

Scripture speaks of a day when Yeshua will be revealed to the entire nation and, as it was in the case of Joseph, the sons of Israel shall morn over him:

> *10:* "And I will pour on the house of David and on the inhabitants of Jerusalem the Spirit of grace and supplication; then they will look on Me whom they pierced. Yes, they will mourn for Him as one mourns for his only son, and grieve for Him as one grieves for a firstborn."[8]

The enigma is that Yeshua has promised not to return until he is welcomed back by the very ones who at this time do not recognize him, the greater part of the Jewish nation and the inhabitants of Jerusalem.

> *37:* "O Jerusalem, Jerusalem, . . . How often would I have gathered your children together as a hen gathers her brood under her wings, and you would not! . . .
> *39:* For I tell you, you will not see me again, until you say, 'Blessed is he who comes in the name of the Lord.'"[9]

How then will he be revealed to the nation of Israel so that they can welcome him back? It is clear that it Yeshua can only be revealed by those who already know his true identity, the Messiah of Israel. But for so very long, so many who know him have tried to tell the Jewish people of his true identity and have failed. So deep are the wounds of the Jewish people, so often they have been deceived and betrayed, that it is impossible for them to believe that this one who appears as a stranger, this foreigner, is truly the Redeemer of Israel. Who then can reveal Yeshua to the Jewish people and what possible language can they use to do so? It can only be by those who are of the nation of Israel themselves and who have already come to know and trust him, those "who keep the commandments of God and bear testimony to Yeshua."[10] The language that they will use is the common ancient tongue of the Jewish people, the Torah. For not only do these bear testimony to Yeshua, but they use the Torah as a schoolmaster, by teaching and keeping the commandments of God.

The purpose of this chapter is to propose a new approach to Messianic Judaism. The idea is to create a worldwide community, based in Jerusalem, of those "who keep the commandments of God and bear testimony to Yeshua."[11] This community will have the potential to form the kernel of

---

8. Zech 12:10 (NKJV).
9. Matt 23:37, 39 (RSV).
10. Rev 12:17.
11. Rev 12:17.

Jewish believers who will bring the entire nation of Israel to accept Yeshua. The nation will then, by their cry, "*Baruch ha ba b'shem Adonai*," bring Yeshua back to earth.

As we have seen, in the final stage of the restoration, two prophetic individuals will be key to strengthening God's ancient covenant with Israel, based on scriptural Torah. Using the Torah, with its crowning jewel, the restored Temple, as a schoolmaster, they will succeed in convincing all Israel that Yeshua is indeed the Messiah. These two individuals will themselves most likely arise from the Messianic Jewish community. They will lead the Messianic Jewish body, headquartered in Jerusalem, in restoring God's Torah covenant with all Israel.

PRACTICAL STEPS

When Theodor Herzl laid out his blueprint for the modern Jewish state of Israel, he proposed practical steps intended to bring the great dream to reality. Likewise, the goal of restoring biblical Torah and creating the community that will act as a catalyst to bring all Israel to know redemption through Yeshua requires a well-planned, pragmatic course of action.

1) Returning and Making Aliyah to the Land

The restoration includes the return of the Jewish people to the land.[12] We are witnessing this part of the restoration occurring in our own day with the regathering of the Jewish people in the state of Israel. In order to become a biblical Torah-based community, Messianic Jews should consider moving to and settling in the land. Christian Zionists should consider spending extended periods in the land. The future capital of the restoration will be Jerusalem. The covenant between God and his people requires God's dwelling in the Temple, in their midst at Jerusalem (see chapter 6). It is to the Mount of Olives to the east of the Old City of Jerusalem that Yeshua himself will return. As we have seen, Yeshua said that his return is dependent on Jerusalem welcoming him.[13]

It is important for Messianic Jews to become familiar with the land of Israel; its history, its politics, and the seasons of its year. One of the signs of the redemption and the soon return of Messiah is that God's people will fall in love with the land.

12. Pss 102; 126.
13. Matt 23:37–39.

> *13:* Thou shalt arise, and have mercy upon Zion: for the time to favor her, yea, the set time, is come. *14:* For thy servants take pleasure in her stones, and favor the dust thereof. *15:* So the heathen shall fear the name of the Lord, and all the kings of the earth thy glory. *16:* When the Lord shall build up Zion, he shall appear in his glory.[14]

Only with a significant number of Messianic Jews in Israel can there be hope to restore the Torah covenant that God established with his people in the land. It is written that in the redemption the sons of Israel will "marry" the land.

> *4:* You shall no more be termed Forsaken, and your land shall no more be termed Desolate; but you shall be called My delight is in her, and your land Married; for the Lord delights in you, and your land shall be married. *5:* For as a young man marries a virgin, so shall your sons marry you, and as the bridegroom rejoices over the bride, so shall your God rejoice over you.[15]

A decision to move to Israel should be a carefully well-thought-out process. The best way to begin such a venture is probably with a visit to scout out the country. The first visit to Israel is in itself is an exciting life-changing experience for all believers in Yeshua.

2) Intensive Study of the Scriptures

It is important to learn how each facet of biblical Torah observance points to Yeshua the Messiah and his sacrifice. It is necessary to search out and discuss the truths of Scripture and how they each point to Yeshua. Messianic institutions, with this in mind, should develop centers of learning and research with the appropriate curriculum. They must be able to demonstrate how every element of the Torah points to Yeshua and his redemption. It is important that they become skillful, just as Yeshua himself was with the disciples after his resurrection, to open minds to the true meaning of the Scriptures.

> *44:* Then he said to them, "These are my words which I spoke to you, while I was still with you, that everything written about me in the law of Moses and the prophets and the psalms must

---

14. Ps 102:13–16 (KJV).
15. Isaiah 62:4–5 (RSV).

> be fulfilled." *45:* Then he opened their minds to understand the scriptures . . .[16]

Likewise, it is important to be able to interpret the Scriptures in the same manner that Yeshua made the disciples on the road to Emmaus to understand them.

> *27:* And beginning with Moses and all the prophets, he interpreted to them in all the scriptures the things concerning himself.[17]

Removing the Veil

Paul speaks of a veil over the eyes of the people of Israel regarding the Torah:

> *7:* Now if the dispensation of death, carved in letters on stone, came with such splendor that the Israelites could not look at Moses' face because of its brightness, fading as this was, *8:* will not the dispensation of the Spirit be attended with greater splendor? *9:* For if there was splendor in the dispensation of condemnation, the dispensation of righteousness must far exceed it in splendor. *10:* Indeed, in this case, what once had splendor has come to have no splendor at all, because of the splendor that surpasses it. *11:* For if what faded away came with splendor, what is permanent must have much more splendor. *12:* Since we have such a hope, we are very bold, *13:* not like Moses, who put a veil over his face so that the Israelites might not see the end of the fading splendor. *14: But their minds were hardened; for to this day, when they read the old covenant, that same veil remains unlifted, because only through Messiah is it taken away. 15:* Yes, to this day whenever Moses is read a veil lies over their minds; *16:* but when a man turns to the Lord the veil is removed.[18]

Right from the beginning at Sinai, the true meaning of the Law became concealed from the eyes of the Jewish people. We have seen that Israel and its constitution, the Torah, are linked with this present creation and will eventually pass away with the coming of the imperishable new heaven and new earth founded on Yeshua's atonement (chapter 7). Because of the glory that surrounds Israel and the Torah, it is easy to see the Torah, and its purity,

---

16. Luke 24:44–45(RSV).
17. Luke 24:27 (RSV).
18. 2 Cor 3:7–16 (RSV), emphasis added.

perfection, and righteousness,[19] as an end in and of itself, rather than for its true purpose, which is to serve as a schoolmaster to lead us to Messiah. It says that the minds of the people of Israel were hardened. This is evidently the reason Yeshua needed to *open the minds* of his disciples to the Scriptures concerning himself.[20] To lift this veil from the eyes of the Jewish people requires not only intimate knowledge of the Scripture but also expert skill in using the Scriptures and the empowerment of God's Spirit. The two leaders of the restoration movement, the two witnesses, will indeed possess these abilities; so must those who hope at this time to begin to reveal Yeshua to the Jewish people.

3) Keeping the Biblical Commandments That Are Currently Possible to Observe without the Existence of the Temple

These include, for instance, keeping the Sabbath and feasts of the Lord at their appointed times (see below), eating only foods permitted in Leviticus 11, and observing so-called family purity.[21] It must be emphasized once again that the purpose for Jewish believers observing the Torah is not for their own salvation or justification. Rather, as a part of the Jewish people, they will be able by their actions to show how the scriptural Torah points to Yeshua. For Messianic Jews to teach scriptural Torah by words alone is not enough. It must be taught by example. It is only by participation in actually keeping biblical Torah and continuing to be an integral part of the Jewish people that Messianic Jews will reveal Yeshua to the nation of Israel. It is not enough for Messianic Jews to keep the commandments of the Torah outwardly to be seen. They must be observant consistently (see chapter 9).

> *19:* "Whoever then relaxes one of the least of these commandments and teaches men so, shall be called least in the kingdom of heaven; *but he who does them* and teaches them shall be called great in the kingdom of heaven."[22]

Thus Messianic Jews will reveal Yeshua to the nation even as Joseph was revealed to his brothers.

---

19. Ps 19:7–11.
20. Luke 24:45.
21. Lev 18:19.
22. Matt 5:19 (RSV), emphasis added.

4) Observing the Biblical Calendar as It Was Kept before the Destruction of the Second Temple

God commanded that his annual festivals be kept precisely at their appointed time of year:

> "These are the appointed feasts of the Lord, the holy convocations, which you shall proclaim at the time appointed for them."[23]

It will come as a profound shock to many people that the calendar kept by Jews today is not the calendar of the Bible. Rather, the Jewish calendar was invented by the rabbis in the fourth century. While it is largely based on the biblical feasts, the days and seasons of the rabbinical calendar, like those of the Gregorian calendar or the Julian calendar, are fixed on set dates that can be intercalated and planned for many years in advance.

God's calendar is different. It is based on observation of naturally occurring phenomena in the land of Israel. The difficulty with all calendars is that while the months are determined by the moon, the seasons are governed by the sun. The discrepancy between the two systems is usually overcome by making some months shorter or longer than others and by the inclusion of a leap year (or in the case of the rabbinical calendar a leap month).

Because the biblical calendar relies on observation of nature, it is the most accurate calendar ever employed by man. In this way the times and seasons of the biblical calendar are set by God himself. In order to know when a holy day would occur or when a convocation of the people was to take place, the Israelite had to continually watch the signs and depend in faith on the hand of God.

The Day

The day begins at sunset, not at sunrise; thus each of the days of creation began with the evening, not the morning:

> 5: God called the light Day, and the darkness he called Night. *And there was evening and there was morning, one day.* 6: And God said, "Let there be a firmament in the midst of the waters, and let it separate the waters from the waters." 7: And God made the firmament and separated the waters which were under the firmament from the waters which were above the firmament.

---

23. Lev 23:4 (RSV).

And it was so. *8:* And God called the firmament Heaven. *And there was evening and there was morning, a second day.*[24]

The Week

The first day of the week is Sunday, however, since days start in the evening rather than in the morning, the week actually begins with sundown on Saturday evening and ends with sundown on the following Saturday. Thus, the New Testament informs us that Yeshua was raised on the first day, the day following the Sabbath.[25] In Hebrew, the days are simply numbered first day, second day, third day, etc. Only the Sabbath, the seventh day (Saturday), has its own unique name.

> *8:* "Remember the sabbath day, to keep it holy. *9:* Six days you shall labor, and do all your work; *10:* but the seventh day is a sabbath to the Lord your God; in it you shall not do any work, you, or your son, or your daughter, your manservant, or your maidservant, or your cattle, or the sojourner who is within your gates; *11:* for in six days the Lord made heaven and earth, the sea, and all that is in them, and rested the seventh day; therefore the Lord blessed the sabbath day and hallowed it.[26]

The Month

The month begins on the evening when the crescent moon is first visible. This "new moon" is not the astronomical new moon, when its surface is dark and thus invisible to viewers on earth, but rather the actual appearance of the first sliver of the moon.

> *14:* And God said, "Let there be lights in the firmament of the heavens to separate the day from the night; and let them be for signs and for seasons and for days and years, *15:* and let them be lights in the firmament of the heavens to give light upon the earth." And it was so.[27]

---

24. Gen 1:5–8 (RSV), emphasis added.
25. Matt 28:1–6.
26. Exod 20:8–11 RSV.
27. Gen 1:14–15).

In the days of the Second Temple, it required the testimony of two witnesses who had actually seen the moon to proclaim the beginning of the new month.[28]

The Year

The biblical year is made up of twelve months (with an occasionally added thirteenth leap month). The beginning of the year, like the day and the month, is also determined by observation of naturally occurring phenomena, in this case, primarily the ripening of barley in the land of Israel. At the end of the twelfth month of the old year, a search is made and if there is enough ripening barley found in the land, the new year is proclaimed. If, however, not enough ripening barley is found, then the thirteenth leap month is added before the new year can be proclaimed. The new year is proclaimed not in the fall, as in the rabbinic calendar, or in the dead of winter, as in the Gregorian calendar. The change of year usually occurs toward the end of March or at the beginning of April of the Gregorian calendar. On the fourteenth day of first month (called Aviv and, since the return from Babylon, also Nissan) of the biblical year, at evening, the Passover lamb was to be sacrificed (Exod 12) and *Hag ha Matzoth* (the Feast of Unleavened Bread, (Exod 12; Lev 23:5–8; Luke 22:7–12) was enjoined. Of this month it is written:

> *1:* The Lord said to Moses and Aaron in the land of Egypt, *2:* "This month shall be for you the beginning of months; it shall be the first month of the year for you."[29]

This first month is known as Aviv, which refers to the maturation of grain. It is at this time the barley reaches maturation. With regard to one of the plagues brought upon Egypt leading up to the Passover, the plague of hail, it is recorded in Exodus 9:31–32.

> *31:* The flax and the barley were ruined, *for the barley was in the ear* [Hebrew: *aviv*] and the flax was in bud. *32:* But the wheat and the spelt were not ruined, for they are late in coming up.[30]

This dependence on the barley ripening to determine the beginning of the new year serves to keep the monthly calendar, which is based on the observation of the moon, in perfect synchronization with the solar year.

---

28. Reches, "Witnessing the New Moon."
29. Exod 12:1–2 (RSV).
30. Exod 9:31–32 (RSV), emphasis added.

Corroborating Signs

Besides the state of the barley crop, there were, it seems, corroborating signs indicating the arrival of the first month of the year at the beginning of spring that were also watched for. Among these was the fig tree beginning to put forth leaves. This may help us to understand more clearly Yeshua's parable of the sign of the fig tree.

> *30:* "then will appear the sign of the Son of man in heaven, and then all the tribes of the earth will mourn, and they will see the Son of man coming on the clouds of heaven with power and great glory; *31:* and he will send out his angels with a loud trumpet call, and they will gather his elect from the four winds, from one end of heaven to the other. *32:* "From the fig tree learn its lesson: as soon as its branch becomes tender and puts forth its leaves, you know that summer is near. *33:* So also, when you see all these things, you know that he is near, at the very gates."[31]

It might seem strange that Yeshua proclaimed that the leafing of the fig tree heralded the beginning of the summer (rather than the spring, when the fig tree actually begins leafing), however, in the warm Mediterranean climate of the Middle East, only two seasons were perceived, summer and winter. When winter ended, summer began. Today in Israel, when the winter rains taper off and the weather becomes warmer, everyone speaks about summer having arrived. The leafing of the fig tree heralds the end of the cold, rainy winter and the beginning of sunny, warmer days.

There was, however, another reason for paying close attention to the signs of approaching spring. It was very important to know when the month of Aviv started in order to make preparations for the Passover and *Hag ha Matzoth* (the Feast of Unleavened Bread). This included diligently cleaning out every corner of the house of leaven,[32] getting ready for the family trip to Jerusalem,[33] and the making of an elaborate annual feast.[34] It was imperative to know whether it was necessary to make ready immediately or whether it was possible to postpone preparations for another month. The end of the twelfth month was consequently a time of watchful anxiousness. It may well be that this is the background to Yeshua's comparison of observing the leafing of the fig tree with the vigilant watching for the signs that in the last days will herald his impending return.

---

31. Matt 24:30–33 (RSV).
32. 1 Cor 5:6–8.
33. Deut 16:16; Luke 2:41.
34. Exod 12:6–14.

You Shall Proclaim at the Time Appointed for Them

> *4:* "These are the appointed feasts [Hebrew: *moedim*] of the Lord, the holy convocations, which you shall proclaim at the time appointed for them."[35]

Why is it important to keep the holidays precisely according to the biblical calendar? We have seen that the Torah and the Prophets paint an accurate likeness of Yeshua and his redemption (see chapter 3). If a single element of that image is missing, the entire picture becomes distorted.

This is the reason why, in order to try to put an end the restoration movement, the man of sin, in addition to killing the two leaders and interrupting the Temple sacrifice, will attempt to "change times."

> *25:* He shall speak words against the Most High, and shall wear out the saints of the Most High, and shall think to change the times and the law; and they shall be given into his hand for a time, two times, and half a time.[36]

The Redemption of Israel in the Cycle of the Year

Each of the biblical feasts reveals an aspect of God's redemptive plan for Israel accomplished through Yeshua's atonement: In the first month, the Passover sacrifice[37] recalls Yeshua as the paschal lamb who died to take away sin.[38] *Yom Hanufa*, (the waving of the first fruits)[39] (see below in this chapter), celebrates Yeshua, who was raised for believers' justification.[40] Shavuot (Pentecost)[41] commemorates the coming of God's Spirit to effect the new creation.[42] In the seventh month, *Yom Ha Truah* (Day of Trumpeting)[43] looks forward to the sounding of the last trumpet, the return of Messiah, and

---

35. Lev 23:4 (RSV).
36. Dan 7:25 (RSV).
37. Lev 23:5–8.
38. John 1:29.
39. Lev 23:10–14.
40. 1 Cor 15:20; Rom 4:25.
41. Lev 23:15–21.
42. Acts 2; Rom 8:11; 2 Cor 5:17.
43. Lev 23:24–25.

the fulfillment of the mystery of God.[44] *Yom Kippur* (Day of Atonement)[45] recalls the atonement of Messiah for the sins of the nation and looks forward to the mourning of the tribes of the land, when they "... look on him whom they have pierced..."[46] Finally, *Succoth* (the Feast of Tabernacles)[47] anticipates the restoration of the kingdom to Israel, when Yeshua the king will tabernacle among us, taking up his throne on Mount Zion, and all the nations come up to Jerusalem to honor him.[48]

Thus the *moedim* (the feasts of the Lord) need to be kept on the precise days appointed for them in order to reveal to the people of Israel Yeshua's redemption for them in the Scriptures.

The Rabbinic Calendar

Again, today's Jewish calendar is not the biblical calendar. The rabbinical calendar that Jews observe today does not fully point to the redemption in Yeshua. This is because the rabbinical calendar does not proclaim the *moedim* at the appointed time. The observance of the biblical calendar was replaced with the rabbinical calendar in the fourth century.[49] One reason given for this was to make it possible for all Jews in the diaspora to keep the feasts at the same time. Nevertheless, the rabbis agree that when the redemption comes, the Temple is rebuilt, and the Messiah arrives, they with all Israel shall return to keeping the dates of the biblical calendar. By observing the biblical calendar now, Messianic Jews witness to the fact that Messiah has already come, that he is about to return, and that the redemption has in fact already begun.

The Waving of the Omer

The calendar is the synchronization factor that runs the entire Law. It puts us on God's schedule. A single well-known example will suffice to point out the importance of staying "in sync" with the Torah: *Yom Hanufa*, the Day of Waving (of the first fruits). God spoke to Moses in Leviticus 23:10–14:

44. 1 Cor 15:52; 1 Thess 4:16; Rev 10:7; 11:15–19.
45. Lev 23:26–32.
46. Zech 12:10.
47. Lev 23:33–43.
48. Zech 14:16–17. There are many references that discuss in depth the subject of the good news of the Messiah in the feasts of Israel, for instance, Buksbazen, *Gospel in the Feasts of Israel*.
49. Belenkiy, "Jewish Calendar in the Roman Period," 3.

10: "Say to the people of Israel, When you come into the land which I give you and reap its harvest, you shall bring the sheaf of the first fruits of your harvest to the priest . . ." *11:* and he shall wave the sheaf before the Lord, that you may find acceptance; on the morrow after the sabbath the priest shall wave it. *12:* And on the day when you wave the sheaf, you shall offer a male lamb a year old without blemish as a burnt offering to the Lord. *13:* And the cereal offering with it shall be two tenths of an ephah of fine flour mixed with oil, to be offered by fire to the Lord, a pleasing odor; and the drink offering with it shall be of wine, a fourth of a hin. *14:* And you shall eat neither bread nor grain parched or fresh until this same day, until you have brought the offering of your God: it is a statute for ever throughout your generations in all your dwellings.[50]

In Yeshua's day, there were two understandings of what the *sabbath* is in this passage. According to the more literal view, the sheaf was to be waved on the day after the first Saturday Sabbath after the Passover sacrifice, that is, on the Sunday following Passover. The priest was to take an *omer* (approximately 2.2 liters or about 2 quarts) of the first barley harvested and wave it before the Lord in the Temple. This day is known as *Yom Hanufa*, the Day of Waving (of the first fruits). As such, it was always celebrated on a Sunday.

However, the Pharisees (and later the rabbis) interpreted the *sabbath* to mean the day of Passover itself. This was based on the day of Passover being a day of rest (Yom Kippur, a day of total rest, for instance, is called a "sabbath of sabbaths" in the Scripture[51]). Consequently the Pharisees kept the command of waving of the *omer* on the day after the day of Passover, no matter what day it happened to fall on. Today, since the Temple is not standing, the waving of the *omer* is not performed, however, the rabbis commemorate the Day of Waving every year on the day following Passover.

If the Saturday=Sabbath interpretation is correct, then the waving of the *omer* may fall on any calendar date between the fifteenth to twenty-first day of the first month, but it *must always* be on a Sunday.

If the pharisaic/rabbinic interpretation of Passover Day=Sabbath is correct, then the *omer* may be waved on any day of the week but *must always* be on the calendar day following the day of Passover, the sixteenth day of the first month. Which one is correct? A story in the Scriptures tells us the answer.

In Joshua 5:10–12, after crossing over the Jordan into the promised land, but before bringing down the walls of Jericho, the Israelite people encamped at Gilgal. There they celebrated their first Passover in the land of Israel:

50. Lev 23:10–14 (RSV).
51. See Lev 23:28–32.

> *10:* While the people of Israel were encamped in Gilgal they kept the passover on the fourteenth day of the month at evening in the plains of Jericho. *11:* And on the morrow after the passover, on that very day, they ate of the produce of the land, unleavened cakes and parched grain. *12:* And the manna ceased on the morrow, when they ate of the produce of the land; and the people of Israel had manna no more, but ate of the fruit of the land of Canaan that year.[52]

According to Leviticus 23:14, they were forbidden to partake of any of the new grain of the land until they had waved the *omer* and brought the offering that went with it:

> *14:* And you shall eat neither bread nor grain parched or fresh until this same day, until you have brought the offering of your God: it is a statute for ever throughout your generations in all your dwellings.[53]

Given all these circumstances, there is only one possible way this scenario can work: The people of Israel sacrificed the paschal lamb on the evening of the fourteenth, which must have been on Saturday, and they waved the *omer* on the next morning, the fifteenth, which had to have been on Sunday. Thus we have a clear scriptural example in which they waved the *omer on a Sunday and not on the sixteenth*. This makes it clear that the correct understanding is the Saturday=Sabbath interpretation.

Yeshua ate his Last Supper on the eve of Passover (the fourteenth) and died precisely on the day of Passover itself (the fifteenth). He rose from the tomb on the Sunday following Passover (Matt 28:1–6), the day of the first fruits.

> *20:* But in fact Messiah has been raised from the dead, the first fruits of those who have fallen asleep.[54]

When Yeshua rose from the dead on the Sunday after Passover, the meaning became clear to those who held to the literal Saturday=Sabbath understanding of this verse: Yeshua is the first fruits of those raised from the dead and his resurrection promised that all who put their faith in him will likewise be raised from death. Those who held to the incorrect interpretation of the Pharisees and the rabbis got the day wrong and missed the significance of its meaning. Moreover, the Day of Waving of the first fruits was to be the

---

52. Josh 5:10–12 (RSV).
53. Lev 23:14 (RSV).
54. 1 Cor 15:20 (RSV).

starting point for the countdown to the Feast of Weeks, *Shavuot* in Hebrew, otherwise known as Pentecost (meaning "fiftieth day" in Greek).

> *15:* "And you shall count from the morrow after the sabbath, from the day that you brought the sheaf of the wave offering; seven full weeks shall they be, *16:* counting fifty days to the morrow after the seventh sabbath; then you shall present a cereal offering of new grain to the Lord. *17:* You shall bring from your dwellings two loaves of bread to be waved, made of two tenths of an ephah; they shall be of fine flour, they shall be baked with leaven, as first fruits to the Lord."[55]

From the day of the first fruits when the barley sheaf was waved by the priest, the people of Israel were to count seven full weeks, forty-nine days. The fiftieth day was the day of Shavuot (Pentecost), on which the priest was to wave two loaves of the new wheat harvest.

Shavuot was of course the day on which the Holy Spirit was poured out on Yeshua's disciples. It is no coincidence that the starting point for countdown for Pentecost was the Day of Waving of the first fruits, the day of Yeshua's resurrection. On the day of the First Fruits, a symbolic *omer* of barley was waved the beginning of the grain harvest in faith that God would bless and multiply the harvest. The resurrection of Yeshua was the beginning of a work that was completed on Pentecost, when the Holy Spirit entered those who had put their trust in Yeshua and received his atonement. Again, those who held the wrong interpretation of Passover Day=Sabbath in Leviticus 23:10–11 would have missed the day of Pentecost and the coming of the Holy Spirit.

5) Turning Israel back from Diaspora (Rabbinic) Judaism to Scriptural Judaism

It is no easy task to separate biblical Torah from rabbinic tradition. This is one reason why the two leaders of the restoration must be prophets.[56] They will need to hear directly from God himself to be able to solve some of the knotty problems of separating Scripture from tradition and knowing how to restore many aspects of Temple worship. Messianic Jewish scholars need to be trained not only in the Bible but also in the Mishnah, Talmud, and other rabbinic literature in order to be able to divide between Scripture and tradition.

55. Lev 23:15–17 (RSV).
56. Rev 11:3.

The Karaites

In the task of separating the Written Torah from rabbinic tradition, much work has been accomplished over the centuries by the Karaite Jews. The term "Karaite" means "Scripturalist." Karaites are Jews who have accepted the *Tanakh* (Old Testament scriptures) as authoritative above the rabbinical tradition (though they may follow rabbinical tradition as long as it does not contradict Scripture). It may well be that Karaism had its start when remnant Jewish parties that rejected pharisaical authority and the reformation of Yavneh in 70 CE came together following the destruction of the Temple (see chapter 10). These Jewish parties included the Sadducees,[57] the Boethusians,[58] and the Essenes[59].

Traditional Karaites and the Saga of Annan Ben-David

An important personage in Karaite history was Anan Ben-David.[60] Anan and his brother Josiah (Hassan) were accounted as descendants of the family of King David and were in the line of succession for the office of exilarch (the representative of the Jews in the exile) around 760 CE. Anan, the older of the two, was passed over and his younger brother Josiah was appointed to the exalted office of exilarch. When Anan attempted to establish an alternate exilarchy, the caliph of Baghdad, Al-Mansur (754–775), who had confirmed Josiah's appointment, took offense and threw Anan into prison to be executed. Providentially, Anan met there another prisoner who advised him to proclaim himself the founder of a new religion at his trial before the caliph. Taking this other prisoner's advice, Anan claimed that his followers held to beliefs different from those of Rabbinic Jews. Anan was acquitted. His followers became known as Ananites. Anan's famous dictum was "Search thoroughly the Torah and don't rely on my opinions."[61]

In the ninth century Ananites joined with other groups that rejected rabbinical authority to become the community that is known as the Karaites. At first Karaism was a vital movement within Judaism, posing a significant philosophical challenge to Rabbinic Judaism. Great debates arose between Karaite and rabbinic champions. The greatest of rabbinic debaters was Rabbi

---

57. See above chapter 10.
58. "Boethusian."
59. "Essene."
60. Harkavy, "Anan Ben David."
61. Harkavy, "Annan Ben David."

Saadia Gaon,[62] who wrote epistles and *responsa* (answers to queries sent by Jewish communities) attacking the Karaites. He went to the extent of claiming that Karaites were not Jews at all. However, it was only when Karaite leaders decided to restrict marriage within the Karaite community that the movement stagnated and became a sect within Judaism.[63] The Karaites were among the first Jews to return to the land. One community returned to Jerusalem in the ninth century. Calling itself "Mourners of Zion,"[64] its members established a synagogue inside the walls of the Old City of Jerusalem, which has been restored and can still be visited today.[65] Despite their emphasis of relying solely on Scripture, the Karaites themselves ended up developing many of their own traditional practices.

The Neo-Karaites

Modern Karaite Jews have not forgotten their historical roots. Notwithstanding, they are interested in restoring Karaism again to being a vital movement within Judaism. They have widened their tent to include all those of Jewish parentage who accept the primacy of the Scripture over rabbinical tradition.[66]

What is important for our concerns is that the Karaites have been about the business of discerning the differences between scriptural practice from that of rabbinical tradition for many centuries. They have striven to keep the biblical calendar and to proclaim the feasts of the Lord at their appointed times. Now, with the Jewish people returning to the land, Karaites have established reliable witnesses who observe the earliest appearance of *aviv* barley and monthly sightings of the new moon from all over *Eretz Israel* (the land of Israel).[67]

Distinguishing between Scriptural and Rabbinical Practice

In order illustrate the principal of preferring written Scripture over rabbinic tradition, let us take a look at two intriguing, often-discussed examples of Jewish practice of daily life: firstly, that of men's head coverings and,

62. Newman, "Karaite Jews in Israel," 22–24.
63. Newman, "Karaite Jews in Israel," 26.
64. Newman, "Karaite Jews in Israel," 14–15.
65. Newman, "Karaite Jews in Israel," facing p. 88.
66. Karaite Korner, "Karaite 'Declaration of Faith.'"
67. Karaite Korner, "Biblical Holidays."

secondly, the separation of milk and meat. To some, the debates arising from these two issues may appear trivial and irrelevant, however, since both matters greatly affect the day to day lives of many Jews in general, they also have consequences for Messianic Jews as well. In both cases, we will see how the principal of relying on the authority of written Scripture may be used to determine the proper course of action.

Head Coverings

Undoubtedly, one of the most distinctive elements of Jewish apparel for men is the skull cap, in Hebrew *kippa*, in Yiddish *yarmulke*. An absolute requirement to be worn during prayer by orthodox Jews, it can be seen everywhere in the streets of Israel on the heads of the observant and less observant alike. Notwithstanding, nowhere in the *Tanakh* (Old Testament scriptures) is a Jewish man required to cover his head when he prays. In fact, the rabbinical obligation of all men covering their heads during prayer only began after the Second Temple Period. During Second Temple times, some Jews covered their head in prayer, while others did not.[68] Many Jews today would be shocked if they were to travel back in time to the Second Temple Period and step into a *beit midrash* (house of study) and find the students as well as the teachers all with bare heads. Paul, however, was emphatic when he asserted that a man should not cover his head while praying:

> 4: Any man who prays or prophesies with his head covered dishonors his head . . .[69]
> 7: For a man ought not to cover his head, since he is the image and glory of God.[70]

There has been much debate among Messianic Jews whether or not to wear *kippas*. On the one hand, Messianic Jews wish to identify with the Jewish people, who traditionally wear *kippas*, but on the other, they desire to be faithful to the New Testament writings. If, however, we stay true to principal of preferring Scripture above rabbinical tradition, and we recognize that Paul's words are indeed Scripture,[71] then there is no contention: it is clear that Messianic Jews should *not* cover their heads (at least not while praying).

---

68. Rothacker, "Men's Head Covering."
69. 1 Cor 11:4 (RSV).
70. 1 Cor 11:7a (RSV).
71. See Peter's endorsement of Paul in 2 Pet 3:15–16.

Separating Milk and Meat

Another well-known example illustrating the distinction between rabbinical and scriptural practice is the separation of milk and meat. Some Jewish households go to the extent of having separate kitchens for milk and meat dishes. Strict tradition demands a waiting period of no less than nine hours after eating meat before dairy products may be consumed.

The rabbinic injunction against mixing milk and meat arises from the pronouncement of Deuteronomy 14:21b: "You shall not boil a kid in its mother's milk."[72] This commandment is very specific. What is forbidden according to this verse is the act of boiling a kid in its mother's milk. It is thought by some scholars that the reason for the prohibition was because this practice was a Canaanite fertility ritual.[73] Another possibility is that it may be a commandment along the same lines as Deuteronomy 22:6–7:

> 6: "If you chance to come upon a bird's nest, in any tree or on the ground, with young ones or eggs and the mother sitting upon the young or upon the eggs, you shall not take the mother with the young; 7: you shall let the mother go, but the young you may take for yourself; that it may go well with you, and that you may live long."[74]

It seems that it is unethical to destroy an animal along with its prodigy. Arguably, according to the same principal, there is revulsion in boiling a kid in the very substance from its mother that was intended to give it life. Whatever the case, there is nothing said here at all about separating milk and meat. It is obvious that the prohibition against mixing milk and meat is the result of the rabbinical practice of encompassing the commandment of the Law with a fence (see chapter 10). It is well known that Abraham served his guests (one of which was no less than the Lord himself) milk and meat together (Gen 18:1–8). It is argued by Rabbinic Jews however that this was before the giving of the Torah. The truth is that there is no prohibition in Scripture against eating or even cooking milk and meat together, so long as one does not boil a kid in its mother's milk.

Using the principal of choosing the written Scripture above rabbinical authority, Messianic Jews can determine the best way to live their lives as witnesses to Yeshua. By paying close attention to the straightforward understanding of the Scriptures, it is possible to slowly chip away the barnacles

---

72. Deut 14:21b (RSV).
73. Dewrell, "You Shall Not Boil a Kid in Its Mother's Milk."
74. Deut 22:6–7 (RSV).

that rabbinical tradition has encrusted onto the Torah, and so reveal the glory and beauty of its true meaning.

6) A Time to Rebuild: Showing the House to the House of Israel

We have seen that the two leaders of the restoration movement will use the Torah with its crowning jewel, the restored Temple, as a schoolmaster, with great power, to convince all Israel that Yeshua is the Messiah. The restoration of all things[75] can only take place fully when the Temple is rebuilt. Political and religious considerations, not the least of which concerns the Dome of the Rock standing over the holy of holies, do not permit the Temple to be rebuilt at this time. Nevertheless, as the time for the restoration of all things approaches, an opportunity will, in the not-too-distant future, undoubtedly present itself for the rebuilding. While it is not at all clear how this will come about, Messianic Jews must be ready. It is important in the meantime to master the skill of showing the house (the Temple) to the house of Israel.

> *10:* "And you, son of man, describe to the house of Israel the temple and its appearance and plan, that they may be ashamed of their iniquities. *11:* And if they are ashamed of all that they have done, portray the temple, its arrangement, its exits and its entrances, and its whole form; and make known to them all its ordinances and all its laws; and write it down in their sight, so that they may observe and perform all its laws and all its ordinances."[76]

It is important even now for Messianic Jews take an interest in things of the sanctuary. In this time, before the Temple is actually standing, it is possible to study the Scriptures diligently in order to show how each detail of the Temple points to Yeshua and his atonement (see chapter 6).

The Western Wall

We have seen that the Western Wall (also called the Wailing Wall) is ironically a most appropriate symbol of Rabbinic Judaism (see chapters 6 and 10). Known in Hebrew as the *ha Kotel ha Maaravi*, the Western Wall was the outer retaining wall of the Temple. Much as Rabbinic Judaism itself, which has exchanged the true faith of the patriarchs for human traditions, those

---

75. Acts 3:19–21.
76. Ezek 43:10 (RSV).

who worship at the *Kotel* have forfeited the inner courts of the Temple, the true place of worship, for a courtyard outside, a mere retaining wall.

The ancient Temple today lies in ruins as it has for two thousand years. Israelis for the most part, however, have become complacent with this situation. They see little reason to return to the Temple Mount. Nearly all Israelis would in fact prefer that the Temple Mount, with the knotty political and religious problems encompassing it, would simply go away. Some years ago, then–Prime Minister Ehud Barak of the left-leaning Labor Party proposed a peace deal that would have included giving permanent ownership of the upper areas of the Temple Mount along with the Dome of the Rock and Al-Aqsa Mosque to the Arabs, while Israel would retain ownership of the Western Wall.[77] Only the obstinacy of Yasser Arafat against calling an end to the so-called Israeli-Palestinian conflict prevented the deal from going through. Not long ago, I saw a bumper sticker written in Hebrew that proclaimed, "the Western Wall is the holiest place on earth." Rabbinic Jews are quite satisfied with the Western Wall. The Temple Mount and the Temple itself have been forgotten by most of the nation. We are living in a time that is very similar to that of the prophet Haggai, when the people of Israel were returning from Babylon. God spoke through the prophet Haggai to the Jewish people:

> *2:* "Thus says the Lord of hosts: This people say the time has not yet come to rebuild the house of the Lord." *3:* Then the word of the Lord came by Haggai the prophet, *4:* "Is it a time for you yourselves to dwell in your paneled houses, while this house lies in ruins? *5:* Now therefore thus says the Lord of hosts: Consider how you have fared. *6:* You have sown much, and harvested little; you eat, but you never have enough; you drink, but you never have your fill; you clothe yourselves, but no one is warm; and he who earns wages earns wages to put them into a bag with holes. *7:* "Thus says the Lord of hosts: Consider how you have fared. *8:* Go up to the hills and bring wood and build the house, that I may take pleasure in it and that I may appear in my glory, says the Lord. *9:* You have looked for much, and, lo, it came to little; and when you brought it home, I blew it away. Why? says the Lord of hosts. Because of my house that lies in ruins, while you busy yourselves each with his own house. *10:* Therefore the heavens above you have withheld the dew, and the earth has withheld its produce. *11:* And I have called for a drought upon the land and the hills, upon the grain, the new wine, the oil,

---

77. Barak's peace deal.

upon what the ground brings forth, upon men and cattle, and upon all their labors."[78]

Some believers in Yeshua, both Jewish and Gentile, consider that since the atonement of Yeshua has been accomplished there is no need for the Temple or sacrifices. They fear that a rebuilt Temple would be "an offense to the Gospel." We have, however, taken great pains to show that the rebuilt Temple will not be in competition with the good news of the Messiah, but will be parallel to it, complementing and making the Gospel more understandable (see chapter 6). It is also widely taught that the Third Temple will be the Temple of the antichrist, rebuilt and possessed by him. However, as we have seen, the man of sin will oppose the restoration movement headed by the two Messianic Jewish leaders and will do his utmost to halt the operation of the Temple by taking up his seat in it[79] and putting an end to the continual sacrifice.[80] The future Temple will be the very key to opening the eyes of the nation of Israel to the fact that Yeshua is indeed the Messiah.

Messianic Appearance and the Redemption

Very slowly, Messianic Jews are gaining recognition in Israel. Today when someone says that he is "Messianic" it is usually perceived that he is a Jew who believes in Yeshua, but not much more is understood of what that really means. The body of believers in Yeshua is intended to act as his hands and feet in this world. Messianic Jews have a special responsibility to witness to their own nation. There is currently such wide diversity of belief and practice among Jewish believers that no specific characteristics make them a visible witness to the reality of Messiah. Often Messianic Jews are dismissed by other Jews because of their apparent distain for the Torah and disregard of the dietary laws. However, the day may come when Messianic Jews are rather known for their careful observance of biblical Torah. They will stand out as eating foods that are "biblically kosher" and keeping the biblical calendar, which is not the same as that of Rabbinic Judaism. In these ways Messianic Jews can begin to reveal Yeshua to the nation of Israel. As we have seen, the biblical calendar that the Messianic Jews will keep is the very same calendar to which the rabbis intend to return, but only when Messiah arrives, the Temple is rebuilt, and the Sanhedrin is sitting in Jerusalem. As they observe the biblical calendar and adhere to other biblical practices,

78. Hag 1:2–10 (RSV).
79. 2 Thess 2:5.
80. Dan 9:27; see above chapter 12.

Messianic Jews as a body will witness by their lives, in a very practical way, to all Israel that the Messiah has *already* come, is soon returning, and that the redemption has *already* begun. More and more Israelis will be attracted to Messianic Judaism as they come to see it as a genuine, viable alternative form of Jewish practice to Rabbinic Judaism. They will eventually come to realize that it is the "real thing," the culmination of all Jewish history and aspirations. The climax of this process will of course be that the two Messianic Jewish leaders, the two witnesses, who will initiate the rebuilding of the Temple on Mount Moriah and succeed in revealing Yeshua to the entire nation of Israel.

17

It Is No Dream

PUTTING IT ALL TOGETHER

IN OUR TRAVELS WE have covered much ground. It is now time to step back and have a look at the whole picture. Let us take a moment as if to climb up to a high mountaintop from which we can view the entire road on which we have journeyed.

THE PURPOSE OF ISRAEL'S NATIONAL REJECTION OF YESHUA

The redemption of the Jewish people is of a spiritual nature but is also of a national character as well. The reception of the kingdom that Yeshua offered to Israel was conditional on its being accepted *by the nation* willingly. The rejection of Yeshua as Messiah and king by the Jewish people as a nation postponed the kingdom of Israel and Jewish national redemption to a later time.

With the national rejection of Yeshua, the criterion for reception into the kingdom became personal acceptance of Yeshua as king. Thus the basis of redemption narrowed from national to individual. This made it possible for not only Jews but also non-Jews to enter the kingdom on an individual basis. The inclusion of non-Jews made possible the redemption or reconciliation of the world one person at a time.

This door of individual acceptance of Yeshua will remain open until the future time when Israel will accept Yeshua as a nation and then "all Israel shall be saved." As a result of Israel's national acceptance of Yeshua in the future, Yeshua will return. Those among the Gentiles along with those of Israel who have as individuals accepted Yeshua over the centuries will experience at that time literal resurrection from the dead.

THE LAW A SCHOOLMASTER TO LEAD THE JEWISH PEOPLE TO YESHUA

The Law (Torah) was given as a schoolmaster that leads to Yeshua. The Law was never intended to provide salvation in and of itself to anyone, but only to point to Yeshua. Firstly, the Law makes us aware of our need by making us conscious of our sin, and secondly, it points to the only provision for the forgiveness of sin, Yeshua's death and resurrection. The Law will be the primary means by which God will draw Israel to accept Yeshua as a nation in the future.

THE TEMPLE SACRIFICE AS A CONTACT POINT TO YESHUA'S REDEMPTION

One of the most important ways that the Torah points to Messiah is through the Temple sacrifice, which symbolized Yeshua's sacrificial death for sin. By reversing man's rebellion through his obedience and submission to death on a cross, Yeshua reestablished God's rule, canceling the legal right of Satan's authority over mankind and the earth. The death he suffered once for all time has immense power that is effective throughout the ages, past, present, and future, to bring forgiveness and to undo the consequences of sin: sickness, pain, and death. It was thus possible in the time before Yeshua's death and even before his birth to receive the promise of salvation through the power of Yeshua's sacrifice. God gave the people of Israel Temple sacrifices as a contact point to make the power of Yeshua's sacrifice accessible to them by means of a two-sided faith equation. On the one side of this equation, God commanded animal sacrifices be brought to the Temple. God was fully aware that they symbolized the sacrifice that his Son, Yeshua, would one day accomplish. On the other side of the equation, an Israelite brought a perfect, unblemished animal in faith and obedience to God's commandment (though not entirely understanding its symbolism) to be slain as an atonement for his sin.

THE NEW CREATION

God has promised that a future day is coming when he will make a new heaven and a new earth. This new creation already began within the very cells of Yeshua's body in the tomb at the moment of his resurrection. The substance of his resurrected body will serve as the very blueprint from which the new heaven and the new earth of the future will be formed.

IN MESSIAH

The believer in Yeshua, being "in Messiah," has died with him, is raised with him, and has already become part of the new creation. The believer is hidden with Yeshua. He awaits Yeshua's return and "the adoption of sons" when he will receive a new, imperishable body and inherit the fullness of the earth of the new creation to rule and reign over it together with Yeshua. In the meantime, the believer lives in two realms simultaneously, that of the present creation and that of the new creation, the Spirit of God within his body assuring him of his future joint inheritance with Messiah.

THE TORAH GOD'S COVENANT WITH THE WHOLE HOUSE OF ISRAEL

While the Torah is useful in pointing an individual to Yeshua, the Torah was not given to individuals. Rather, it was delivered by God at Mount Sinai to the entire nation of Israel as a special covenant with him. At the very heart of the covenant was God's promise to dwell among his people. He accomplished this through his Spirit inhabiting the Tabernacle and later the Temple at Jerusalem. The Law is designed in such a way that it can only be fully observed within the framework of the Jewish community as a whole with the Jerusalem Temple at its center. The Temple, through its symbolism of Yeshua's sacrifice, is the most essential element of the Torah in drawing the Jewish people to Yeshua. The ultimate purpose of the Mosaic Law, with the Temple at it center, is to serve as a schoolmaster to lead Israel as a nation to Yeshua the Messiah.

THE LAW HAS NOT PASSED AWAY

Yeshua did not come to take away the Torah but to fulfill it. The Law did not pass away when Yeshua died on the cross. It will continue in its entirety to remain in full force as long as the present heaven and earth continue to exist. The destruction of the Second Temple in the year 70 CE did not change the validity or effectuality of the Law any more than the destruction of the First Temple in 586 BCE. As we have seen, the Temple will one day again be rebuilt on Mount Moriah. Israel and its covenant, the Torah, are inextricably connected with the present creation. The Torah will only come to an end when Israel welcomes back Yeshua, the present heaven and earth pass away, and the new creation fully comes.

THE BELIEVER IS FREE FROM THE LAW

The believer in Yeshua is free from the Law! The Law has not passed away or in any way changed. Rather, it is the believer who changes the moment he puts his faith in Yeshua. For the believer, the new creation has already come. In Yeshua the believer has died and has risen with him, and is already part of the new creation. Yeshua, through his death and resurrection, has effected a new covenant that supersedes that of the Torah, which only foreshadowed it. Unlike the Torah, this new covenant is able to make a person righteous and has the power to deliver him from death, spiritually and physically. The new covenant does not rely on human frailty as does the Torah, whose blessings are conditional on a person obeying *all* its commandments perfectly. Rather, it relies exclusively on the power of the finished work of Yeshua's death and resurrection. Neither Paul nor any of the other writers of the Scriptures ever intimate that the Torah has passed away. Whenever the Scriptures speak of the Torah having been in any way annulled, superseded, or ended, it is only with regard to the believer, who, being in Messiah, has been transformed and who is already part of the new creation.

ISRAEL—THE EXAMPLE NATION

Israel as the example nation took the burden of keeping the Torah for all mankind. The Law was not given to Gentiles or even to individual Jews but to the whole house of Israel. A Gentile, the moment he becomes a believer in Yeshua, has no obligation whatsoever to the Law. He cannot break the commandments of the Law even if he tried, with one exception: if he does so when he comes into contact with the Jewish people or the land of Israel (see chapter 9). The Gentile believer in Yeshua is not grafted into the Israel that is connected with the present creation. Rather, he is grafted into what the remnant of Israel that accepts Yeshua in the future will become: fellow inheritors of the kingdom in the new creation. As such, Gentile believers in

Yeshua do not become Jewish and have no part in Israel. However, they do have a shared destination with "all Israel" that will be saved when Yeshua returns.

REMAIN AS YOU ARE CALLED

Jewish believers in Yeshua are at present saved as individuals and are personally free from the Law. However, inasmuch as they still belong to the Jewish people, they have an obligation to the Law because it is through the Law of Moses that God will point the Jewish people as a nation to Yeshua. For this reason, Paul taught that every man should remain as he was called. If he is Jewish when he comes to faith in Yeshua, he should remain Jewish and continue to live a Jewish lifestyle, keeping the commandments of the Torah. By the same token, if he is a Gentile when he comes to faith, he should continue to live a non-Jewish lifestyle, free from the Law.

RABBINIC JUDAISM

After the destruction of the Temple and Jerusalem in 70 CE, the sages at Yavneh came up with Rabbinic Judaism, founded largely on the oral tradition of the Pharisees. This Temple-less Judaism bears similarities to the Judaism of the Scriptures but has an entirely different basis. Instead of being based on the Temple sacrifice, it is based on prayer, doing *mitzvoth* (good works), and giving charity as a means of righteousness. Its purpose was to keep the Jewish people separate from the Gentiles, hold the Jewish people together as a nation during the diaspora, and to eventually restore them to Jerusalem and the land of Israel. In line with keeping them separate from the Gentiles, they especially opposed gentilized Christianity, which they perceived as the main threat to their religious beliefs. Moreover, the oral tradition intentionally provided loopholes in the Law to prevent having to face the problem of sin and the need for the forgiveness provided by Yeshua. Thus, in effect, a primary aim of Rabbinic Judaism is to block Jews from believing in Yeshua and accepting him as the Messiah. In preventing the Jewish people from accepting Yeshua as a nation until the right time, Rabbinic Judaism unwittingly delays the return of Yeshua as Messiah. In so doing, it continues to hold the door open for the salvation of the world until the time of Messiah Yeshua's return.

ON THE THRESHOLD OF THE RESTORATION OF ALL THINGS

When we assess the times we live in, the general picture is that we are standing on the threshold of the moment spoken of by Scripture as "the time of the restoration of all things."[1] At that time, Israel will be restored to the land and scriptural Torah will be restored with a rebuilt Temple. At its culmination, the Davidic kingdom will be reinstated to Israel with the return of Yeshua to earth (chapter 13).

MESSIANIC JUDAISM

Messianic Jews are individuals who have accepted Yeshua as Messiah but continue to be a vital part of the Jewish nation. As such, they uniquely have the potential to reveal Yeshua as the Messiah to the Jewish nation, much as Joseph was revealed to his brothers, the sons of Israel. The Jewish people at this time, like the dry bones in the vision of Ezekiel 37, have indeed been gathered together from all over the world back into the land of Israel. However, like the restored bodies in the vision, they await life from the Spirit of God. Messianic Jews represent the portion of the Jewish people who having put their faith in Yeshua, and are *already* filled and enlivened with God's Spirit. They are, as it were, the toes wiggling. Only a small part of Israel is currently messianic. However, when scriptural Torah is presented rightly as a schoolmaster to lead the nation to Messiah, the entire people will be transformed!

THOSE WHO KEEP THE TORAH AND BEAR TESTIMONY TO YESHUA

Revelation 12:17 envisions a Jewish community, in the end times, "who keep the commandments of God [biblical Torah] and bear testimony to Yeshua." This group will form the kernel of the Israel that will eventually accept Yeshua and so will act as the catalyst that causes all Israel to be saved! An embryonic form of this community already potentially exists in the worldwide body of Messianic Jews.

---

1. Acts 3:21 (Christian Standard Bible).

THE TWO WITNESSES

Two leaders will eventually emerge from this community. In the spirit and power of Moses and Elijah, they will restore scriptural Torah, turning the children of Israel to the true and original faith of the fathers. They will use scriptural Torah with the rebuilt Temple to point to Yeshua and his sacrifice. They will thus succeed in convincing the Jewish people that Yeshua is indeed the Messiah and turn them as nation to him. The man of sin will oppose these two leaders, kill them, and put an end to the Temple operation. At the same time, the man of sin will initiate a worldwide persecution and holocaust of Jews and Gentile believers in Yeshua, with the aim of wiping them both out. In response to the united cry of Jewish and Gentile believers, Yeshua will return to destroy the man of sin and establish his kingdom on earth.

RESTORING SCRIPTURAL JUDAISM

Mimicking Rabbinic Judaism is counterproductive to Messianic Jews attempting to point their nation to Yeshua, since a primary objective of Rabbinic Judaism is to prevent Jews from believing in Yeshua. Instead, Messianic Jews should promote scriptural Judaism, using it to point to Yeshua the Messiah. It must be taught that the Law has not passed away, since it is still God's covenant with Israel and still convicts all men of sin and points to Yeshua. Moreover, it yet has an important role in turning Israel as a nation to Yeshua. The Jewish believer in Yeshua is free to observe scriptural Torah (as Paul himself did) as a member of the "Israel of God."

Intensively Studying the Scriptures

It is essential to learn how each facet of biblical Torah observance points to Yeshua the Messiah and his sacrifice.

Keeping the Biblical Commandments

As we await the appearance of the two witnesses, it is possible to observe the commandments that do not require the existence of the Temple.

Observing the Biblical Calendar

By keeping the biblical calendar (as opposed to the rabbinic calendar), Messianic Jews witness to the fact that Messiah has already come, that he is about to return, and that the redemption has already begun.

Turning Israel Back from Diaspora (Rabbinic) Judaism to Scriptural Judaism

This will prepare the nation as a whole to recognize Yeshua in the same way the sons of Israel recognized Joseph.

Making Aliya

Messianic Jews should consider moving to the land of Israel. Christian Zionists should visit and, if possible, come for extended stays.

Getting Ready to Build!

Messianic Jews and Christian Zionists must in every way possible promote Israel's preparation to rebuild the Temple on Mount Moriah. Getting ready includes studying every detail of the Temple and sacrifices and how they point to Yeshua.

Not only will these steps prepare Israel as a nation to accept Yeshua in the future and give unified purpose and identity to the Messianic Jewish community, they will in the meantime prove to be the most effective means of sharing the good news of Messiah with Jewish individuals and leading them to faith in Yeshua today.

THE ROLE OF CHRISTIAN ZIONISTS

Christian Zionists, while not observing the Torah themselves, will play an important role in supporting Israel and teaching scriptural Torah. In so doing, they will bring the winds of the Holy Spirit from the four corners of the earth back to Jerusalem to enliven the Jewish people.

THERE IS NO "PLAN B"

It is important to realize that this plan is not the initiative of man. This is *God's* master design for the redemption of the Jewish people (and through them all mankind) as he revealed it in the Scriptures right from the beginning. There is no alternate "plan B." This program has continued throughout the ages and is rapidly drawing to its finale in our day with the regathering of the Jewish people in the land of Israel and the restoration of Jerusalem. God's Spirit is working at this very hour to bring his plan at last to its completion. It is important that we do our part and get with God's program, his master plan for the redemption of Israel. Our part is using scriptural Torah as a schoolmaster to open the minds and hearts of the Jewish people, causing them to seek and turn to their Messiah

THE REVIVAL THAT WILL NEVER END

There is coming a last-day revival that will shake the world, turning many people to faith in Yeshua. This awesome revival will be attended by great miracles the likes of which mankind has never seen. The Scriptures speak of a great outpouring of God's Spirit yet to come upon Israel.

> *10:* And I will pour on the house of David and on the inhabitants of Jerusalem the Spirit of grace and supplication; then they will look on Me whom they pierced. Yes, they will mourn for Him as one mourns for his only son, and grieve for Him as one grieves for a firstborn.[2]

Throughout history, beginning with Shavuot (Pentecost), the fire of revival, with miracles and manifestations of God's Spirit, has ignited in one city or region, only to die out and then burst forth in a new region or in another part of the world altogether. As Zechariah 12:10 indicates, the revival that is about to take hold of Jerusalem and the Jewish people in the last days will not end, but will consummate with the return of Yeshua himself. Indeed, we have seen how the signposts indicate that we are standing on the threshold of the era spoken of in Scripture as the time for "the restoration of all things" that will culminate with the physical return of Yeshua to the earth.[3]

---

2. Zech 12:10 (NKJV).
3. Acts 3:20–21.

NO MERE DREAM

When, under Moses, the people of Israel stood at the threshold of the promised land,[4] their entering into the land depended on their willingness to follow God's plan for them. Because of their failure to listen to the advice of Joshua and Caleb and their lack of faith, they could not at that time enter into their inheritance. They were doomed to wander about for another forty years in the wilderness.

In a similar way, when Theodore Herzl laid out his blueprint for the modern state of Israel, he wrote to the worldwide Jewish community of his day, "If you will it, it is no dream."[5] The return of the Jewish people to their land and the establishment of the state of Israel was a giant step toward realizing their redemption.[6] Its coming to reality was dependent on the will of the worldwide Jewish community to take the initiative.

Likewise, the goal of revealing Joseph (Yeshua) to the nation of Israel is dependent upon the will of the worldwide Messianic Jewish community. If there are enough of those among Messianic Jews and Christian Zionists who are willing to act according to the plan laid out in Scripture, it may, in fact, become a reality in our day.

CLEAR THE LANDING STRIP!

Imagine that an airline pilot is attempting to land his plane when he looks down on the runway and finds that it is littered with service vehicles, airplane parts, and rubbish. To try to land the plane under these circumstances would be hazardous. He must rely on the ground crew to clear the landing strip before he can take his airliner down. He has little choice but to put his plane in a holding pattern, circling above the airport until the obstructions are cleared away. In a similar manner, the time has come for Yeshua to touch down on the Mount of Olives, but he must wait for his ground crew on earth to clear away the obstacles that now prevent him from making his landing. Until they do, he must remain in a holding pattern, even as Peter proclaimed when admonishing the people of Jerusalem in his day,

> *19:* Repent, then and turn to God, so that your sins may be wiped out, that times of refreshing may come from the Lord, *20:* and he may send the Messiah who has been appointed for you—even Yeshua. *21: He must remain in heaven* until the time

---

4. Num 13:1—14:10.
5. Herzl, *Altnuland*.
6. Ezek 37.

comes for God to restore everything, as he promised long ago through his holy prophets.[7]

That time of restoration has indeed arrived, but before Yeshua can touch down his ground crew must clear the tarmac. They must get rid of the deception that the Torah has passed away or changed (see chapter 7) and the false idea that the antichrist will build the Third Temple (see chapter 12); they must correct the errors of supersessionism (replacement theology) and Galatianism and clear away the obstructions of Rabbinic Judaism that obscure the true meaning of the Law. Even as John the Baptist made ready for Yeshua's first coming, it is now our task to prepare the way for his return

> *3:* "... prepare the way of the Lord, make straight in the desert a highway for our God. *4:* Every valley shall be lifted up, and every mountain and hill be made low; the uneven ground shall become level, and the rough places a plain. *5:* And the glory of the Lord shall be revealed, and all flesh shall see it together, for the mouth of the Lord has spoken."[8]

PREPARE YE THE WAY

The time has come when the veil over Israel's eyes is already being lifted. Even now, God's Spirit is calling individuals to come to partner with him in the work of completing his plan for the redemption of Israel. The toes have already begun to wiggle! He is seeking both Messianic Jews and Christian Zionists who can catch the vision and who are willing to make the sacrifices needed to see the dream become a reality. In doing so they will be preparing the way of the Lord, making straight before him the path for his return.

> *16:* When the Lord shall build up Zion, he shall appear in his glory.[9]
>
> *13:* Thou shalt arise, and have mercy upon Zion: for the time to favor her, yea, the set time, has come.[10]

---

7. Acts 3:19–21 (NIV), emphasis added.
8. Isa 40:3–5 (RSV).
9. Ps 102:16 (KJV).
10. Ps 102:13 (KJV).

Bibliography

Amiran, Ruth. *Ancient Pottery of the Holy Land: From Its Beginnings in the Neolithic Period to the End of the Iron Age*. Ramat Gan, Israel: Massada, 1969.
Anderson, Robert. *The Coming Prince: The Marvelous Prophecy of Daniel's Seventy Weeks Concerning the Antichrist*. London: Createspace, 2017.
Anwarul, M., and Zaid F. A. Islam. "The Dome of the Rock: Origin of Its Octagonal Plan." *PEQ* 139/2 (2007) 109–28.
Augustine. *City of God*. Translated by John Healey. Everyman's Library, London 1956.
Avigad, Nahman. *Discovering Jerusalem*. Jerusalem: Shikmona, 1980.
Barr, Eitan, and Golan Brosh. *Rabbinical Judaism Debunked: Debunking the Myth of Rabbinic Oral Law*. Netanya, Israel: One Israel, 2019.
Belenkiy, Ari. "Jewish Calendar in the Roman Period: In Search of a Viable Calendar System." https://u.cs.biu.ac.il/~belenka/roman.pdf.
Ben-Dov, Meir. *In the Shadow of the Temple: The Discovery of Ancient Jerusalem*. New York: Harper & Row, 1985.
Bivin, David, and Roy Blizzard. *Understanding the Difficult Words of Jesus*. Dayton, OH: Center for Judaic-Christian Studies, 1995.
"Boethusian." *Encyclopedia Britannica*, October 19, 2011. https://www.britannica.com/topic/Boethusian.
Borschel-Dan, Amanda. "Ancient Cloth with Bible's Purple Dye Found in Israel, Dated to King David's Era." *Times of Israel*, January 28, 2021. https://www.timesofisrael.com/ancient-cloths-with-royal-purple-dye-found-in-israel-dated-to-king-davids-time/.
Bourgel, Yonatan. "Jewish Christians and Other Religious Groups in Judea from the Great Revolt to the Bar-Kochba War." PhD thesis, Tel Aviv University, 2009. https://humanities.tau.ac.il/sites/humanities.tau.ac.il/files/media_server/all-units/%D7%91%D7%99%D7%AA%20%D7%A1%D7%A4%D7%A8%20%D7%9C%D7%9E%D7%93%D7%A2%D7%99%20%D7%94%D7%99%D7%94%D7%93%D7%95%D7%AA/%D7%A2%D7%91%D7%95%D7%93%D7%95%D7%AA%20%D7%93%D7%95%D7%A7%D7%98%D7%95%D7%A8%D7%98/%D7%99%D7%95%D7%A0%D7%AA%D7%9F%20%D7%91%D7%95%D7%A8%D7%92%D7%9C-%20%D7%93%D7%95%D7%A7%D7%98%D7%95%D7%A8%D7%98.pdf.
Buksbazen, Victor. *The Gospel in The Feasts of Israel*. Bellmawr, NJ: Friends of Israel. 2004.

Carlebach, Shlomo. "'Od Avinu Chai." Music and lyrics (Hebrew). In *Israel In Song*, by Velvet Pasternak. Cedarhurst, NY: Tara and Board of Jewish Education, 1974.

Chernoff, Joel. "Messianic Jewish Revival and Liturgy." In *Voices of Messianic Judaism: Confronting Critical Issues Facing a Maturing Movement*, edited by Dan Cohn-Sherbok, 11–18. Baltimore: Messianic Jewish, 2001.

"The Constantinian Creed." In *Acta Sanctorum Martyrum Orientalium et Occidentalium*, by Stefano Assemani, vol. 1, 105. Rome, 1748.

Danby, Herbert, trans. *The Mishnah*. Oxford: Oxford University Press, 1933.

Dehann, M. R. *Law or Grace*. Grand Rapids: Zondervan, 1965.

Dewrell, Heath. "You Shall Not Boil a Kid in Its Mother's Milk: The Dietary Law That Wasn't." Paper presented at the meeting of the Society of Biblical Literature, 2012. https://biblicallaw.files.wordpress.com/2013/07/dewrell.pdf.

Dunetz, Jeff. "Moshe Dayan: The Hero and Villain of Jerusalem Day." The Lid with Jeff Dunetz, *Jewish Press*, May 24, 2020. http://www.jewishpress.com/blogs/the-lid-jeffdunetz/moshe-dayan-the-hero-and-villain-of-jerusalem-day/2020/05/24/

"Essene." *Encyclopedia Britannica*, April 3, 2008. https://www.britannica.com/topic/Essene.

Flavius Josephus. *Josephus: With an English Translation By H. St. J. Thackeray*. Vol. 2, *The Jewish War*, books 1–3; vol. 3, *The Jewish War*, books 4–7. Loeb Classical Library. London: Heinemann, 1927.

Fructenbaum, Arnold G. *Israelology: The Missing Link in Systematic Theology*. Tustin, CA: Ariel Ministries, 1994.

———. The Three Sabbath Controversies between Jesus and the Pharisees." Study 19: Ariel Ministries' Messianic Bible Study #036. http://www.messianicassociation.org/ezine50-af-sabbath-controversies-messianic.htm.

Garr, John D. *The Hem of His Garment: Touching the Power in God's Word*. Atlanta: Golden Key, 2007.

Gilor, Dov. "The Sanhedrin Reestablished (Part III)." InDepth, *Jewish Press*, June 7, 2006. https://www.jewishpress.com/indepth/columns/the-sanhedrin-reestablished-part-iii/2006/06/07/.

George, Bob. *Growing in Grace*. Eugene, OR: Harvest House, 1991.

Gordon, Nehemia, *The Hebrew Yeshuah Vs. the Greek Jesus: New Light on the Seat of Moses from Shem-Tov's Hebrew Matthew*. Atascosa, TX: Hilkiah, 2005.

Harkavy, Abraham de. "Anan Ben David, Founder of the Karaite Sect." *JewishEncyclopedia.com*. http://www.jewishencyclopedia.com/articles/1460-anan-ben-david.

Herzl, Theodor. *Altnuland*. Leipzig: Seemann Nachf, 1902.

Howard, George. *The Hebrew Gospel of Matthew*. Macon, GA: Mercer University Press, 2005.

Ice, Thomas D. "Is It Time for the Temple?" May 2009. Liberty University Article archives, 124. https://digitalcommons.liberty.edu/pretrib_arch/124.

Imber, Naphtali H. *Hatikva*. Lyrics. In *Sepher Barkai*. Jerusalem: M. Meuchas (Mordechi Edelman), 1886.

Inbari, Motti. *Jewish Fundamentalism and the Temple Mount: Who Will Build the Third Temple?* Albany: State University of New York Press, 2009.

Juster, Daniel. *Jewish Roots: A Foundation of Biblical Theology for Messianic Judaism*. Pacific Palisades, CA; Rockville, MD: Davar, 1986.

The Karaite Korner. "Biblical Holidays." https://www.karaite-korner.org/holidays.shtml.

———. "The Karaite 'Declaration of Faith.'" https://www.karaite-korner.org/declaration_of_faith.shtml.
Kim, Kyu Seop. "Another Look at Adoption in Romans 8:15 in Light of Roman Social Practices and Legal Rules." *Biblical Theology Bulletin* 44/3 (2014) 133–43.
Knarud, Silje B. "'Bringing God's Chosen People Home': A Study of Christian Zionist Strategies Used to Support and Assist the State of Israel." MA thesis, University of Oslo, 2014.
Levin, Edward, trans. *The Mishnah*. Vol. 3. Edited by Bezalel Rappaport. Eliner Library; Everyman's Mishnah Series. Jerusalem: Department for Torah Education and Culture in the Diaspora of the World Zionist Organization, 1992.
Levine, Lee I. *The Ancient Synagogue: The First Thousand Years*. New Haven, CT: Yale University Press, 2005
Lindsey, Robert L. *Jesus, Rabbi and Lord: The Hebrew Story of Jesus behind Our Gospels*. Oak Creek, WI: Cornerstone, 1990.
Linfield, Harry S. "The Relation of Jewish to Babylonian Law." *American Journal of Semitic Languages and Literatures* 36/1 (October 1919) 40–66.
Mazar, Eilat. "Hadrian's Legion Camped on the Temple Mount." *Biblical Archaeology Review* 32/6 (November–December 2006) 53–56, 58, 82.
Mulder, Martin J. *Mikra: Text Translation, Reading and Interpretation of the Hebrew Bible in Ancient Judaism and Early Christianity*. Philadelphia: Van Corcum, 1988.
Napier, B. D. "Prophet, Prophetism" In *Interpreter's Dictionary of the Bible, K–Q*, edited by George Arthur Buttrick, 896–919. Nashville: Abigdon, 1962.
Newman, Albert R. "The Karaite Jews in Israel." MA thesis, University of South Africa, November 1996.
Paul, Shalom, and Dever William. *Biblical Archaeology*. Jerusalem: Keter, 1973.
Philo. *Quis Rerum Divinarum Heres Sit*. In *The Works of Philo*, edited by F. H. Colson and G. H. Whitaker, vol. 4. Loeb Classical Library. Cambridge, MA: Harvard University Press; London: William Heinemann, 1929–1953.
Price, Randall. "Daniel's Prophecy of the Seventy Weeks." In *Exploring Bible Prophecy from Genesis to Revelation: Clarifying the Meaning of Every Prophetic Passage*, by Tim LaHaye and Ed Hindson. Tim LaHaye Prophecy Library. 243-258. Eugene, OR: Harvest House, 2011. https://www.researchgate.net/publication/332652460_Daniel's_Prophecy_of_the_Seventy_Weeks.
Prince, Derek. *The Destiny of Israel and the Church: Understanding the Middle East through Biblical Prophecy*. New Kensington, PA: Whitaker House, 2016.
Rabinovich, Abraham. "No Temple Mount Prayers by Jews till Regulations Issued Court Rules." *Jerusalem Post*, July 1, 1976.
Rahmani, Levi Y. "Stone Synagogue Chairs: Their Identification, Use and Significance." *Israel Exploration Journal* 40/2–3 (1990) 192–214.
Rausch, David A. *Messianic Judaism: Its History, Theology and Polity*. New York: Mellen, 1982.
Reches, Yonathan. "Witnessing the New Moon: What Our Calendar Tells Us about the Jewish Soul." *Dallas Jewish Monthly*, 2020. https://dallasjewishmonthly.com/djm/moon1/.
Reich, Ronny, and Yaacov Billig. "The Robinson's Arch Area." In *The New Encyclopedia of Archaeological Excavations in the Holy Land*, edited by Ephraim Stern, 5:1809-11. Jerusalem: Israel Exploration Society, 2008.

Rothacker, John. "Men's Head Covering." Hope of Israel Ministries. https://www.hope-of-israel.org/Mheadcover.html.
Schechter, Solomon. *Abot de-Rabbi Nathan*. London: D. Nutt; Vienna: Ch Lippe; Frankfurt: D. Kauffman, 1887.
Shiloh, Yigal. *The Proto-Aeolic Capital and Israelite Ashlar Masonry*. Jerusalem: Hebrew University of Jerusalem, Institute of Archaeology, 1979.
Sigal, Phillip. "Aspects of Dual Covenant Theology: Salvation." *Horizons in Biblical Theology* 4/1 (1982) 1–48.
Simmons, Michael B. "The Emperor Julian's Order to Rebuild the Temple in Jerusalem a Connection with Oracles." *ANES* 43 (2006) 68 –117.
"The Six-Day War: The Liberation of the Temple Mount and Western Wall." June 7, 1967. Jewish Virtual Library. https://www.jewishvirtuallibrary.org/the-liberation-of-the-temple-mount-and-western-wall-june-1967.
Stern, David H., trans. *The Complete Jewish Study Bible*. Peabody, MA: Hendrickson, 2017.
———, trans. *Jewish New Testament*. Clarksville, MD: Messianic Jewish Publishers and Resources, 1997.
———. *Messianic Jewish Manifesto*. Jerusalem: Jewish New Testament, 1988.
———. *Messianic Judaism: A Modern Movement with an Ancient Past*. Jerusalem" Jewish New Testament, 1992.
Student, Gil. *The Religious Zionism Debate: Essays Regarding the Religious Significance of the Modern State of Israel, in Honor of Israel's Sixtieth Independence Day*. 2008. https://www.academia.edu/33625561/The_Religious_Zionism_Debate.
Swanson, Ron. *Earth's Final Hours: A Look at What's Just Ahead, and How to Prepare for It*. Calgary, Alberta: Victory Churches International, 2014. https://static1.squarespace.com/static/57840c5ab8a79b20f4331363/t/57b1e33a725e255199513336/1471275844041/Earth%27s+Final+Hours.pdf.
Tari, Mel, *Like a Mighty Wind*. Green Forest, AR: New Leaf, 2008.
Viljoen, Francois. "The Foundational Statement in Matthew 5:17–20 on the Continuing Validity of the Law. *Die Skriflig* 45 (2011) 385–408.
Vine, W. A. *Vine's Expository Dictionary of New Testament Words*. Iowa Falls, IA: Riverside Book and Bible, 1952.
Weaver, Joel A. *Theodoret of Cyrus on Romans 11:26: Recovering an Early Christian Elijah Redivivus Tradition*. New York: Peter Lang, 2007.
Weiss, Moshe. *Rabbi Isaac Jacob Reines: Founder of Mizrachi, the World Religios Zionist Organiztion*. New York: Religious Zionist Oganization of America, Mizrachi Hapoel Hamizrachi, 1965.
Wright, Katherine. "After the Star: The Bar Kokhba Revolt of 132–136 CE and Its Significance for Jews, Christians and Romans." MA thesis, University of Southampton, 2019.

Subject Index

Abd al Malik, 96
Abraham the Patriarch, xi, xiii, 2–8,
    11, 16, 55, 65, 91, 102, 108,
    184, 250
adoption of sons, 62, 63–67, 72, 257
Al Mansur, 247
Al-Aqsa Mosque, 96, 203, 252
American fundamentalists, 212
Annan Ben-David, 247–48
Antichrist, 175, 179, 192, 253, 265
Antioch, 115, 116, 130–31, 132
Antiochus IV Epiphanes, 94, 175, 183
Arafat, Yasser, 252
ark of the covenant, 81–88, 94, 188,
    196
Ateret ha Cohenim Yeshiva, 202

Barak, Ehud, 252
Bar-Kochba Revolt. *See* Second Jewish
    Revolt against the Romans,
barley, ripening of, 37, 240, 241, 244,
    246
Ben Dov, Meir, 202
Billig, Ya'akov, 203
Brotman, Manny, 213, 215
Byzantines, 95

calendar, biblical, 205, 238–40, 242–43,
    244, 248, 253,262
calendar, rabbinical, 243, 244, 253
Chanukah, 94, 174, 183
Chernoff, Joel, 223, 224
Chernoff, Martin, 214
Cherubim, 80, 81, 86–88

International Christian Embassy, 206
Christian Friends of Israel (CFI), 206
Christianity, legalization of, 160
Christianity made the official religion
    of the Roman Empire, 160
Christians United for Israel (CUFI),
    206
Constantine the Great, 160
continual sacrifice (the *tamid*), 42, 98,
    191–92, 193, 253
Covenant, 11, 12, 25, 73–77, 85–86, 88,
    104, 113, 114, 126, 162, 166,
    172, 184, 185, 187, 190–92,
    193, 196, 203, 220, 226, 228,
    234, 235, 258, 261

Daniel xi–xii, 49, 66, 100–1, 183–86,
    207-08
David, King of Israel, 6, 47, 48–49,
    89–92, 187–90
destruction of Jerusalem and the
    Temple in 70 CE, 19, 84, 95,
    146, 168–70, 202, 259
dividing wall of hostility, 78, 111,
    125–27
Dome of the Rock, 96, 97, 203, 251,
    252,
Dual Covenant Theology, 11

eis Chistos, See in Messiah,
Elijah the prophet, 164–72, 176–77
Even Shytia (foundation stone of the
    Temple), 94, 96

Ezekiel's vision of the Temple, 93–94, 172–73
Feast of First Fruits (*Yom Hanufa*), 37–38, 242–46
Feast of Tabernacles (*Succoth*), 243
Feast of Weeks (Shavuot, Pentecost), 48, 116, 185, 220, 242, 246, 263
fig tree, the budding of as a corroborating sign, 100–101, 141
Finkelstein, Joe and Debbie, 213–14
first council of Jerusalem, 115–16, 187–88
First Jewish Revolt against the Romans (70 CE), 19, 146
First Temple, 79, 81, 85–88, 92, 147, 151, 169, 173, 188, 258
four winds, 209, 217, 220–222, 262
Frey, Joseph Samuel, 212
Fruchtenbaum, Arnold, 158, 225

Galatianism, 137, 265
Gamara, 152–53
Gentiles, age of, 21, 200
Gentiles, fullness of, 22
Gentiles, no obligation to the Law, 115–17, 119–20
Gentiles, the salvation of, 15–16
Gentiles, times of, 21–22, 170, 200, 214–15
Great Tribulation, 194–95, 197
Gush Emunim Movement, 206
Gyllenberg, Kevin, 62

Ha Tikvah, The Hope, 9
Hadrian, 19, 95, 178
Hebrew Christian Alliance, 212, 213, 215
Hebrew Christianity, 211–13, 216
Hechal (the Temple hall), 80
Herod the Great, 94
Herod's Temple, 78, 94, 97, 174
Holy Spirit, the guarantee of our inheritance, 67–68, 71

in Messiah, 59–68, 70–72, 107–11, 112, 113, 126, 130, 143, 208, 229, 257, 258

Inheritance, believer's, 58, 63–68, 71–72, 257
Isaac, the binding of, 1–8
Israel, the example nation, 73–76, 119, 120, 186, 258–59
Israel of God, 128, 143–44
Israel, establishment of the modern Jewish state of, 9, 13, 200, 206, 213, 218, 264
Israel, national redemption of, 12–13
Israel, restoration of the kingdom to, 14–15, 19, 199, 200, 243

Jerusalem restored sovereignty to the Jewish People, 21, 97, 199–201 210
Jeshua son of Jozadak the high priest, 94–95
Jesus Movement, 213–14
John the Baptist, 81, 167–72, 265
Joseph the patriarch, 231–33, 262, 264
Judaism, branches of, 153
Julian the Apostate, 178
Juster, Daniel, 226–27, 226,12; 227

Karaites, 247–48, 247
Kingdom of God, 15, 52–55
Kingdom of Heaven. *See* Kingdom of God,
kippa (yarmulka), 249
Kook, Abraham Yitzak, 206
Kook, Zvi Yehudah, 206

Lamb singing group, 215
Lamb, the, 3, 5–6, 7, 8, 42, 43, 50–51, 66, 182, 242
Lamb's Book of Life, 197
Laws of Noah, 116
Lions, chastened by, 123–24
Logos, 43–44

Man of Sin, 175, 179, 183, 192–95, 242, 253, 261, 175, 179, 192–94
Mazar, Benjamin, 202
Menorah (seven-branched lampstand), 80, 82, 105, 174
Messianic Jewish Alliance, 215, 216
Messianic Jewish synagogue, 224, 230

SUBJECT INDEX   273

Messianic Judaism, xii, 202, 210, 211–13, 215, 216, 223–30, 260
milk and meat, separation of, 150, 249, 250
Mishnah, 40, 152, 153
Moses, 35, 104, 261, 154–55, 157, 165
Moshe Dayan, 178, 41, 97
Mount Horeb. See Mount Sinai,
Mount Moriah. *See* Temple Mount,
Mount of Olives, 18, 61, 79, 201, 234, 264
Mount Sinai, 24, 73, 81, 85, 89, 149, 165, 166
Mount Zion See Temple Mount,
murex marine snails for making blue (techelet) dye, 204
Mystery of God, 186–87, 190, 195, 242
Mystery of Messiah, 186, 201

Neo-Karaites, 248
New Covenant, 12, 109, 138, 231, 253
new creation, 6, 14, 46, 58–59, 61, 67–72, 101, 105–6, 107–15, 126, 128, 130, 137, 140, 143–44, 186, 219, 228, 229, 257, 258

'Od Avinu Chai, popular Israeli song, 13
Oral Law, 149–51, 152, 157, 158

Paidagogos. See schoolmaster,
Palm tree and Ibex Motif, 86–88
parochet (the Temple veil), 80, 150, 174
Passover, 37, 39–41, 240, 241, 242, 244–45, 246
Paul the Apostle, 10, 11–19, 64–65, 76–77, 116–18, 128–30, 132–33, 186
Peter the Apostle, 130–32
Pharisees, 147–49, 150–59, 259
Prophecies, messianic, 6, 47, 184

Rabbinical Judaism, 145–62
Reich, Ronny, 202, 203
Reines, Yitzak Ya'kcov, 205–6
Religious Zionists, 205–7
Replacement theology. *See* Supersessionism,

resurrection from the dead, 6, 7, 17, 19, 46, 50, 51–52, 57, 58, 59, 60–61, 109, 174–75, 196–97 208, 246, 257

Saadia Gaon, 248
Sabbath, 120–21, 158–59, 239
Sadducees, 147–49, 155, 160, 247
Samaritan Passover, 39–41
Samaritans, 39, 124
Sanhedrin, 149, 155, 205
Satan rulership of, 27–28, 182, 194
schoolmaster (*paidagogos*), 25
Seat of Moses, 153–57
Second Great Awakening, 212
Second Jewish Revolt against the Romans (the Bar-Kochba Revolt, 132–36 CE), 178
Second Temple, 81, 88, 94, 95, 132, 174
Second Temple, building of, 93
seventh trumpet, 195–97
seventy elders, 155, 177
sheaf (*omer*), waving of, 243–46
Shekina (residing presence and glory of God), 97
shofar, the ram's horn, 1–2, 7, 8
Six-day War, 21, 96, 178, 206, 214–15, 223
Sojourner, 65, 84, 121, 123, 124, 125
Solomon's dedication of the Temple, 92
Stern, David H., 216, 225–26
Supersessionism (Replacement Theology), 11, 141, 160, 265
synagogue, 77, 146–47, 155, 224, 226, 248,

Tabernacle of David, 91–92, 187–90
Tabernacle, the, 38, 41, 77, 81, 82, 89, 92, 105, 122, 146, 196, 257
Table of Shewbread, 80, 82, 105
takanot (rabbinical changing of commandments out of expediency), 151
Talmud, 152–53, 225, 245
Tari, Mel, 218
Temple altar of sacrifice, 56, 79, 82, 85, 172
Temple Court of Israel, 79

Temple Court of the Gentiles, 126, 78–79, 126
Temple iconography, 81, 86
Temple Institute, 202
Temple laver, 79, 82
Temple Mount Faithful, 178, 202
Temple of God in heaven, 81–82, 196
Temple sacrifice, 38, 41–42, 55–57, 82, 84, 89, 98, 104, 105, 117, 146, 177, 185, 191, 192, 256
Temple Women's Court, 79
Temple, the Debir, the Holy of Holies, 79, 80, 82, 87, 88, 105, 251
Theodosius I, 160
Tradition of the Elders, 152
transfiguration, 165
Tree of the Knowledge of Good and Evil, 27
the two realms, 58–72
The Two Witnesses, 164–67, 171, 173–76, 177–80

tzitzit (tassels at the corners of a garment), 203, 227

ulam (the Temple Porch, 79–80; 105

The Wailing Wall, *See* Western Wall,
The Western Wall (*Kotel*), 2, 96–97, 251–52

Yachin and Boaz (Temple, pillars), 79
Yavneh Academy, 146
Yeshua, 6-8, 14-15, 18, 37-38, 41, 42-49, 149, 150, 153, 156-59, 194, 233, 245
Yohanan Ben-Zachai, 145
Yom Kippur (the Day of Atonement), 80, 94, 105, 120, 121–22, 242, 244

Zerubbabel son of Shaltiel, 95, 174

Scripture Index

Genesis

1—2	26
1:5–8	239
1:14–15	239
3	85
3:4–5	44
3:4	30
3:6	27
3:22–24	87
6:1—9:19	59
12:1–3	2
15:6	7
15:13–14	24
22:1–18	2
22:7–8	3
22:12	3
22:14	5, 91
22:15–18	4
22:17	102
22:18	16
37, 39—47	231
37:3, 31–33	232
37:9–10	102
42:8, 23	20
44	231
49: 9–10	47
50:20	232

Exodus

2:23	194
7:20–21	165
9:31–32	240
12	37, 240
12:1–2	240, 241
12:6–14	241
12:6	39
12:8–9	40
12:17–20	121
12:46b	40
16:33–34	84
18:13–26	148, 154
18:21	155
19	85
19:3–6	110
19:5–6	74
19:8	32
19:11	73
20:1–26	73
20:8–11	121, 239
24:3	132
25—27	89
25:10–22	81
25:17–21	88
25:18–20	81
25:21	85
25:22	81
25:23–30	80
25:31–40	80
26:31–33	80
29:1	40
29:38–42	98, 191, 192
29:41	148
29:45–46	77
30:1–10	80
30:12 (text)	90
30:17–21	79

Exodus (continued)

30:18–21	82
34:10, 27	12
35:3	121
40:35	78, 179

Leviticus

10:11	148
11	237
16:1–2	80
16:29–31	122
17:11	85
18:19	237
18:24–28	122
20:24–26	110
23	185, 193,
23:4	138, 142, 193, 238, 242
23:5	37
23:5–8	240, 242
23:10–11	246
23:10–14	37, 242
23:14	245
23:15–21	116, 242, 243–44
23:15–17	246
23:24–25	242
23:26–32	243
23:28–32	244
23:33–43	243
25:1–6, 8	184

Numbers

6:1–21	117
6:21	79
11:16–17	154
11:16	155
13:1—14:10	264
15:37–38	203
15:38–39	204
17:10	85
27:1–8	134

Deuteronomy

4:34–38	74, 110
5	85
6:4	35
6:21	13
10:4–5	85
11:18–21	103
12:5–7	89
14:21b	150, 250
16:16	241
18:3	40
18:18–19	37
22:6–7	250
22:8	79
30:19–20	104
32:46–47	35

Joshua

5:10–12	245
8:31–34	39
17:3–6	134
23:8–13	123

2 Samuel

6:17	92
7:4–17	921
7:16	14, 47, 188
20:25	148
24:24	92

1 Kings

5—6	92
6:23–28	87
6:29, 32, 35	86
6:29,32	86
6:29	86, 87
7:5–21	80
8:6–7	87
8:27	92
8:38–43	92
17:1	165
18:21	166
18:36–39	167
19:13–14	166

2 Kings

1:9–12	164
17:24–28	124
25:1–21	93

1 Chronicles

15:1	92
16:1,4–38;	92
17:1	92
21:1–8	90
21:9–24	91
21:18—22:1	169
21:25	92

2 Chronicles

3:10–13	81
5:13–14	78, 179
36:15–20	93
36:20–21	93
36:22–23	94

Ezra

1:1–4	94
3:7–12	94

Esther

4:14	220

Psalms

2	182
2:1–9	15
2:6–12	49
2:6–9	37
2:6	63
2:7–9	16
14:1–3	35
18:26	18
19:7–11	237
19:7a	34
22	37
40:6–8	57
47:1–5	1
51:17	56
80:1	81, 82
90:1	81
99:1–2	82
100:4	82
102	234
102:13–16	200, 235
102:13	265
102:16	265
116	37
118:22–23	23
118:22	83
118:26	18
120—134	79
126	234
126:1–6	163

Isaiah

1:2–31	93
1:11–17	56
5:1–4	76
6:4	78, 179
7:14	6, 37, 43
9:6–9	6
9:6–7	12, 47, 189
11:1–16	13
11:10	16
11:11	9, 143
11:12	217
25:6–9	13, 17
25:7–8	4, 46
29:13–14	151
40:3–5	265
42:6	16
43:1–2	74
49:6	16
53:3	23
53:4–12	6
53:5	45
53:6,12	184
53:10a	45
53:11–12	37
53:12b	46
59:20	17
60:1–22	13
62:4–5	235

Jeremiah

3:19	63
10:25	15
17:9	27
25:11–12	93, 173, 183
25:12	185
29:10	93, 173, 183

Jeremiah (continued)

31:31–35	12
31:31–34	138
31:31	12
31:33	227
31:35–37	104
32:42	8

Ezekiel

1:5–7	81
10:3–4	78, 179
36:26	227
37	9, 13, 17, 143, 264, 210
37:1–14	
37:9–10	217
37:9b	222
37:21	199
37:22–24	12
37:24–28	14
37:24–25	48, 189
37:26–28	15
40—43	172, 174
40:1–4	94
41:17b–18a	86
41:18–20	87
43:7	46
43:10–11	172
43:10	251
48:11–12	148
48:15	46

Daniel

2:44	49
7:2	217
7:8–11, 23–26	175
7:21–22	66
7:25	193, 242
9:2	xi, 173
9:24	195
9:24–27	183, 184
9:24–26	6
9:25–26	37
9:27	190, 192, 253
9:27a	185
9:27b	192
11:5–45	175
11:31	192, 193
12:1–2	15
12:1	194
12:1b–3	197
12:1b–2a	17
12:4	207
12:6–9	101
12:6–7	195
12:8–10	208
12:11	191, 192, 193

Joel

3:16–31	15

Amos

9:1	188
9:11–12	188
9:11	14, 16, 92, 188

Micah

4:2	84
5:2	6, 37
5:2–4	12
11:1–16	12

Habakkuk

1:13	30

Haggai

1:2–10	253
1:14	174

Zechariah

2:8b	123
4:1–5	173
4:11–14	173
4:14	174
4:16–19	94
8:23	22
12	17
12:10	233, 243, 263
14:3–4	18
14:4	61
14:16–17	243

SCRIPTURE INDEX 279

Malachi

3:1–4	95
4:4–6	166
4:5–6	170

Matthew

1:16–18	94
3:2	171
3:7–12	169
5—7	136
5:5	66
5:17–19	99, 136, 225, 228
5:17–18	99
5:18	102
5:19	114, 120, 237
5:21–22	33
5:23–24	56
5:27–28	28
7:14	88
7:28–29	150
8:16–17	52
11:13–15	171
12:1–7	158
12:40	41
15:2–3	157
15:6–9	152
15:15–20	112
16:1–3	198
16:6–12	157
17:10–13	167
18:3	53
18:20	53
19:16–22	33
19:23–24	54
22:37–39	136
23:1–3	153, 155
23:2–3	157
23:4	150
23:34–36	170
23:37–39	18, 143, 169, 233, 234
24	190
24:1–2	78, 169
24:14	201
24:15–18	101, 194
24:21–22	194
24:27, 30	200
24:29–35	208
24:30–33	241
24:31	217
24:32–34	100, 101
27:51	80
28:1–6	239, 245

Mark

7:14–23	111–12
7:19	112
7:21–23	27

Luke

1:6	171
1:9	80
1:13–17	168
1:32–33	48
1:34–35	43
2:41	241
4:5–8	28
6:7–11	158
6:20	54
9:52	124
10:27	136
10:33	124
11:20–22	52
11:29–30	170
11:49–51	170
12:1	157
12:32	66
13:11–16	159
13:35	18
16:19–20	204
17:16	124
17:20–21	52
18:17	53
18:24–25	54
18:38–39	48
19:41–44	170
19:44	198
20:41–44	49
21:20–24	170
21:20–24a	199
21:22–24	214
21:23b–24	21
21:24	19, 21–22, 200

Luke (continued)

21:29–32	101
22:20	12, 231
22:27	45
22:42	232
24:27	236
24:44–45	236
24:45	273

John

1:1–3	43
1:10–13	64
1:11–12	15
1:19–23	168
1:29	6, 41, 242
2:17	83
2:18	83
2:19	83
2:24	43
4:4–42	124
5:53–57	41
6:35	82
7:15	149
8:12	82
8:56	6
10:7–9	36
10:23	78
13:34–35	139
14:6	88
19:2–3	204
19:23–24	232
20:21–22	221

Acts

1:5	201
1:6–8	14
1:6–7	199
1:6	189
1:7–8	14, 19
1:8	201, 221
1:9	180
1:9–12	18
1:10–11	201
2	242
2:1–2	220
2:29–32	48
3:11	78
3:17	143
3:17–21	18
3:19–21	171, 251, 265
3:20–21	263
3:21	61, 163, 260
3:23	37
4:1	148
5:12	78
5:16	189
5:17	148
9:1–30	10
10:9–16	112, 113
10:9–11	115
10:17	113
10:28	113
15:9–11	115
15:13–18	187, 188
15:19–20	115
15:21	156
15:22–29	116
16:1–3	132
18:18	117
20:16	116
21:17–25	128, 129
21:19–26.	117, 133
22:3	10

Romans

1:16	12, 23
1:19–32	15
3:10–12	35
3:19	115, 119
3:19–20	36, 74, 140
3:20	26, 119
3:28–29	77
3:31	141, 228
4—5	2
4	11
4:13	65
4:15	184
4:23–25	7
4:25	242
5:12	30, 42
5:12a	28
5:14	31
5:18–21	2

6:1–2	139
6:3	59, 71
6:4–5	60
6:5	72
6:6–7	60
6:15–16	139, 43
6:23a	30
7:10–15	34
7:13	26
7:14	28
7:22–25	69
8:1–2	60, 71, 107
8:10	68, 71
8:11	60, 67, 72, 242
8:15–17	64, 71
8:17	65, 67, 68
8:19–24	30
8:19–23	62, 106
8:19–22	46
8:20	29
8:22–24	63
9—10	19, 23
9:2–3	10
9:4–5	64, 126
9:6–8	127
10:1	10
10:1–12	15
10:4	108, 109, 229
10:9–13	15
10:9	12
11:1	11
11:1–2a	142
11:2a	11
11:11	14
11:12	16
11:15	17, 229
11:15a	161
11:17–24	125
11:17–19	11
11:18b	11
11:25–26a	10, 22
11:25	21, 201
11:26–27	12, 187
11:26	17, 195
11:29	13
12:2	69

1 Corinthians

2:9	58
5:6–8	241
5:7–8	41
5:7	37
6:19	83
7:17–20	118, 129, 134
9:19–23	129
9:20–21	135, 136, 139
10:11	74
10:20	135
10:27	117
11:4	249
11:7a	249
11:25	12
15:20	38, 242, 245
15:42–56	17
15:51–56	196
15:52	8, 243

2 Corinthians

3:4–6	140
3:7–16	236
5:14	60
5:17	59, 61, 67, 72, 242

Galatians

1:15–16	10
2:11–16	131
2:14	118
2:16	132
3:1–5	137
3:10	32
3:19	25
3:23	36, 140
3:24–26	76
3:24	25
3:26	71
3:28	110
4:4	45
4:9–10	135
5:1–5	137
5:1	109, 117
5:2–4	132
5:13	139
6:2	140

Galatians (continued)

6:14–16	143
6:16	128

Ephesians

1:3–4	51
1:3	71
1:13–14	68, 71
1:19–20	12
1:20–21	70
2:4–6	68, 71
2:11–22	78, 125, 126
2:12–13, 18–19	65
2:12	15, 127
2:13–16	111
2:13	71, 127
2:13–16	111
2:19–22	84
2:20–22	127
3:1–12	187
3:9	44

Philippians

2:5–8	45
2:7	45
3:17–21	62

Colossians

1:15–17	44
1:15	44
2:9	83
3:1–4	61
3:3	71, 229
3:9–11	110

1 Thessalonians

4:13–18	17
4:14–17	62
4:16	8, 71, 196, 242

2 Thessalonians

2:1–8	200
2:2–8	190
2:3–4	193
2:3	183
2:4	84, 143
2:5	253
2:8	175, 194

1 Timothy

1:15	12
1:17	43
4:8	70
6:17	70

2 Timothy

2:15	148

Titus

2:11–14	12
2:14	12

Hebrews

6:4–5	67
7:27	50
8:5	82, 105
8:6–8	12
8:6	109
8:13	109
9:6–10	104
9:7	80
9:8	105
9:9	70, 105
9:10	105
9:22	85
9:24	82
9:26	51
10:4–8	42, 57, 71
10:11–12	42
10:20	83
11:17–19	4

James

2:10	32
4:1–3	29
5:17	165

1 Peter

2:4–8	23
2:5–8	84

2 Peter

3:15–16	249

1 John

2:27	138

Revelation

1:7	61
2:11	30
3:5	17, 197
3:21	66
4:6–8	81
5:4–5	47
5:6–10	50
5:8	82
10:5–7	190
10:7	8, 195, 242
11:1–2	84, 143, 172
11:2	21–22, 203, 19
11:3–6	164
11:3	165, 192, 246
11:4	173
11:6	164
11:7	192
11:7–13	175
11:10	179
11:15–19	196, 242
11:15	40, 63
12:1	163
12:7–12	182
12:12b–13a	103
12:16	103
12:17	179, 194, 219, 233, 260
13:8	17, 51, 197
13:14	193
13:14–15	194
20:6, 14	30
20:12, 15	17, 197
21:7	17, 67
21:27	197
22:3–5	66

THE APOCRYPHA

2 Maccabees

2:21	54

www.ingramcontent.com/pod-product-compliance
Lightning Source LLC
Chambersburg PA
CBHW050338230426
43663CB00010B/1911